THE HISTORY OF

WORKING-CLASS HOUSING

A Symposium

The History of
WORKING-CLASS HOUSING

A Symposium
Edited by STANLEY D. CHAPMAN

Contributors:
A. S. Wohl
John Butt
M. W. Beresford
S. D. Chapman
J. H. Treble
J. N. Bartlett
W. J. Smith
F. J. Ball

 DAVID & CHARLES: NEWTON ABBOT

ISBN 0 7153 5233 4

Set in Baskerville
and printed in Great Britain
by Clarke Doble & Brendon Limited Plymouth
for David & Charles (Publishers) Limited
South Devon House Newton Abbot Devon

CONTENTS

LIST OF ILLUSTRATIONS

PLATES

IN THE TEXT

INTRODUCTION

THE history of working-class life is notoriously difficult to write. For any period before the beginning of this century the number of authentic working-class autobiographies, letters, pamphlets, news sheets, and other material are so scarce that the historian can seldom feel confident the sample is representative. For the most part we have had to rely on middle-class observers— magistrates and government officials; social idealists like Kay-Shuttleworth, Owen, Cobbett, Engels, and Cooke Taylor; novelists like Dickens, Mrs Gaskell, and Disraeli; and amateur statisticians from Dr Percival and Sir John Sinclair in the 1790s to the early contributors to the transactions of the London and Manchester Statistical societies in the 1830s and 1840s. The study of the anatomy of the crowd in political history has acquired new methodology and significance in recent years, trade unions and early democratic movements have attracted a succession of eager researchers to the archives at the Public Record Office, and the impact of religion on people on the lower rungs of society is becoming a serious area of historical study. But the more humdrum and everyday problems of food and shelter, which necessarily occupied the working-class mind more than any other matter, have attracted much less scholarly attention. The first explorations into the history of working-class diet have now been published, but there has been nothing on housing beyond an article or two in academic journals and a few pages in more general works like the recent volumes of the *Victoria County History*. The reason for this gap has not so much been lack of interest as the implicit recognition that the history of housing was only marginally covered in the familiar sources, and the only adequate source material was scattered through any quantity of estate papers, local deeds, maps, official reports, reformers' pamphlets, provincial newspapers, builders' accounts, fading photographs, and many other sources, and in addition demanded street-by-street familiarity with the twilight areas of our great cities. The slum-demolition programmes of recent years are steadily destroying the physical evidence, but while something remains of the first major phase of urbanisation, and the housing situation promises to retain its position as Britain's most intractable social problem, the time is clearly ripe to attempt to study in depth the development of working-class housing in the last two centuries.

The pioneers of economic and social history derived much of their evidence from published investigations, more particularly Parliamentary papers and political literature on social problems, but it is increasingly realised that this kind of source material may be prejudiced insofar as it was written to demonstrate the need for particular reforms, often taking the normal practice for granted and ignoring significant regional variations except to examine a selection of the most offensive cases. Moreover, some social problems, of which housing is one, were not investigated by central government agencies until the 1840s, and then only as a by-product of inquiries into poverty, health of towns, and other pressing issues. However, Britain is rich in local records, and an increasing number of researchers are seeking their source material in the growing collections of county and borough record offices and libraries. The present collection of studies of working-class housing finds its origin in the contributors' conviction that an adequate appreciation of the subject must be founded on a series of local studies of the problem in the major centres of population in the country.

At this stage of our knowledge of the history of working-class housing, it is not feasible for an editor to attempt to prescribe a schedule of topics to be covered by his contributors, or a pattern to be adhered to. The most superficial inquiry is sufficient to show that the nature of the housing problem varies between different regions. Moreover, archive and secondary sources offer varying opportunities from one town to another, not only because of different degrees of interest in and measurement of social problems in the nineteenth century, but also because of significant differences since that time in the care of business and local authority archives and in opportunities given to researchers to consult them. Given this diversity of materials and methods, the editor has taken the view that the essays composing this volume should illustrate a variety of interests and approaches to the subject. In the contributions that follow, some authors lay more emphasis on the economic aspects, others on the social or architectural; one finds deeds of clearance property as his most valuable source, another the physical survivals, another business records, and others local authority reports, newspapers and other local chronicles. It is hoped that these eight essays will be recognised as an early sample of a 'grass roots' approach to the housing problem in its historical context.

Despite some divergence of approach, there is a large degree of accord between the essays in this volume, and some common themes clearly emerge. In the earlier (industrial revolution) period the most recurrent theme is the response of the artisan élite to new economic opportunities and higher earnings. Individually, or in co-operative enterprise, the skilled beneficiaries of industrial change can be seen striving to reach superior standards of accommodation and domestic comfort, and the studies of Leeds, Birmingham, Nottingham and Manchester examine this process in detail from several distinct angles. In the new industrial settlements (for which Ebbw Vale provides an unusually well documented case study) a better class of dwellings provided the incentive for the migration of labour, but it is clear that the successive companies who exploited the mineral resources of the valley frustrated housing progress at a later date. Another contrast is provided by the almost uniformly low standard of Liverpool, and by some evidence of the plight of the framework knitters in the essay on Nottingham. The restricted area within which 'self-help' could operate is analysed in the contribution on Birmingham, the classic home of the small master and prospering artisan.

The other theme that comes out strongly is the endless difficulties involved in the improvement of working-class housing in the second half of the nineteenth century. Reformers, philanthropists, and local-authority officials struggled to set and maintain adequate standards of sanitation and ventilation, and to provide accommodation at rents which working-class families could regularly afford, but unemployment, widespread casual employment, low earnings and desultory habits frustrated repeated attempts to reach better standards. The problem was exacerbated by relentless demographic pressure, by hordes of immigrant Irish inured to primitive conditions, by the mass destruction of cheap property for building central railway termini and, more generally, by lack of education and failure to appreciate elementary cleanliness. In comparison with the magnitude of the problem, the contribution of the voluntary and municipal reformers seems marginal. Up to the period of the Royal Commission of 1885, the improved dwellings companies housed only 4 per cent of the population of London, and Glasgow Corporation, more active than most municipal authorities, provided accommodation for no more than 1 per cent of its population in 1914. Until 1905, back-to-back houses never fell below 60 per cent of the total number of houses completed year by year in Leeds. It also seems that the advances made in the building boom of the 1880s and 1890s were not so solid as the monotonous terraces of cobbled streets might suggest; jerry-building was by no means dead, and more rooms were only to be had at the sacrifice of an increasing proportion of family income. The story is not one to give much comfort to optimistic historians of the standard of living issue, but it may offer some consolation to present-day welfare economists, architects and town-planners, to know that the heritage with which they wrestle presented no less difficult problems to their predecessors a century and more ago.

S. D. CHAPMAN

University of Nottingham

CHAPTER I

THE HOUSING OF THE WORKING CLASSES IN LONDON
1815-1914

A. S. Wohl

THE gigantic growth of London between the reigns of George III and George V created many serious social and economic problems. Of these, none was more pressing than the provision of adequate dwellings for artisans and labourers. The 'housing question', as it came to be known, taxed the ingenuity and energies of reformers throughout the nineteenth century, but despite the lengthy political debates, varied experiments, and attempted solutions, working-class housing still constituted a grave social problem when World War I began. Many reasons were advanced for the poor sanitary state and inadequate supply of working-class homes, but essentially the problem could be reduced to two principal causes : demographic pressures and economic factors, and neither of these allowed for facile solutions.[1]

Between the late eighteenth century and early twentieth, London grew enormously, both in physical extent and in population. At the beginning of the nineteenth century, London was still a city which one could walk across comfortably. From the Thames a 2-mile journey, either north or south, would bring one to the periphery of built-up London. From the most westerly to the most easterly built-up area was about 5 miles. By the middle of the century London had about doubled its physical size, and by the end of the century had grown to a city 18 miles across, from Edmonton in the north to Croydon in the south. This physical growth was somewhat erratic, a mixture of swallowing-up of already existing communities, such as Hampstead and Chelsea, and slow growth along new or established paths of communication.[2]

Extensive as was the geographical expansion of London, the astounding growth of its population was of greater significance; unless the demographic pressures are constantly borne in mind, it is impossible to understand the seriousness of the housing problem. Between 1801 and 1881, London's population grew from under 1 million to almost 4 million, and by 1911 that of Greater London was well over 7 million.[3] But such figures, coldly stated, do not convey the amazing speed and bewildering persistency with which the population spiralled. Horace Walpole, as early as 1791, drew attention to the fact that Lord Camden was dividing up his property in Kentish Town for building plots, and commented, 'London is, I am certain, much fuller than I ever saw it. I have twice this spring been going to stop my coach in Piccadilly to enquire what was the matter, thinking there was a mob—not at all; it was only passengers.'[4] A hundred years later, Andrew Mearns, the author of the immensely influential protest pamphlet, *The Bitter Cry of Outcast London*, considered demographic trends to be of vital significance to London's social ills. Writing in 1885, he emphasised that Kensington's population was equal to the combined populations of Bradford, York, and Scarborough; that Fulham's inhabitants were as numerous as those of Lincoln, Coventry, and Exeter; Islington's as numerous as those of Newcastle and Leicester; while Finsbury's and St George's, Hanover Square, were, respectively, greater than Manchester's and Newcastle's.[5] In each of the three decades between 1871 and 1901, Greater London increased its population by over 850,000 people, so that in the last decades of the nineteenth century over 85,000 additional people *each year* were increasing the strain upon accommodation. With the centrifugal movement of the population to the suburbs, it was the outer areas of London that were recording the greatest gains by the end of the nineteenth century. Indeed, the last gain in population for the central districts (the City, Westminster, St Marylebone, St Pancras, Holborn, Finsbury, Shoreditch, Bethnal Green, Stepney, Southwark, Bermondsey and Lambeth) was during the decade 1861–1871. In each of the first five decades of the nineteenth century, the central district experienced growths of population of over 12 per cent; the County of London area experienced a population increase of over 10 per cent in every decade of the century except the last (7.3 per cent increase—the highs were in 1811–21 with a 21·1 per cent increase and 1841–51 with a 21·2 per cent increase); while Greater London, with the exceptions of 1831–41 (+17·4 per cent), 1891–1901 (+16.8 per cent), and 1901–11 (+10·2 per cent), had a population increase of over 18·0 per cent in every decade between 1801 and 1911.[6] Despite the general slow decline in central London's population after 1871, many central areas continued to grow right down to the end of Victoria's reign. Battersea, Bethnal Green, Bermondsey, Lambeth, Southwark, Stepney, and St Pancras, were all crowded districts which continued to experience an increase in population down to the end of the nineteenth century.[7]

The pressure created by the rapidly multiplying population was greatly aggravated, especially in the central districts, by two factors —the necessity of many working men to live near their work, and the numerous displacements caused by various improvements and building. To live close to their employment was absolutely imperative for certain men : porters, market workers, men in the building trades, dock hands, tailors, jewellers (who often shared tools), and most of the casually employed. This necessity, of course, imposed a great burden upon house accommodation. 'The crowding', wrote John Hollingshead in his *Ragged London in 1861*, 'arises from the desire of the working population to be "near their bread" as they express it; and the high rental of the tenements . . . arises naturally from this rush upon a particular spot. An empty room', he added, referring to Westminster, 'is a novelty.'[8] In the 1880s almost one half of those living in the dwellings of the Metropolitan Association for Improving the Dwellings of the Industrious Classes lived under one mile from their place of employment.[9] A statistical survey, conducted by the London County Council's (LCC) Housing of the Working Classes Committee just before World War I, revealed that in Bethnal Green, Southwark, Westminster and Holborn, a large number of working men gave their reason for enduring the high rents as 'convenience to their work'. Even at this late date, when transport facilities were much improved, over 24 per cent of the total wage-earning population of Bethnal Green had to live near their work; in Westminster the percentage was as high as 40 per cent (due to the large number of costermongers, hawkers, office cleaners and charwomen living there); in Holborn 21 per cent; and in Southwark, 25 per cent.[10] For these men the suburbs were of little use : 'I might as well go to America as go to the suburbs', one casually employed workmen told the Select Committee on Artisans' Dwellings in 1882.[11] Thus centred around the great food markets, the docks, railways, workshops, and homes of the wealthy were great aggregations of working-class dwellings. It is important to notice in this connection that one urban historian has recently defined the slum as representing 'the presence of a market for local casual labour'.[12] Lower food prices, better work opportunities for women and children, easy credit at local pawnshop or pub, and sense of community and tradition also served to make many centrally located working-class families less mobile than reformers would have liked.[13]

The second factor complicating the housing problem in central London was the continual dislocation caused by street, commercial, and railway building. The social costs, measured in terms of higher rents and lower standards, of the transformation of central London into commercial and financial areas, were enormous, and go far to explain why overcrowded conditions prevailed right through this period. The activities of the railway companies in pushing their lines through, and building their termini in central London attracted the greatest attention and probably created the greatest amount of displacement and hardship. Ultimately, of course, the trains helped to relieve central congestion by transporting thousands of workers to the suburbs, but railway construction wrought such havoc that one must conclude that in human costs the railways were responsible for as much harm as good. So many houses were torn down during the railway boom, which lasted down to 1867 and picked up again after 1875, that contemporaries likened the coming of the railways to the invasion of the Huns. Although the companies were required to rehouse those displaced, they were easily able to evade their obligations, and thousands were evicted in central London without any provision being made for their rehousing.[14] In the 1870s, for example, the whole of Somers Town, a densely populated working-class district, was torn down to make way for the railway construction north of St Pancras. Despite the protests of such groups as the Somers Town Defence League, the working classes were helpless in the face of the onslaught. In fact, in a period when men somewhat naively, but understandably, rejoiced in anything that assisted the demolition and aeration of dense slums, railways were often regarded as the panacea to solve the housing question. They were viewed as a double blessing, cutting through the slums and whisking the evicted inhabitants off to the fresher air, lower rents and higher morality of suburban living. Thus they were permitted throughout the nineteenth century to continue their construction with the minimum of effective interference from Parliament.

Adding to house demolitions in central London was a rash of commercial, street, and school-board building, and other improvements. Many of the wide new thoroughfares cut through working-class districts : Farringdon Street, Southwark Street, New Cannon Street, New Oxford Street, Commercial Street, Bethnal Green Rd, Wapping High Street, Clerkenwell Rd, Holborn, and Queen Victoria Street, all cut their way through rookeries.[15] As with the railways, so with the new street building, contemporaries were generally more aware of the fact that disgusting eyesores were being torn down than they were of the social costs to the unfortunate inhabitants of the demolished buildings.[16] A great number did in fact suffer eviction : New Oxford Street displaced some 5,000 people, Farringdon Street 40,000, and the construction of Holborn Viaduct, the Embankment, the Law Courts, the enlargement of Smithfield, and the docks (completed in the main by mid-century) all added to the pressure upon housing in neighbouring districts. Of the fifty improvement schemes carried out by the Metropolitan Board of Works only thirteen provided for rehousing.[17] Though the great damage done by the conversion of the City into a place exclusively of commerce and finance, and by street and railway building, took place largely before the 1880s, improvements continued to lead to demolition and evictions. The London County Council estimated that in the period between 1902 and 1913 over 45,000 rooms in central London and some 70,000 working-class rooms throughout London were destroyed to make way for various 'improvements', and of these only 15,073 rooms were demolished to make way for new working-class dwellings.[18]

The immediate result of this wholesale demolition and eviction was not the broad dispersion throughout London of the working classes, so much hoped for by reformers, but (due largely to the need to live near their work) increased crowding together in adjoining areas. Paradoxically, sanitary and housing legislation resulted in a similar undesirable increase in density of population in streets adjoining those recently demolished. The Torrens Act, 1868, which gave local authorities the power to demolish individual unsanitary houses, and the Cross Act, 1875, which extended the power to large areas, often aggravated rather than alleviated overcrowding. Pushed out from their homes and unable to move far afield or afford the rents of the model dwellings that arose on the sites cleared under the Cross Act by the Metropolitan Board of Works,[19] the evicted thronged into the already crowded back streets and courtways, where, until the next round of slum clearance or street building, they remained in densely crowded dwellings. 'I came to London twenty-five years ago', one poor woman told an East End clergyman, 'and I have never lived in any room more than two years yet : they always say they want to pull the house down to build dwellings for poor people, but', she complained, 'I've never got into one yet.'[20]

Had the sanitary acts been vigorously enforced, there can be little doubt that great discomfort and overcrowding would have resulted. Perhaps somewhat fortunately, it was largely up to the local medical officers of health to recommend the demolition of unsanitary houses to the vestries, and although these local bodies generally needed little encouragement to be inactive, it was more due to the sensitivity of the medical officers than to vestry apathy that the Torrens and Cross Acts were not employed more vigorously. For similar reasons legislation against overcrowding[21] was not enforced, for medical officers were extremely reluctant to initiate any proceedings which might result in eviction without provision for rehousing. Clerkenwell, for example, was a vestry with a justifiably bad reputation for inactivity and overfondness of economy, yet the medical officer in his report for 1862 gave as the most pressing reason for not interfering with overcrowding and unsanitary dwellings : 'if the occupation of rooms throughout the district were regulated, there would not be sufficient accommodation for the inhabitants'.[22] If to so many contemporaries the slum problem could be solved by the wholesale sweeping away of rookeries, those more informed attacked purely destructive legislation. The medical officer of health for St Marylebone argued that to the working classes 'sanitary improvement is a very car of juggernaut, pretty to look at, but which crushes them. Not a house is rebuilt, not an area cleared, but their possibilities of existence are diminished, their livings made dearer and harder.' Had the Torrens and Cross Acts been used thoroughly, he continued, 'an appalling amount of misery, of overcrowding, and of poverty would have been the result', and voicing an opinion common to medical officers, he concluded that 'until tenements are built in proportion to those demolished at low rents, it is not humane to press on large schemes'.[23]

Thus while the great improvements and slum-clearance schemes carried out by the Metropolitan Board of Works certainly destroyed the infamous and fever-ridden courts and alleys of central London (such as St Giles, Clare Market, and Wild's Rents), they did little to solve the housing problem. 'All improvements recoiled on the poor', one medical officer sadly proclaimed in 1883, echoing the discovery, a few years earlier, by the special Charity Organisation Society's Committee on the Housing of the Working Classes, that 'all social changes must tell first and most heavily, on the poorer classes'.[24] The correlation between the increasing density of people per house in certain central London districts, and demolition in or near those districts is very close indeed, and the impact of demographic pressures and house demolition upon working-class housing standards may be calculated from the fact that only seven of the twenty-nine registration districts of London witnessed a decrease in person to house density between 1851 and 1881.[25] As the festering slums were slowly torn down, so the population became more compressed.

But throughout much of the nineteenth century, and certainly during the first half century, overcrowding attracted less attention than sanitary problems. Until the 1880s the housing question was seen largely in the light of broader problems of general public health. Descriptions of working-class housing in the early part of Victoria's reign are uniform in their portrayal of filth, stench and inadequate water and sanitary facilities. The local Committee of Health and Sanitary Improvement, describing a street in central Westminster at mid-century presented a picture which could be multiplied a thousandfold throughout London :

> Although there is a sewer, the houses are not drained into it, but into cesspools in surrounding premises. The rooms are crammed with occupants, irrespective of number, age, or sex, are most horridly dirty, as is also the scanty furniture, and many of the houses are very dilapidated, and without a semblance of ventilation. The cisterns or water butts are NEVER cleaned out; front kitchens, without any areas at all, are used as dwellings; the houses are let and underlet two, three, four times deep; and the privies are so filthily dirty on floors and seats as to prohibit their natural use and at the south-end of the street are large premises filled with cows on the basement and upper floors, from which the stench at times is unendurable. None of the houses are provided with ashbins, and such are the filthy habits of the inhabitants that the street would be impassable, but for the daily cleaning of it by the scavengers.

The report concluded, perhaps not surprisingly, that 'the morality of the inmates is unfortunately on a level with its sanitary conditions'.[26] The first reaction of many sanitary officials on entering the dwellings of the poor was to force, or even break open the windows and try to relieve their heaving stomachs with the comparatively fresh outside air. Visitors to working-class homes often commented on the boarded up or shut windows. While health enthusiasts and housing reformers like Octavia Hill advocated thorough ventilation, the undernourished inhabitants of unheated rooms had different ideas about fresh air. In addition to the lack of furniture (for much of the century 'furnished' labourers' dwellings had only a few broken sticks), total lack of decoration and colour, peeling walls, overflowing privies, rickety stairs, and blocked drains, contemporary descriptions stressed the foetid atmosphere and stench of the houses in which the labourers and poorer artisans were forced to crowd. Smell is one of the many intangibles with which the social historian of this period must deal.[27] Victorians, well used to the heady odours of street and stable, repeatedly commented upon it. John Hollingshead, whose *Ragged London in 1861,* is one of the most accurate and compelling descriptions of working-class London, could hardly bring himself to enter some of the houses. 'The stench throughout the house,' he wrote of one dwelling off Regent Street, 'although the front and back doors were wide open, was almost sickening; and when a room-door was opened this stench came out in gusts'.[28]

The miserable and dangerous sanitary condition of working-class tenements was not confined to the homes of the casually employed or poorer type of labourer, but applied also to the dwellings of thousands of skilled artisans, who, despite regular employment, sober habits, and adherence to the precepts of Smilesian self-help, were forced by the housing shortage to live, more often than not, in just one room in wretchedly unsanitary surroundings.[29] Nor were the fever-nests to be found only in the relatively obscure alleys and by-ways of Whitechapel, Ratcliff, Shadwell, Poplar, Limehouse, Rother-hithe, and Southwark. Dickens, Hollingshead, Cardinal Wiseman (who first popularised the word 'slum') and others pointed out that Westminster and the West End had some of the worst slums in London, and one writer correctly pointed out that 'from Belgravia to Bloomsbury—from St Pancras to Bayswater—there is hardly a settlement of leading residences that has not its particular colony of ill-housed poor hanging on to its skirts'.[30]

The poorly-built sewers, the irregular supply of fresh water, the lack of toilet facilities,[31] and the density both of houses and people, made keeping a clean home a most arduous task during most of the first half of the nineteenth century, but certainly the habits of the very poor did nothing to assist general sanitary standards. While medical officers and sanitary officials were often sympathetic towards the plight of the poor, they were quick to condemn their behaviour. 'When these poorer people, especially the labourers, enter a house, at once begins a course of dirt and destruction', wrote the Clerken-well medical officer in 1883. He continued :

The locks and handles of doors become toys for the children, and are soon demolished. The drain taps are sold at the bone and bottle shops, those left are never kept on; the closets are stopped up and the pans are broken. The chimneys are never swept, so that the rooms become blackened and disfigured. The paper is torn off the walls; the floors and passages are never washed, and there are no mats, so that the whole place becomes a mass of dirt and destruction. The water-butt lids and the dust-bin lids are used for firewood, the ball-cocks are broken off, so that there is great water-waste which floods the yards and washes away the cement from the paving.

The very hand-rails of the staircases are broken away and even the walls are picked with nails, or something of the kind so as to leave large holes. The windows are constantly broken and stopped up with brown paper; in fact, there exists in every parish a juvenile window-breaking club, the members of which demolish every pane of glass they can, especially in empty houses.[32]

Little wonder that so many argued that it was the pig which made the sty, and not *vice versa*. Many placed the best chance of an improvement in housing conditions in compulsory education; certainly as the century progressed working-class habits improved, partly in response to better sanitary facilities and to lessons learned in hygiene classes in school, partly as a consequence of increasingly strict enforcement of the nuisance removal and other sanitary acts.[33]

The annual reports of the local medical officers of health and sanitary inspectors reveal a clear picture of slowly improving sanitary conditions. One must admire, and wonder at, the energy and determination of these officials who, in the face of great hostility from all sides (landlords, tenants, slum-owning vestrymen and rate-payers), went about their task with such grim enthusiasm. The number of annual inspections conducted by the local authorities was remarkable, a testimony to Victorian energy.[34] The improvement in the sanitary condition of working-class homes was hindered, however, by the reluctance of so many local authorities to take advantage of the power to place tenements on a register, control them by strict byelaws and place them under a system of regular inspections,[35] and by the inadequate number of sanitary officials for the ever-expanding population.[36]

Nevertheless improvements were made constantly, although what the cost to the poor was, in increased rent, it is difficult to say. Certainly the opposition of tenants to sanitary improvements indicates where the cost often fell.[37] As late as the 1890s it is clear that the enforcement of sanitary standards in the homes of the working classes presented a constant battle against petty offences. Taking at random, for example, the annual report of the Mansion House Council's dwellings committee (one of several bodies assisting local authorities in spotting and correcting sanitary abuses) for 1894, there is a steady stream of complaints about drinking cisterns without covers, imperfect taps, bad gulleys, poorly-paved yards, defective drainage, wcs cut off from the water supply, overcrowded conditions, inadequate dustbins, dangerous or defective brickwork, illegally occupied dwellings (attics and cellars primarily), and dangerous roofs.

In the face of such persistent sanitary defects, so often of a seemingly petty nature and so often leading to arguments over ultimate responsibilities and ownership, the quiet optimism of sanitary officials was quite remarkable. After years of aiding and activating local authorities, the Mansion House Council on the Dwellings of the Working Classes concluded at the end of the century that its labours had been rewarded with 'a fruitful record of victories achieved in a quiet, unobtrusive way and without sensationalism . . .'[38] All the available evidence points to a steady improvement in sanitary conditions throughout working-class London. It was not due to the advance in medical science alone that the working-class quarters of central London were, by the last quarter of the nineteenth century, no longer feared as fever-breeding haunts of depravity and contagion.

Unlike the problem of sanitary defects, the problem of overcrowding became more serious as the century wore on. By 1885 the Royal Commission on the Housing of the Working Classes was quite correct to stress in its *First Report* that overcrowding was 'a central evil around which most of the others group themselves'. Lord Shaftesbury's evidence before the Commission, based upon sixty years' experience, that 'overcrowding has become more serious than it ever was', was corroborated by almost all witnesses.[39] Statistics of overcrowding and person-to-house density are always misleading, for both landlord and tenants had very good reasons for concealing the amount of subletting, and most local authorities were extremely reluctant, for a variety of reasons, to employ night inspections.[40] Behind the bare figures of an increase in person-to-house density from 7·03 (1801) to 7·72 (1851) to 7·85 (1881)[41] there is a clearly discernible trend towards overcrowding, which reached an extremely critical and dangerous level in the 1880s. By 1896 London's person-to-house density had reached 8·02, the highest of the century.[42] The LCC for statistical purposes considered more than two persons to each room to constitute overcrowding. By this measure, in 1896, over 56,000 one-roomed tenements, over 55,000 two-roomed tenements, over 24,000 three-roomed tenements, and nearly 10,000 four-roomed tenements were overcrowded; out of a total of 632,148 tenements, 145,844 were considered overcrowded.[43] These figures represent all London, and all classes; the figures for working-class houses would reveal an even greater amount of density and distress.

Overcrowding was certainly increasing both in intensity and in extent throughout London up to at least the census year 1891. After that there is contradictory evidence, but overcrowding did not significantly increase, and probably decreased somewhat, between 1891 and World War I. During this period significant decreases in overcrowding took place in the densely populated central districts —Holborn, St Marylebone, Westminster and the City of London.[44] The four most crowded working-class districts of central and eastern London (Shoreditch, Finsbury, Bethnal Green and Stepney) all experienced a decline in overcrowding between 1891 and 1911. Taking the percentage of inhabitants living in one- to four-roomed tenements who were living in overcrowded conditions, we get the following figures for 1891, 1901 and 1911 respectively : Shoreditch, 43·9 per cent, 39·7, and 36·6; Finsbury, 52·4, 45·6, and 39·8; Bethnal Green, 45·0, 38·9 and 33·2; and Stepney, 45·3, 47·4 and 35·0. Taking London as a whole, the respective percentages of overcrowding (for those living in one- to four-roomed tenements) were : 35·5, 29·6, and 17·8.[45] Between 1891 and 1901 overcrowding decreased in every metropolitan borough within the County of London except Stepney;[46] but over the next decade overcrowding in central London districts appeared to increase again, and in only eight boroughs (Chelsea, Hampstead, Holborn, St Marylebone, St Pancras, Stepney, Westminster and Woolwich) did overcrowding decrease between 1901 and 1911.[47] The degree of high density living was still staggeringly high in the early twentieth century. In 1911, of the single-roomed tenements in London, 43·8 per cent were overcrowded, and of the two-roomed, 41·3 per cent : in Stepney, Bethnal Green, Shoreditch, St Pancras, St Marylebone, and Southwark, over 30 per cent of the population were living in one- or two-roomed tenements, while in Holborn and Finsbury the percentage was over 40.[48]

As overcrowding in London increased, so too, naturally, did the rents. Rents had always taken a large slice out of the working-man's wages and constituted, with food, the largest item in his budget. The Royal Commission on the Housing of the Working Classes discovered in the course of its comprehensive investigations that the London artisan and labourer classes were spending much too much on much too little. Over 85 per cent of the working classes paid over one-fifth of their income in rent, and almost one-half paid between one-quarter and a half.[49] After the Commission's Report in 1885 rents began to rise even more steeply than before,[50] and proved to be the great exception to the general trend of falling prices during the late nineteenth century 'great depression'. The price of accommodation thus held back whatever gains in real wages those working men who remained steadily employed were able to make in the last two decades of Victoria's reign. In the East End accommodation was so difficult to find that a system of key money was introduced,[51] making still further demands on the workmen's pocket.

Whereas in the 1850s 2s 6d for a single room was the average rent in central London, by the 1880s it had crept up to 4s 9d or so, and the cost of two rooms—7s 6d to 10s was often beyond even a semi-skilled artisan's wages.[52] One observer, complaining about the lack of single rooms for under 4s in Kensington and Lambeth, cautioned that 'rents of less than six shillings a week are generally danger-signals, unless the amount is for a single room'. 'The chief item of every poor budget,' she added, 'is rent . . .'[53] Official figures for London in 1905 revealed a clear pattern of steeply rising rent for houses with a gross annual value of £50 and under. Taking the year 1900 as the base year of 100, working-class rents rose in the following manner : 1880 (87), 1885 (92), 1890 (90), 1895 (96).[54]

As rents soared so the cry for fair rents, first raised after the 1881 Irish Land Act, became more prevalent. Not only did left-wing groups, such as the Social Democratic Federation, press for fair-rent tribunals, but several medical officers of health took up the demand, and the Hackney Borough Council asked the other borough councils to join it in pressuring the government to apply the Irish Land Act to London.[55] *Justice*, which frequently criticised the apathetic attitude of the London working man to his surroundings, felt that the increase in rents might achieve some good, for it might drive tenants to demand better, more sanitary, accommodation and awaken him from his political stupor. The medical officers were uncomfortably aware that the sanitary legislation they were enforcing was pushing up rents, and in 1883 their president, Dr Dudfield, argued that 'he could not free his mind from the belief that before this question was solved there would have to be fixity of fair rent'.[56]

The high rents were the product, primarily, of the relentless pressure of people upon houses, and the increasing costs of land and house building. The medical officer for Hackney, disturbed by the alarming rent rise of 33 per cent in his area between 1894 and 1901, produced figures which revealed that in Hackney the cost of building materials had increased by 40 per cent, and that of labour by 18 per cent between 1880 and 1900. Summarising his research we get the following figures :

1880–1900

MATERIALS	AVERAGE INCREASE PER CENT
Bricks	39
Timber	30
Lead	54
Iron	80
Stone	27
Lime	30
Cement	20
Average	40

LABOUR	AVERAGE INCREASE PER CENT
Bricklayer	16
Carpenter	16
Plasterer	16
Plumber	16
Painter	14
General Labourer	30
Average	18[57]

If the hours worked per week are taken into account, bricklayers in 1914 were earning about 8s 6d more per week than in 1873, and labourers about 8s per week more.[58] In the London County Council's experience, brickwork rose from £11 per rod in 1890 to £20 15s per rod in 1898, and, in the same period iron and steel rose 20 per cent and labourers' wages 27 per cent.[59] Combined with new building regulations, these costs made it extremely difficult for even the model dwelling companies and trusts, operating on a dividend of 3 per cent to 5 per cent, to build blocks of dwellings in central London which could be let at rents the working man could afford. To these costs must be added the inability of housing interests to compete with business and commercial interests for centrally situated land. Land in central London became so expensive as to make the building of working-class housing there an almost impossible task.[60] The Metropolitan Association for Improving the Dwellings of the Industrious Classes had spent about £41 per room at mid-century: by 1881 the cost of its buildings worked out at over £60 per room.[61] The London County Council's Boundary Street Scheme in the East End worked out at between £67 and £79 per room, and if the baths, bakery, clubrooms and workshops are included the cost was over £90 per room.[62]

Given rising costs of land, materials and labour, and more stringent building codes, it is small wonder that little large-scale working-class house construction was undertaken in central London after the 1880s. By 1890, of the model dwelling companies, only the Peabody Fund was pursuing a policy of extensive building, and although it was joined by the Sutton and the Guinness Trust, and many new, impressively well constructed, blocks went up in Westminster, Chelsea, and other central districts, the overall total of rooms provided by the philanthropic societies down to 1914 was not impressive, and generally the rents were such that only the better paid artisans could afford them.[63] In 1905 the *Economic Journal* was forced to observe that

> the increased cost of building, due partly to greater expense in labour, material, and land, but also to the far higher standard of house accommodation required by modern hygienic laws, had made it almost impossible for the ordinary builder to provide dwellings at low rents.[64]

Faced with the realities of rising costs, two alternatives, partly complementary, suggested themselves: to encourage the natural movement of the population from central London to the suburbs where land values and building costs were lower and to accept the tendency for London to subdivide itself into heavily concentrated commercial and residential areas; and, for those who could not be encouraged by cheap transport and lower rents to move into the suburbs, to provide housing in central London through the various local authorities or the central London government. Suburbs or subsidised housing appeared to be the only solutions to an over-whelmingly difficult housing situation.

The infinitely cheaper land outside the built-up areas of the metropolis presented an opportunity to develop large working-class estates, if only cheap transport facilities could be provided. As early as 1857 the *City Press*, acknowledging economic realities, argued that overcrowding would never be conquered so long as there was an insistence upon building in central London. 'Cannot some plan be devised', it inquired, 'for bringing the suburbs nearer to the metro-polis? We mean, of course, by railways.'[65] In the 50s and 60s pleas for 'suburban villages' or 'railway villages' connected by radial arms to a continuous railway belt round London were frequently raised.[66] Working men occasionally joined in the cry: 'Why don't they build us a great village or town out Epping Way . . . and then let the railways bring us backwards and forwards for a trifle. They take our homes; let them give us something in return.'[67]

In fact, not until the Cheap Trains Act of 1883 were the railway companies compelled to give 'something in return'. Before this Act there were several companies running workmen's trains, either be-cause they were discovered to be profitable, or because special train acts required their use.[68] Nevertheless, before 1883 the number of working men carried by trains to the suburbs was negligible. In 1882 only 25,671 tickets were issued daily to workmen. After 1883 the number of workmen's trains increased, although not as fast as housing reformers would have liked.[69] Railway companies were still able to evade their statutory obligations, but from 1883 onwards constant pressure was put upon the companies to provide a more effective, thorough, and extensive service. Of several pressure groups, the National Association for the Extension of Workmen's Trains, a group with several left-wing affiliations, was the most powerful.[70] Its president, George Dew, was also a member of the LCC's Hous-ing Committee, and partly under Dew's guidance, the LCC strongly supported the demand for an extension of transport facilities to the suburbs.

The central London government kept up constant pressure upon the railway companies and Board of Trade, and it was in more or less permanent session with the railway companies, negotiating an extension (both of time and distance) of workmen's trains which would be acceptable to the railway board and other interested parties. By steady pressure, but partly as a natural consequence of the great growth of the suburban population, which made work-men's trains more of a paying proposition, the number of workmen's tickets issued daily greatly increased from the 26,000 issued just before the 1883 Act. By 1902 almost 325,000 daily tickets were issued, and while in 1883 there were only 106 workmen's trains running daily in London for a total distance of 735 miles, in 1897 there were 466 such trains (3,248 miles), and by 1914, 1,966 work-men's trains, covering 14,060 total miles.[71] Equally instrumental in opening up the suburbs, was the rapid development of an efficient, if somewhat slow, tram service. The Board of Trade in 1908 dis-covered that the best and cheapest facilities from the centre to the suburbs were provided by the South London electric tram system. As early as 1884 the chairman of the London Tramways Company, which served South London, calculated that accommodation for 20,000 people had been provided along its routes and, he argued, his company had 'relieved London of an immense number of poor people' by carrying them out to the suburbs.[72] John Burns, the President of the Local Government Board, argued in 1907 that 'the taking of the tramways over Westminster and Vauxhall Bridge did more to open up the minds of the industrial classes of the big city than twenty-five years' previous housing agitation'.[73]

The vast improvement in transport facilities greatly assisted the development of the suburbs, although it is extremely difficult to correlate exactly the development of any particular area and work-men's transport facilities to that area.[74] As early as 1852 Dickens, lamenting the invasion of London by 'Brigadier Bricks' and 'Field Marshal Mortar', drew attention to the fact that 'in no part of London is the invasion . . . so perceptible as on the line of railways . . .'[75] The astounding growth of working-class suburbs[76] after 1850 (between 1851 and 1891 Willesden leapt from under 3,000 people to over 114,000; West Ham from under 19,000 to over 267,000, and Leyton from under 5,000 to over 98,000[77]) was certainly facilitated by the availability of cheap and rapid transport. Although as Dr Dyos has shown,[78] the suburbs began to build up their own corporate identities, and were becoming self-sufficient communities which were attracting workers from both central and extra-London areas, the suburbs were still essentially dormitory com-munities, dependent upon good communications with various parts of central London. The connection between working-class subur-ban growth and cheap transport may be seen in the case of North

East London, which attracted many more working men, and grew far more rapidly, than the western or southern suburbs, largely because of the policies of the Great Eastern Company, which provided the most comprehensive service of workmen's trains.[79] At the end of the century, the Valuer of the LCC, speaking for that body's housing committee, commented :

> The Great Eastern Railway Company ⁊ . . . is the only company which offers reasonable facilities for the travel of the working class; and the result is that ever-increasing numbers of the working class population are practically forced along the lines of the Great Eastern Railway; so that while there is an enormous working-class population in that one direction, there are, in the north, west, and south of London, within a much less distance from the Bank of England, large tracts of land not developed for the erection of houses—sometimes within the county boundaries.[80]

The LCC's statistical office pointed out that of all the working-class rooms built during the years 1902 to 1908 well over one-third were situated in the north-eastern suburbs.[81]

The LCC, which after 1900 embarked upon a policy of building working-class estates in the suburbs, was fully aware of the value of low-cost transport, and argued that even if suburban cottages were provided by municipal authorities at the very lowest rents, there would be 'no relief to the overcrowded districts of the centre until proper means of cheap and rapid transit were supplied'.[82] But the Council's Housing of the Working Classes Committee realised that it was working under the great handicap of a vicious circle, for 'the railway companies cannot be compelled to provide workmen's trains until the dwellings are occupied in a particular district and . . . the people will not occupy the dwellings until workmen's trains have been provided'.[83]

In fact, despite the number of workmen's tickets sold, the range of the workmen's trains was disappointing, and not until the twentieth century did the railway companies satisfy the demands of the housing reformers. In 1905 the limit of the twopenny ticket (the fare which, in the estimation of the London County Council was 'within the reach of the largest body of workpeople') was eleven miles from the centre in North London, twelve miles in West London, twenty-one miles in East London, and only eight miles in South London.[84] By 1913 the 2d return workmen's fare extended beyond the County of London on certain lines, while the 4d fare ('the maximum within the reach of any considerable number of persons of the working class') extended beyond the boundary at practically all points in the North. On the south side of the Thames, the 2d limit was still very confined, and even the 4d fare did not include much of Woolwich and Lewisham.[85]

Suburban rents were so much cheaper than central rents (in 1890 a workman's cottage in the suburbs—two rooms on the ground floor and three rooms above—could be had for only 6s 6d, little over half the cost of a comparable flat in the centre) that where cheap transport facilities did exist, the suburbs obviously offered the working man the chance to enjoy a much higher standard of living. In 1900 the LCC carried out a survey of the 'relation between wages, rents, and fares of workmen resident within half a mile of each station of the London and South-Eastern Railway to a distance of about twenty miles from Waterloo'. The study was deliberately made of South London, and of a company which had a very poor record of running workmen's trains, and the LCC based its figures, not upon workmen's fares, but on ordinary third-class travel. The investigation revealed that those workmen living near Waterloo Station paid an average weekly rent of 8s 1d for two or three rooms (24·8 per cent of weekly wages consumed in rent), and they had no travel expenses. Those workmen (average wage 35s 4d per week) living near Vauxhall Station, 1·36 miles from Waterloo, were paying 6s 9d for two or three rooms (19 per cent of wages), and 1s per week on fares. At Wandsworth, 4·174 miles from Waterloo, labourers earning 34s 11d per week were paying an average weekly rent for two or three rooms of 7s 2d (20·5 per cent of weekly wage), and 2s per week on fares. In Sunbury, over sixteen miles from Waterloo, the labourers were paying an average rent of only 5s 6d per week for their cottages, but were spending 5s per week in fares.[86] Certainly in the north-east the total cost of rent and travel offset the slightly higher general cost of living in the suburbs.

Despite the claims that cheap transport would be self-defeating, since, with the coming of workmen's trains, landlords would put up rents and thus 'the extension of travelling facilities "crystallises into rent" ',[87] and in spite of the argument of one prominent housing reformer that 'directly cheap trains are established to a district the jerry builder sets to work and rents were exacted which made the cheap transit of no advantage',[88] the suburbs, from the 1880s onwards, attracted an increasing number of labourers and artisans who wished to better their standard of living without greatly increasing their cost of living. In 1890 the LCC's Housing of the Working Classes Committee noticed that 'in strong contrast to the cessation of building of workmen's dwellings in the centre of London is the very remarkable increase in the number of cottage dwellings which have lately been erected on some districts outside the county'.[89] A few years earlier the model dwelling companies operating in central London started to complain that the migration of workmen was such that there was little use in building large blocks in the centre, where, in any case, they could not provide tenements as cheaply as the speculative builder could provide cottages in the suburbs.[90] By 1907 the hard-pressed medical officer for Finsbury could write, thankfully, 'an immense improvement in the means of transit is fast revolutionising Finsbury and central London generally', and in the same year the Mansion House Council on the Dwellings of the Poor (which was always more concerned with sanitary rather than overcrowding problems, and which tended to be somewhat sanguine about overcrowding) felt that decentralisation of population with the great movement of working men to the suburbs had now reached the stage where hardly a centrally located borough was seriously in need of further working-class accommodation. It attributed the increased willingness to live in the suburbs to improved travelling facilities, shorter hours of labour, cheaper rents in the suburbs, and a marked decentralisation of industry.[91] John Burns stated in 1907 that the lines of cheap communications had so improved that 13,000 families a year were leaving the inner circle for the suburbs : in the official estimation of the LCC, based upon both railway returns and tramway figures, at least 251,000,000 workmen a year, or 820,000 a day, were making extensive journeys to their work in 1913.[92]

Thus, by the end of the century, cheap transport had completely changed the habits and mobility of the working classes, and thus the face of London. In addition to the thousands of working men the trains carried each day, we should add the thousands of middle-class families who, deserting the centre for the suburbs, left behind large houses which, converted or unaltered, were quickly occupied by the working classes. Yet it would be incorrect to regard the rapidly mushrooming suburbs of London as a totally benign solution to London's overcrowding problems. Suburban rents were lower because suburban builders not only had the advantage of relatively inexpensive land but also enjoyed considerably less harassment from sanitary officials, and thus could build with the most shoddy materials. Rarely were suburban builders hampered by the stringent building and sanitary codes which were vigorously enforced in central London. Walthamstow, which trebled its population between 1861 and 1871, did not see fit to appoint a building inspector until 1884, and Willesden, one of the fastest-growing suburbs, did not adopt byelaws governing houses let in lodgings until 1893, and had still to place a single house on the register in 1914![93] So notorious were building practices in the working-class suburbs that the *Lancet* was incredulous that anyone who had the working classes' interests at heart could seriously suggest suburban living. 'It is difficult', it wrote in 1874,

> to understand the argument of those who contend that the labouring classes ought to live in the suburbs—i.e. in unhealthy, cheap, undrained districts, often beyond the pale of sanitary legislation, and in adulterated houses whose foundations were rotten, whose walls were scarcely weatherproof, and whose owners but too often belong to the most unscrupulously dishonest class to be found among us.

The journal rightly considered the suburbs to be a 'no man's land, where the most glaring breaches of hygiene and of sanitary Acts of Parliament are allowed, in a great measure, to go unchecked'.[94] As early as 1860 the *Tottenham Advertiser* remarked upon the 'rapid replacement of well-built houses by rows of jerry-built dwellings', and five years later it sadly reflected that 'some of our speculative builders have seriously succeeded in disfiguring some portions of our district with a new type of hovel—not only unsightly but unsafe'.[95] In Willesden jerry-built houses were being run up everyhere and 'bats' (broken fragments of brick) and mortar composed of road sweepings mixed with lime were used as building materials.[96]

Of course it was not in the suburbs alone that the jerry-builders operated, but it was mainly in the outer districts of London that low cost speculative building operations prevailed. Indeed, the suburban builder of working-class houses often operated under a system which almost dictated the process of jerry-building. This system was so well analysed by the journal of the medical officers of health, *Public Health*, that it bears quoting in full :

> The evolution of the jerry-built house appears to be somewhat as follows: some green fields, or some mansion with a few acres of pleasure or garden ground, conveniently situated in the suburbs, are advertised to be sold, or let on building leases. Timber is forthwith cut down, roads formed,

and sewers built; plans are prepared by which the ground is cut up into plots containing a few feet of frontage and a great number of feet for depth. These plots, if not sold, are let at ground rent at so many pounds each, the lessee undertaking to put a house of specified value upon it. By these means it is intended that a field, which at the time of letting brings in a few shillings per annum as grazing ground, shall, when covered with houses, bring in as many pounds, and that, moreover, the houses erected thereon shall revert to the ground landlord at the termination of the lease. But to get the house built something more is needed. The capitalist, often the owner of the land, now comes forward with loans, to enable a class of small builders to undertake the work. These builders, for the most part men with little or no means, but with a certain knowledge and experience, have to build the houses and to support themselves and their families during the period in which the loans can be made to last. A surveyor is appointed to protect the advances of loans, and if he proves faithful to his employer the brick, lime and timber merchants, and others, will probably suffer by the bankruptcy of the builder. But if the builder is not to fail, it follows that he must go to the cheapest market for the materials. His bricks will be porous, his timber 'shaky', his mortar deficient in lime, his plaster destitute of hair, his woodwork and joinery of the most unsatisfactory kind, and his sanitary appliances of the cheapest quality. The drainage, supposed for the main part to have been supervised by the sanitary officials, will often be found to be defective, and . . . it may be said, without much fear of contradiction, that in a great part of London the jerry-builder has been content with clay-joined drains which are now leaky.[97]

No wonder, wrote the author, the medical officer for Hampstead, that 50,000 notices for repairs and sanitary defects were annually served in London. Unfortunately, because of the lack of any legal definition and standard of quality of materials, it was extremely difficult for the district surveyors who summonsed the builders to the police courts, to get a conviction, and since tenants rarely complained for fear of eviction, or (in the case of enforced improvements) a rent increase, little could be done to halt the process of jerry-building. Indeed, the medical officer for Hampstead rightly concluded, 'It would seem, therefore, that attempts to take the housing of the poor out of the hands of the speculative builder on any large scale are not likely to meet with success.'[98]

One tends too often to think of the suburbs of Victorian London as middle-class retreats. In fact, by 1912 about 25 per cent of all suburban railway passengers were buying workmen's tickets, and within the six to eight mile zone of the centre of London about 40 per cent of the suburban commuters were working-class men.[99] The speculative builders managed to build houses at a sufficient rate to prevent the suburbs becoming unbearably overcrowded : between 1902 and 1911, for example, 278,000 rooms in working-class houses were built in Extra London for a population which had increased by 684,000 people of all classes.[100] Nevertheless, when in 1907 the author of an article on 'The Housing Problem' wrote :

> From day to day the venue for the solution of the problem is changed, yesterday it lay in West Ham, in Streatham, Hackney and Tottenham; to-day it lies in East Ham, in Croydon and Harrow; to-morrow it will be in the belt of country lying beyond.[101]

he was acknowledging less the ability of the suburbs to absorb wave after wave of new population than their tendency to outlive their usefulness as absorbers of population and to become, themselves, overcrowded areas. Contemporaries were shocked when they looked at the forlorn and shabby working-class suburbs that stretched out from London on all sides. By the end of the period working-class suburbs were showing distinct signs of becoming somewhat cleaner (because newer) and healthier (because fresher), versions of the slums of central London : 'embryo slums', in the words of one reformer.[102] It is a sad commentary on urban growth that between 1890 and 1914 central London enjoyed a brief respite from increasing density of population only through the creation of sprawling, ugly, lifeless, and often congested suburbs. Unplanned, unpleasant, and often unsanitary, the working-class suburbs, assisted by cheap means of transport, partially and temporarily eased, though far from cured, London's great working-class housing difficulties.

Whether the artisans and labourers were to be housed in large blocks of tenements in the central districts, or in long terraces of workmen's cottages in the suburbs of London, the crux of the problem was one of costs on the one hand—what was the lowest rent one could profitably charge—and wages on the other—what rent could one reasonably afford to pay? What rent *could* the London working man afford, and what sort of accommodation would it buy him? Booth defined the level of poverty at 21s a week for a moderately sized family, and his strenuous investigations revealed vast stretches of London where the majority of men were earning less, and where, consequently, poverty was the norm. In the central part of East London 44 per cent of the population was living at the poverty level, in the Eastern section of East London, 32 per cent; in the central part of North London, 43 per cent, in the central part of South London 47 per cent, and in West London, 25 per cent. As might be expected, these areas conformed to districts of dense overcrowding and sub-standard housing, though Booth himself was somewhat ambiguous about the connection between poverty and overcrowding.[103] Thus in 1887, when Booth started his monumental study, vast numbers of working-class men were earning under 21s a week, and, since the Royal Commission on the Housing of the Working Classes discovered just two years previously that over 85 per cent of the working classes paid one-fifth of their income in rent, and almost one-half paid between a quarter and a half, it may be gauged that the majority of the working men were paying anywhere between 5s and 10s a week for their accommodation. Other evidence suggests that far more were paying the former rather than the latter figure.[104] And 5s a week rent would buy very little indeed in the 1880s! Thus large numbers were living in one-roomed flats so widely condemned on both moral and physical grounds. The widespread continuance, even expansion, of the one-roomed flat by the end of the nineteenth century, at a time of rising real wages, reveals the seriousness of the housing problem.

When one compares the rents prevalent in various parts of London at the turn of the century, one may say, that, on the average, rents in the inner and middle zones of London in 1900 would run about 5s for a single room, 6s 6d for two rooms, 8s 6d for three rooms, and 10s 6d for four rooms for sparsely furnished flats.[105] With the wages artisans and labourers were earning, the basic economic factors were clearly at the root of the overcrowding situation. Yet contemporaries were slow to awaken to the fact that the housing problem was part of a greater poverty problem. This realisation was slow in dawning, partly because the housing question had always been muddled with matters of public health and sanitation, partly because in an age of slow improvements belief in Smilesian dicta still held firm, partly because general prosperity in the mid-Victorian years partially hid pockets of intense poverty, and partly because the will to believe in the efficacy of free market capitalism to solve most social problems was still immensely strong. With the worsening of the economic crisis, the growth of organised socialism, the re-working of economic theory, the impact of the careful statistical analyses of Booth and Hyndman, and the visits of Henry George, the problem of overcrowding in the 1880s came to be viewed in a much less emotional manner. Instead, for the first time, the housing of artisans and labourers was viewed as only a part of the general problem of standard of living, though a problem which was attracting more and more attention. Gradually, therefore, after 1883 or so,[106] poverty was seen to be at the root of the housing crisis.

Medical officers of health, for example, disillusioned with partial remedies, felt that all along one had dealt only with the symptoms —overcrowding, one-roomed living, poorly constructed houses, high density living—rather than the disease of poverty itself. The medical officer for Hampstead argued that at the root of the housing problem was the overwhelming fact that London was inhabited by a majority of people divided by just one or two weeks' wages from starvation, while the medical officer for Bethnal Green flatly stated that since 98 per cent of all the overcrowding cases that came to his notice were caused by 'poverty and the inability to pay the rent', 'overcrowding, with all its attendant evils, is a poverty problem, nothing more nor less'.[107] Sir John Simon, who had devoted the better part of his life to improving the living conditions of London's working classes, sadly concluded that the problem of better 'house accommodation of the poorer labouring classes' was largely a question of 'how far poverty can be turned into non-poverty, *how far the poor can be made less poor*'.[108] *The Times* argued that 'the housing of the great mass of workers in London, is a question, we say, of wages . . .'—an analysis with which Sir J. P. Dickson-Poynder, the chairman of the LCC's Housing of the Working Classes Committee concurred : 'The Housing problem', he wrote, 'indeed may be said to be the sum and total of all the social and economic problems which await solution', for, he felt that at bottom, 'it provokes the vexed question of the relation between rent and wages, which easily slides into that of capital and labour'.[109]

From the 1850s down to the beginning of the 1880s great trust was put in the ability of the model dwelling companies, such as the Metropolitan Association for Improving the Dwellings of the Industrious Classes or the Improved Industrial Dwellings Company, and in public trusts, such as the Peabody Trust, to provide inexpensive blocks of model dwellings for those who could not afford other forms of workmen's houses in central London. These companies, operating on a low (3 per cent to 5 per cent) return from capital invested, and building very often on land cleared of slums by the Metropolitan Board of Works and sold below full market cost to them, did in fact manage to combine a high standard of living accommodation with rents that were certainly within reach of many artisans. But by 1875 they had housed less than 33,000 people; and at the end of our period, despite the energetic building of the Peabody, Guinness, and Lewis Trusts throughout central London, they had still provided less than a 100,000 rooms, or little more than enough room to absorb two years' addition to the population.[110] In certain areas of London, especially in Westminster and the East End, the model dwellings did have a great impact, and the 'five per cent' philanthropic societies and trusts were virtually the only large-scale builders of dwellings for the working men in these areas. In East Finsbury, for example, at the turn of the century, one-fifth of the population resided in blocks erected by model dwelling companies.[111]

Despite much controversy on the subject, there can be little doubt that the majority of the inhabitants of the model dwelling blocks tended to come from the artisans rather than the labourer class, though far more labouring men were living in the model dwellings by the end of the century than has commonly been supposed.[112] The critics of the Peabody Trust, for example, maintained that only the better paid labourers and artisans could afford to live in the Peabody buildings. Using Charles Booth's poverty line figure of 21s a week (1887) as a guide line, the average wages of Peabody tenants (heads of families only) was: £1 3s 10d (1881); £1 3s 8d (1885); £1 4s 0d (1891).[113] The bulk of the Trust's flats were let out to families whose heads were earning between 20s and 23s per week, or between 25s and 30s per week. By 1891 the average rent paid in the Peabody buildings throughout London was approximately 4s 9d per week. The vast majority of the Peabody tenements were let as two- or three-room flats, and the scarcity of one-roomed flats, coupled to the strict prohibition against subletting, effectively kept out the lower paid workers. In 1885, out of 9,600 rooms, only 692 were single-room flats.[114] The Sutton Estate, in Old St, Shoreditch, placed a wage limit on the heads of families living in its blocks of : 20s per week wages, for one-roomed tenements (3s–3s 6d rent per week); 25s per week for two-roomed tenements (5s 6d–6s 6d per week); 30s per week for three-roomed tenements (7s 6d–8s 6d per week), and an upper wage limit of 35s per week for occupants of four-roomed flats (10s per week).[115] As much as the rents, the conditions of tenancy tended to prevent the very poor and casual labourers taking advantage of the model dwellings. Prohibitions against subletting, the taking in of washing, and the storage of tools were suffi-

cient to frighten away the casual poor.[116] By 1890 it was quite clear
that the activities of philanthropic capitalism, whether on the part
of great companies and trusts, or on the part of individuals, like
Octavia Hill,[117] had failed to reach sufficient working men, or indeed,
the workmen most in need of special assistance. The judgment and
forecast of the Charity Organisation Society in 1881 were both
correct :

> The amount of remedial work in the direction of housing the labouring
> poor in London performed by philanthropic or associated commercial
> enterprise, useful as it undoubtedly is, continues . . . relatively insigni-
> ficant and wholly inadequate in proportion to the needs of the
> population, nor is there reason to expect a large development in this
> direction in the future.[118]

Faced with the failure of philanthropic capitalism to provide an
adequate number of low cost dwellings for the working men in central
London, the LCC, which, from its formation in 1889 had energeti-
cally built large blocks to rehouse those evicted by its slum clearance
schemes,[119] was forced to consider a policy of housing (as distinct
from rehousing) for the working classes. After ten years of energetic
slum clearance and rehousing, the LCC, somewhat reluctantly,
decided to become both builder and landlord; at the same time (in
1900), the metropolitan borough councils were given the power to
build completely new housing for the working classes in addition to
the power they already enjoyed to rehouse those evicted by their slum
clearance schemes.[120] Subsidised housing was still officially frowned
upon, both by the LCC, and the borough councils, and no housing
scheme could be entertained which placed a burden upon the rates.
In fact, both the LCC and the borough councils discovered that
given the terms of loans from the Government, the cost of building,
and the need to reach the labourers as well as better-paid artisans,
it was almost impossible to build in central London without making
a charge on the rates, and usually the amount of the subsidy was
disguised by writing down the real value of the land on which the
houses were erected. For much of the period from 1900 to 1914
the energies of housing reformers were directed towards bringing
down the rates of interest and extending the length of period for the
repayment of the loans to the Public Works Loans Commission.[121]

Though handicapped by the need to repay over a relatively short
period money borrowed from the government, and handicapped also
by widespread popular opposition to municipal socialism in housing,

both the LCC, and the metropolitan borough councils provided a remarkable number of high-quality workmen's dwellings throughout London. By the beginning of the war, the LCC had provided 3,883 dwellings, and eleven borough councils had erected a total of 1,682 dwellings : this is in addition to the provision of 5,610 dwellings by the LCC, and 797 dwellings by the borough councils for rehousing purposes.[122] Thus up to 1914, the LCC and the borough councils had provided (if we include conversions also) over 12,000 dwellings : between 1902 and 1913, the LCC provided 18,000 rooms and the borough councils another 8,000.[123] By 1913 over 55,000 people were living in LCC accommodation : an impressive total for just twenty-five years' work, the first ten of which were devoted mainly to slum clearance.[124]

Over 90 per cent of the LCC rooms provided for those evicted under slum clearance schemes were in blocks, while almost all the other accommodation provided was in cottages, and almost 40 per cent of these cottages were erected outside the County of London. Rents for a four-roomed cottage, built and maintained by the LCC varied from 6s 1d to 8s 11d; rents for a three-roomed LCC flat varied in 1914 from 6s 7½d to 12s 3d.[125] Typical rents charged by the borough councils in central London were, to take the example of Bermondsey, one room (with separate scullery and wc) for 3s 6d, two rooms for 5s 6d to 6s, and three rooms for 7s 6d to 8s per week in 1906.[126] Hammersmith borough council charged from 6s 6d to 7s for its three-roomed tenements in 1904, and from 8s 6d to 9s for its four-roomed flats; in Westminster in the same year, the borough council was providing excellent flats at rents which ranged from 3s for a single room to 12s 6d for four rooms (two rooms cost from 6s to 7s, and three rooms from 8s 6d to 9s 6d).[127]

Like the model dwelling companies before them, the municipal authorities in London found it extremely difficult to provide housing for the more poorly paid labouring class. A combination of the rents and extremely rigid rules and scarcity of single-roomed dwellings tended to put these dwellings beyond the reach of the casually employed or unskilled labourer. Nevertheless the contribution which the municipal authorities made is considerable. Although without exception these bodies accepted the lowest bids on their tenders, their dwellings were generally soundly constructed, often aesthetically pleasing, and certainly beyond minimum standards. Included in the rents would often be electric lighting, modern cooking appliances, washing and drying rooms, window blinds, fitted cupboards, dressers, plate racks, storage areas, and, above all, hot water.[128] They set an example to private builders and often inspired the working classes to higher standards. To many thousands of families, who were prepared to accept rigid and often tedious regulations, council housing represented a great step upwards from the filth, and often despair, of their former habitations. Somewhat ironically, perhaps, one Independent Labour Party representative argued that council housing enabled the working classes to live in a controlled environment, whereas in the houses owned by private landlords, 'the dirtiest and cleanest people . . . were compelled to live next door to each other'.[129] Above all, the LCC, and to a lesser extent the borough councils, continued the work of the model dwelling companies and trusts in proving that high density living need not be harmful to health and morals.

By 1914 municipal socialism in the provision of housing for the working classes had obviously made its mark, and the fear of political bodies playing the role of builder and landlord had weakened considerably. But in 1914 the LCC and the borough councils had just started to scratch the surface. It is perhaps significant that in the LCC's four great suburban housing estates (Norbury, Totterdown Fields, White Hart Lane, and Old Oak), over one-third of the 2,531 families had moved in from *outside* the County of London, and that while the LCC's prime objective had been to relieve overcrowding in the centre, it was, by 1914, performing the function of easing the pressure upon housing accommodation in the outskirts.[130] In the centre, the provision of houses by private enterprise had slowly ground to a halt by 1914, and the borough councils were taking stock of the cost to the rates of their housing experiments. When the war broke out in 1914, only Holborn and Shoreditch had fresh housing schemes afoot.[131] In the suburbs, high land prices, increased demand for housing, and rapidly increasing population density were beginning to have their effect.

Fulham, which in 1861 had had about 2,500 houses for a population of 15,500 had, forty years later, almost 20,000 houses for its population of 137,000, and, by the turn of the century the medical officer was complaining of impossibly high rents, badly located speculative building, and, with only nineteen acres of vacant land suitable for building sites left, and that fetching £2,500 per acre, he held out little hope for the future.[132] As the rows upon rows of badly constructed, jerry-built suburban houses began their inevitable decline, the pattern of London's housing problem began to repeat itself in the suburbs, while not yet solved in the centre. Despite the enormous amount of private building, the provision of houses for the working classes in the rapidly growing suburbs had proved feasible only when cheap land for speculative building existed, and substandard building could escape the notice of authorities. By 1914, cheap vacant land in the suburbs was no longer so freely available, and the authorities along the periphery of Greater London were no longer so tolerant of the methods of the jerry-builder.

As World War I commenced, it was clear that London's housing needs had not yet been met. While the well paid artisan, thanks to his increased mobility and shorter hours, could achieve a reasonable degree of comfort in his suburban house, the casual labourer was in need of cheaper housing than the municipal authorities had yet provided. The Great War simply delayed the inevitable demand for direct treasury grants to municipal authorities, for more completely subsidised housing, for municipal housing projects on a larger scale, for rent controls, minimum wage guarantees, and broader pension and insurance schemes. Perhaps the lesson of the past century was that no housing policy could be successful, unless it could be backed up, either by unprecedented general prosperity or by a full programme of social welfare benefits.

NOTES

1　The housing question was intimately connected to broader problems. In the words of the chairman of the London County Council's Housing of the Working Classes Committee: 'The Housing problem indeed may be said to be the sum-total of all the social and economic problems which await solution. It embraces the land question . . . local taxation, valuation, and rating . . . transit and locomotion.' Sir J. P. Dickson-Poynder, *The Housing Question* (London, 1908), 1.

2　For a description of this growth south of the river see: E. M. Rolfe, *The Growth of South-East London, 1836–1914, with Special Reference to the Development of Communications;* London University, PhD thesis (1968). See also, M. L. Moore, *A Century's Extension of Passenger Transport Facilities (1830–1930) Within the Present London Transport Board's Area and its relation to Population Spread.* London University, PhD (1948).

3　By Greater London is meant the Administrative County of London and the adjacent suburbs (urban districts, rural districts and municipal boroughs).

4   Quoted in D. Mayne, *The Growth of London* (London, 1952), 101.

5   A. Mearns, *London and its Teeming Toilers, Who they are and How they Live* (London, 1885), 3.

6   LCC, *London Statistics,* XXXIX (1934–6), 27.

7   *Ibid,* XXXI (1925–6), 24–5.

8   J. Hollingshead, *Ragged London in 1861* (London, 1861), 118.

9   W. Vere Hole, *The Housing of the Working Classes in Britain, 1850–1914. A Study of the Development of Standards and Methods of Provision.* London University, PhD (1965), 212.

10 LCC, *Minutes of Proceedings* (1913), Vol. I, 654. Similarly, of the inhabitants evicted in Chelsea by the Cadogan and Hans Place Estates in the early twentieth century, over 30 per cent were dependent upon work in the immediate area: LCC, *Housing*/General/2/2, item 69. The men most affected were coachmen, housekeepers, cabmen, busmen, carmen, milk carriers, charwomen, postmen, policemen, packers, porters, and servants.

11 *PP,* 7 (1882), *Minutes of Evidence,* 'Select Committee on Artisans' and Labourers' Dwellings', 128. For similar statements see: A. S. Wohl, *The Housing of the Artisans and Labourers in Nineteenth Century London, 1815–1914,* Brown University, PhD (1966), 415ff.

12 H. J. Dyos, 'The Slums of Victorian London', *Victorian Studies,* XI, No. 1 (Sept 1967), 34. Many of those whose earnings were casual corresponded to Charles Booth's Class B. 'In Class B, we have the crux of the social problem. Every other class takes care of itself, or could do so if Class B were out of the way. These unfortunate people form a quagmire underlying the social structure, and to remove this quagmire must be our principal aim.' Charles Booth, *Life and Labour of the People of London, Poverty Series I* (1903–4), 176.

13 While the London working classes were remarkably mobile over short distances (often moving from house to house within a neighbourhood every two or so years), they were much less mobile over greater distances. Historians have not paid sufficient attention to the sense of local community in London and its effect upon working-class mobility. Booth, for example, noticed that recent immigrants to London were much more willing to move to the characterless suburbs than were old-time residents of the central districts.

14 It has been estimated that between 1853 and 1885 56,000 people were evicted by demolition work under fifty-one separate railway schemes in London: the intensity of railway construction caused great havoc. Between 1859 and 1867 alone, 37,000 displacements occurred. H. J. Dyos, 'Railways and Housing in Victorian London, Pt I', *Journal of Transport History,* II, No 1 (May 1955), 13, 14.

15 For a discussion of this see William Gilbert, *The City* (London, 1877).

16 Even Simon called for the amputation of diseased and congested areas; see, R. Lambert, *Sir John Simon, 1816–1904* (London, 1963), 9. Of the railways, *The Times* wrote in 1861: 'We accept the railways with their consequences and we don't think the worse of them for ventilating the City of London . . . You can never make these wretched alleys

really inhabitable, do what you will, but bring a railway to them and the whole problem is solved.' Quoted in H. J. Dyos, 'Railways and Housing in Victorian London, Pt. II', *Journal of Transport History*, II, No 1 (May 1955), 95.

17 Percy Edwards, *London Street Improvements* (London, 1898), 136–7. The Metropolitan Board of Works began extensive street building and improvements in 1857, but not until the Bethnal Green Road Improvement Scheme, finished in 1879, did the Board begin to rehouse some of the working classes displaced. In all, it rehoused 10,340 members of the working classes, but this represented a small fraction of the number displaced by the creation of 3,000 new streets.

18 LCC, *London Statistics*, XXV (1914–15), 164, 165.

19 The Cross Act was amended in 1879 to reduce compensation paid to owners to the level of the market value of the condemned house; the amendments also simplified procedure, and permitted the Metropolitan Board of Works to rehouse outside the area cleared. For a discussion of the workings of the act see A. S. Wohl, 197ff. The Metropolitan Board of Works generally sold the cleared land to the Peabody Trust, which took care of the rehousing.

20 Rev A. Osborne Jay, *A Story of Shoreditch: Being a Sequel to 'Life in Darkest London'* (London, 1896), 11. Jay, Vicar of Holy Trinity, Shoreditch, was the model for the vicar in Arthur Morrison's *A Child of the Jago*. George Godwin, the editor of the *Builder*, and a man deeply interested in working-class housing, condemned the so-called 'improvements': 'our new street-makers when they are asked where the displaced occupants of the garrets and cellars are to go, shout without thought:—"go to?—Anywhere." ' G. Godwin, *Town Swamps and Social Bridges* (London, 1859), 2–3.

21 The 1855 Nuisance Removal Act, section 28 read: 'When a Medical Officer or two medical practitioners shall certify that a house is so overcrowded as to become dangerous to the health of the inhabitants, and the inhabitants shall consist of more than one family, the local authority shall cause proceedings to be taken before the justices to abate such overcrowding, and the person permitting it shall be fined.' The 1866 Sanitary Act, clause 35, allowed local authorities to draw up byelaws, providing, among other things, for the fixing of the number of persons who could occupy houses let in lodgings. In both acts overcrowding within a single family was not declared illegal.

22 Vestry of St James and St John, Clerkenwell, *Seventh Annual Report (1862–3) of the Medical Officer of Health*, 15.

23 *Transactions of the Society of Medical Officers of Health* (Session 1883–4), 36, 37.

24 *Ibid,* 32; *Dwellings of the Poor*, Report of the Dwellings Committee of the Charity Organisation Society (London, 1881), 141.

25 The seven districts were: St George's, Hanover Square; Stepney; Westminster; Strand; City of London; Marylebone; St Giles'. Price Williams, 'The population of London, 1801–1881', *Journal of the Statistical Society of London*, XLVIII (Sept 1885), 388–96. It was

estimated that between 1851 and 1881 only 181,983 houses were built for a population which had increased by 1,466,956. (LCC, *London Statistics*, XII (1901–02)), x. Representative increases in person-to-house density between 1851 and 1881 are: Islington from 7·05 to 8·31; Hackney from 5·95 to 6·79; Shoreditch from 7·12 to 8·35, and Bethnal Green from 6·78 to 7·65. *Ibid.* These figures should be used with great caution, for not only was the definition of a 'house' most vague, but desire on the part of both landlord and tenant to underestimate the numbers occupying a dwelling mingled with genuine ignorance about the exact numbers to produce most unreliable figures. In the absence of any coherent system of night-time inspection, it is extremely difficult to get accurate figures for person-to-house density, and the figures quoted in the text are used only to show an unmistakable trend.

26   St James, Westminster, *Report of the Proceedings of the Committee of Health and Sanitary Improvement upon the Inquiries made by the Visitors as to the Sanitary Condition of Certain Poor Districts of the Parish* (London, 1848), 10–11.

27   See: H. J. Dyos, 'The Slums of Victorian London', *Victorian Studies*, Vol XI, No 1 (Sept 1967), 5, and also Francis M. Jones, 'The Aesthetic of the Nineteenth Century Industrial Town', in H. J. Dyos, ed, *The Study of Urban History* (London, 1968), 173.

28   J. Hollingshead, *op cit*, 119.

29   The Royal Commission on the Housing of the Working Classes (1884–5) brought to light for the first time for the general public, the extent of one-roomed living. But medical officers had long dwelt upon the moral and physical ills of the one-roomed tenement. Writing in 1842, John Liddle, the medical officer for Whitechapel, stated that 'Nearly the whole of the labouring population there [in Whitechapel and Aldgate] have only one room.' John Liddle, *Sanitary Report (Supplement) for Whitechapel* (1842), 2. The effect of overcrowding upon one-roomed living horrified medical and sanitary inspectors, but when there was a death in the family conditions became even more intolerable. Liddle expressed horror at the 'degree of indifference to the presence of the corpse: the family is found eating and drinking and pursuing their usual callings, and the children playing', *ibid*, 2.

30   J. Hollingshead, *op cit*, 14; see also: *Household Words*, Vol 1, No 13 (22 June 1850), 297.

31   The sanitary condition of London is excellently described, and the improvement in facilities well analysed, in H. Jephson, *The Sanitary Evolution of London* (London, 1907).

32   St James and St John, Clerkenwell, *Twenty-Eighth Annual Report of the Medical Officer* (1883), 14–15.

33   Dorothy George, in her *London Life in the Eighteenth Century* (NY, 1965), mentions the difficulty in trying to gauge the reasons for the change in working-class habits; see 104ff.

34   Hammersmith Borough Council (*Annual Reports*, I, 1901, 277) carried out about 3,000 house inspections each year. This was by no means

exceptional. See Hampstead Borough Council, *Report for 1901*, 91; St Giles', Clerkenwell, *Report of the Vestry* (1859–60), 18; Clerkenwell Borough Council, *Sixth Annual Report* (Medical Officer of Health's report), XXXV. As important as the number of inspections, was the number of inspectors. At one end of the scale, at the end of the nineteenth century, stood the Strand, with one inspector for every 358 inhabited houses and every 4,187 inhabitants (other examples are : the City, one inspector for every 578 inhabited houses and 3,750 inhabitants, and St Martin-in-the-Fields, one inspector for every 738 inhabited houses and 7,308 inhabitants), and, at the other end of the scale, Paddington, with one inspector for every 4,849 inhabited houses, and 39,282 inhabitants, Lambeth, one inspector for every 4,819 inhabited houses and 34,400 inhabitants, and Mile End, one inspector for every 4,689 inhabited houses and 35,864 inhabitants. See: LCC, *Annual Reports of the Medical Officer of Health* (1894), Appendix x.

35   Section 35 of the 1866 Sanitary Act permitted local sanitary authorities to place houses let in lodgings to more than one family on a register, but not until the Public Health (London) Act of 1891 (section 94) was it made compulsory. In 1884 the Royal Commission on the Housing of the Working Classes discovered that only Chelsea and Hackney were employing the 1866 Act vigorously, and in 1889, after considerable agitation, still only half the local London authorities were taking advantage of the Act. By 1908 the number of houses let in lodgings placed on local registers and controlled by local byelaws varied from Hammersmith, with 3,352 houses and Stepney with 2,805 to Lewisham with only fifteen and Greenwich with twenty-three. See: LCC, *Annual Report of the Medical Officer of Health* (1908), tables, 68, 69.

36   See footnote 34 above. Earlier in the century the number of inhabitants to each inspector was very much greater. In 1884 Mile End had only one inspector for every 105,000 people. In 1885 there were only 103 inspectors in the Metropolis, an average of one inspector for every 40,000 people. See: *PP* 30 (1884–5), Royal Commission on the Housing of the Working Classes, *Minutes of Evidence*, 16, and Sir G. Gibbon and R. Bell, *History of the LCC, 1889–1939* (London, 1939), 59.

37   Generally of course the increase in rents more than compensated the landlord for the cost of enforced improvements. But occasionally high rents could lead to improvements rather than the other way round. The medical officer of health for Chelsea considered that 'the high rents now almost universally obtainable for working-class accommodation not only render improved sanitation possible, but also make it remunerative', Chelsea, *Forty-Fourth Annual Report of the Parish, 1899–1900*, 111.

38   *Mansion House Council on the Dwellings of the Poor, Annual Report for the Year ending 1897*, 5. In the 1890s the Council was making over 10,000 annual inspections in London and dealing with over 7,000 houses each year.

39   *PP*, 30 (1884–5), 30, 'Royal Commission on the Housing of the Working

Classes, *First Report*, 16 and 11. The extent of overcrowding was recognised by medical officers and others in contact with the poor, well before the 1880s. In 1860, for example, a contributor to the *Quarterly Review* could argue : 'The philanthropist must never forget that it is more urgent to multiply the dwellings of the poor even than to improve them. Overcrowding would turn a Paradise into a "rookery" and a palace into a "den".' R. H. Cheney, 'The Missing Link and the London Poor', *Quarterly Review*, No CCXV (July 1860), 2.

40   Night inspections smacked of police interference and 'continental despotism'. Only after the pubs closed could the extent of overcrowding really be judged, but the poor were masters at hiding the true extent of the subletting by which they were able to afford their apartments.

41   LCC, *London Statistics*, XII (1901–2), x.

42   *Ibid,* The second highest figure of the century was 1901, when the density was 7·89 persons per house.

43   *Ibid,* 117, table ii.

44   LCC, *Annual Reports of the Medical Officer of Health* (1912), 65.

45   These figures are derived from comparing the statistics contained in LCC, *London Statistics*, XII (1901–02), 111 and *ibid*, XXIV (1913–14), 111.

46   *Ibid*, XII (1901–02), 116. Sanitary sub-districts which experienced an increase in overcrowding between 1891 and 1901 were : Mile End Old Town, St George-in-the-East, and Whitechapel. LCC, *Annual Report of the Medical Officer of Health* (1902), 5–10.

47   LCC, *Annual Report of the Council*, (1912) III, Appendix ii, iv–vi. In addition to these eight boroughs, the City of London witnessed a decrease in overcrowding. *Ibid*, V.

48   *Housing Journal*, 96 (October, 1913).

49   *PP*, 30 (1884–5), Royal Commission on the Housing of the Working Classes, *First Report*, 21.

50   In 1884 it was pointed out in Parliament that 'Since 1844 wages had risen, the taxes in necessaries had been lowered, and the ability of working men to obtain better accommodation had increased. But while that ability had increased, the rents of houses had also risen. Since 1844 house rent had increased by 150 per cent, and consequently, while the condition of the working classes had improved in all other respects, the state of their dwellings had not undergone a corresponding improvement.' Quoted in the *Pall Mall Gazette* (5 March 1884).

51   The great influx of Jewish immigrants into the East End in the last two decades of the nineteenth century certainly exacerbated the housing problem, and led to a great deal of anti-alien feeling. For a discussion of this, and for the introduction of key-money, see Wohl, 450ff.

52   See the survey carried out by the *Pall Mall Gazette* (5 Feb 1884). For typical rents in London see below.

53   Mrs Pember Reeves, *Round About a Pound a Week* (London, 1914), 35, 24.

54   *Housing Journal*, No 51 (January, 1905). These figures should be compared to the movement of real wages (excluding rents) in the late

nineteenth century: using a base figure of 100 in 1900, the real wages of artisans in London were: 1880, 77·4; 1885, 86·7; 1890, 93·4; and 1895, 101·6. See: R. Tucker, 'Real Wages of Artisans in London, 1729–1935', *Journal of the American Statistical Association*, XXXI (March, 1936), 80.

55 Kensington Borough Council, *Minutes of the Council*, V (1904–5) 22 November 1904, 6. Hackney Borough Council argued that in view of the recent rent rises the provisions of the Irish Land Act should apply to London.

56 *Transactions of the Society of Medical Officers of Health* (1883–4), 39. In 1899 *Justice*, the organ of the SDF, wrote in disgust: 'The "ideal slum dweller", . . . burning with revolt against the social conditions which oppress him is nothing but a "fabric of unfact" '; see: *Justice* (2 December 1899).

57 These figures are taken from, J. King Warry, 'On the Housing of the Working Classes in Hackney', *Public Health*, XIII, No 10 (July, 1901), 677. Norman Dearle in his *Problems of Unemployment in the London Building Trades* (London, 1908), 27, estimated that although the numbers employed in the London building trades rose by 20 per cent between 1860 and 1870, wages in a similar period rose 50 per cent. In the estimation of the LCC, the rapid increase in costs was largely responsible for the lag in working-class house-building in the centre of London. LCC, *Minutes of Proceedings* (1898), 1258. Between 1890 and 1899, alone, the cost of iron and steel increased by 20 per cent, and labourers' wages by 27 per cent. LCC, *The Housing Question in London*, 52–3.

58 A. Bowley, *Wages and Income since 1860* (London, 1951), 10ff.

59 Fulham Borough Council, *Annual Reports* (1900–01), 50. See footnote 57 above.

60 In 1902, for example, Chelsea Borough Council was able to buy land for working-class housing projects from Lord Cadogan at a special rate of £12,500, for 1·614 acres. The Borough Surveyor valued the land at £20,000. See Louis C. Parkes, *Description of the Work Carried Out by the Borough Council for the Housing of the Working Classes* (Author's Manuscript, Chelsea Public Library), 2.

61 J. N. Tarn, *Housing in Urban Areas, 1840–1914*, Cambridge University PhD (1961), 75ff.

62 O. Fleming, *Working Class Dwellings: the Rebuilding of the Boundary Street Estate* (London, 1900), 6, 7.

63 See the discussion below, 38ff.

64 L. Fisher, *Economic Journal*, XV (March, 1905), 27.

65 *City Press* (3 October 1857).

66 See *ibid* in the correspondence columns.

67 *The Times* (2 March 1861), quoted in H. J. Dyos, *Journal of Transport History*, II, No I (May 1955), 14.

68 H. J. Dyos, 'Workmen's Fares in South London, 1860–1914', *ibid*, I, No I, (May 1953), 8.

69 See Dyos' articles for a discussion of this. One of the inconveniences

D

of the early workmen's trains was that they arrived at the London termini too early, especially in winter, when many jobs—such as outdoor construction—began at a later hour.

70 This association was intimately linked with the National Workmen's Housing Council and had a powerful voice in the TUC. It felt that workmen's trains ought to be provided on all main lines up to 8 a.m., and that in order to help those workmen whose working hours did not fall within the statutory times for workmen's trains, the companies should issue third-class season tickets with reductions comparable to those of first- and second-class season tickets.

71 See: LCC, Public Health and Housing Committee, *Housing Development and Workmen's Fares* (London, 1913), appendix 4, 19; LCC, *Housing After the War,* Report of the Housing of the Working Classes Committee (London, 1918), 30; LCC, *Housing,* General, 32, pp 34ff.

72 Quoted by H. Pollins, 'Transport Lines and Social Divisions', R. Glass (ed), *London. Aspects of Change* (London, 1964), 43.

73 International Housing Congress, *Report of the VIIIième Congrès International Des Habitations à Bon Marché* (London, 1907), 33.

74 Other factors at work in the development of any particular working-class suburb are: shopping facilities, local industry, work opportunities for youths and women; of course, suburban growth was the product not just of a flow out from the centre but also immigration from outside the Greater London area.

75 *Household Words,* Vol V (1852), 69, 71.

76 See next footnote.

77 For an excellent analysis of the development of the suburbs and the provision of workmen's houses see: LCC, Public Health and Housing Committee, *Housing Development and Workmen's Fares,* especially the appendices. For an interesting comment on the connection between suburban growth and railway communications, see: E. Gwynn, 'The Jerry Builder considered in relation to the Housing of the Poor', *Public Health,* Vol XIII, No 4 (Jan 1901), 252.

78 By 1901, for example, Camberwell had grown to a population of 260,000, and had local industries including: tarpaulins, linoleum, Venetian blinds, leather goods, sacks, bottles, vinegar, sauces, mineral waters, building trades, road services, market gardening, tailoring, shoemaking and many more. See Dyos, *Victorian Suburb. A Study of the Growth of Camberwell* (Leicester, 1961), 55, 62.

79 LCC, *Minutes of the Proceedings of the Council* (1898), 1258.

80 *Ibid.* It is significant that he adds: 'The aggregation of so vast a population of one class in one locality in this way seems likely to be productive of social danger, the best means of avoiding which is to be found in the provision of equivalent travelling facilities for the working classes in other directions.'

81 134,314 rooms out of 381,000 rooms suitable for working-class occupancy. See: Public Record Office, Housing and Local Government, *HLG,* I, 14,676 31/03.

82 LCC, *Minutes of Proceedings of the Council* (1898), 1437.

83 *Ibid* (1900), 468.

84 LCC Public Health and Housing Committee, *Housing Development and Workmen's Fares*, 6.

85 LCC, *Housing After the War*, 32. The importance of good transport facilities may be judged by the areas chosen by the Artisans', Labourers' and General Dwellings Co for its suburban estates. Shaftesbury Park was in South London, near Clapham Junction, Queen's Park was in North-west London, along the Harrow Road and near Westbourne Park station; and Noel Park was in North-east London, near the Hornsey Station of the Great Northern.

86 LCC, *London Statistics*, XI (1900–1901), 384ff.

87 *The Great Problem of our Great Towns* (London, nd).

88 *Housing Journal*, No 15 (October 1901). This was Steadman's statement to the Swansea TUC in 1901.

89 LCC, *Minutes of the Proceedings of the Council* (1898), 1437.

90 *PP*, 7 (1881), 'Select Committee on Artisans' and Labourers' Dwellings Improvement', *Minutes of Evidence*, 141. Gatliff, of the Metropolitan Association for Improving the Dwellings of the Industrious Classes (the oldest of the model dwelling companies) told the Select Committee that the provision by speculative builders of two-family houses in Tottenham let at 8s per week was providing sufficient accommodation to make the work of the model dwelling companies considerably less valuable.

91 Finsbury Borough Council, *Annual Reports*, 1907, 107; *The Dwellings of the Poor*, Annual Report of the Mansion House Council for the Year ending 1907, 26.

92 International Housing Congress, *Report of the VIIIième* . . . , 33.

93 R. Wall, *A History of the Development of Walthamstow, 1851–1901*, London University PhD (1968), 240; Willesden Local Board, *Sanitary Report for the Year* (1893), 1914.

94 *Lancet* (21 November 1874), 739; *ibid* (2 May 1874), 624.

95 Tottenham. *Tottenham's Health*, the Annual Report of the Medical Officer of Health (1950), Appendix, 22. For an amusing attack upon the jerry-builder see *Household Words* (22 Feb 1851), 513, where the houses built by 'Mr Roomy, the builder, of Lumbago Place' are attacked. In the eyes of one Congregational minister, jerry-builders were among the predestined damned and should be driven from church. *Pall Mall Gazette* (9 April 1884).

96 *The Star* (19 May 1888).

97 E. Gwynn, *Public Health*, Vol XIII, No 4 (January, 1901), 248–51.

98 *Ibid*, 251. One must agree with J. M. Mackintosh, who concludes in his *Trends of Opinion About the Public Health* (London, 1953), 103, that 'Before the First World War house-building kept pace with the demand only so long as the private builder was permitted to put up sub-standard houses.'

99 Dyos, *Journal of Transport History*, No I, Vol I (May 1953), 18.

100 LCC, Public Health and Housing Committee, *Housing Development and Workmen's Fares*, Appendix 2, 17.

101 F. W. Lawrence, 'The Housing Problem', *The Heart of Empire*, 80.

102   The Rev Andrew Mearns, 'The Outcast Poor. II.—Outcast London', *Contemporary Review*, XLIV (December 1883), 924.

103   C. Booth, *Life and Labour*, Vol 11, Poverty Series, 25, 26, 29. See also his Presidential address before the Statistical Society of London, *Journal of the Statistical Society of London*, Vol 56 (Dec 1893), 566.

104   See footnote 105 below.

105   In Hampstead, a special inspection of houses in 1901, conducted by the Borough Council, showed that there was an equal number of working-class living in two-roomed flats (6s 6d pw), and three-roomed flats (8s 6d pw); about half as numerous were families occupying one-roomed flats (3s 6d pw), and four-roomed flats (10s 6d pw). Hampstead Borough Council, *Report for the Year 1902*, 48.

106   For a discussion of this and the development of a housing reform agitation see: A. S. Wohl, 'The Bitter Cry of Outcast London', *International Review of Social History*, Vol XIII (1968), Part 2.

107   Bethnal Green, *Tenth Annual Report of the Medical Officer of Health for Bethnal Green*, 7.

108   Sir J. Simon, *English Sanitary Institutions* (London, 1890), 444.

109   *The Times* (26 Nov 1883); Sir J. P. Dickson-Poynder, 2.

110   C. Gatliff, 'On Improved Dwellings and their Beneficial Effect on Health and Morals with Suggestions for their Extension', *Journal of the Statistical Society of London*, XXXVIII (March, 1875), 34–5. See also: LCC, *London Statistics*, Vol XII (1901–02), table II, 117.

111   Finsbury Borough Council, *Annual Report of the Medical Officer of Health* (1901), 140. Of the model dwelling companies operating in the area by far the largest was the Peabody Trust, which housed well over 4,000 people. In Whitechapel alone, in 1891, there were over 3,000 model dwelling flats, housing over 12,000 people: Whitechapel, *Annual Report on the Sanitary Condition of the Whitechapel District, 1891*, 16.

112   See Wohl, *The Housing of the Artisans and Labourers . . .*, chapter 6.

113   See: *PP* 7 (1881), Select Committee on Artisans' and Labourers' Dwellings Improvement, *Minutes of Evidence*, 126; *PP*, 30 (1884–5), Royal Commission on the Housing of the Working Classes, *Minutes of Evidence*, 126; Newsholme, *Journal of the Statistical Society of London*, LIV (March, 1891), 90.

114   *PP* 30 (1884–5). Royal Commission on the Housing of the Working Classes, *Minutes of Evidence*, 401. In 1885 the Peabody Trust numbered among its occupants: 'charwomen, monthly nurses, basket makers, butchers, carpenters, firemen, labourers, porters, omnibus drivers, sempstresses, shoemakers, tailors, waiters, warehousemen, watch finishers, turners, staymakers, smiths, sawyers, printers, painters, laundresses, letter-carriers, artificial flower-makers, dressmakers, carmen, cabinet makers, bookbinders, and others . . .', *Ibid*.

115   Shoreditch Borough Council, *Municipal Reports*, Vol LV (1910–11), 'Report of the Medical Officer of Health', 143.

116   The conditions of tenancy of the St Marylebone Borough Council

dwellings in John St may be cited as typical: rent had to be paid in advance, subletting was prohibited, stairs and landings had to be swept daily and washed every Saturday by the tenants in turn in the order directed by the caretaker, tenants had to wash the floors of their flats once a week, no washing could be hung from the windows, carpets had to be beaten before 10 a.m., windows had to be washed once a fortnight, lights in the staircases had to be turned out at 11 pm (12 on Saturdays), no prams or bikes were allowed in the stairways, and no pets were permitted. See St Marylebone Borough Council, *Minutes*, Vol V (1904–5), 79.

117 Octavia Hill was the most famous housing reformer of the mid- and late-Victorian period. The best biography of Octavia Hill is W. Hill, *Octavia Hill: Pioneer of the National Trust and Housing Reformer* (London, 1956); see also Wohl, *The Housing of Artisans and Labourers . . .* , chapter 5.

118 Charity Organisation Society, *Dwellings of the Poor*, 138.

119 The most famous of the slum clearance schemes was the Boundary Street Scheme in the East End. It involved the clearance of over 700 blocks of dwellings, the vast majority of them working class, the clearance of fifteen acres, and the displacement of 6,000 people. For a short discussion of the work of the LCC in this and other schemes, see: A. S. Wohl, *ibid*, chapter 14.

120 In 1900 the metropolitan borough councils were given permission to employ part three of the 1890 Housing Act, which permitted municipal authorities (in the case of London this had, previous to 1900, referred to the LCC alone) to build houses for the working classes. Most of the borough councils formally adopted the Act, but only eleven took advantage of it: the most energetic were Chelsea, Battersea, Westminster, and Camberwell.

121 Local authorities borrowing from the Public Loans Commissioners had to pay a rate of interest of 3¾ per cent for thirty year loans, 4 per cent for loans over forty years and four and a quarter per cent for over fifty years. In the 1903 Housing of the Working Classes Act the reformers, after years of agitation, achieved a partial victory when the period for loans was extended to fifty years. The LCC and metropolitan borough councils complained bitterly about the terms of government loans, and argued that they were the cause of their reluctance to engage upon large-scale housing schemes. The Workmen's National Housing Council sponsored legislation in Parliament, generally through its president, W. C. Steadman, from 1900 to 1914, with the view of bringing down the rate of interest to two per cent over 100 years. By 1912 demands for direct treasury grants, rather than loans, were being made with greater frequency in Parliament.

122 See LCC, *London Housing Statistics* (1955–6), 22.

123 See H. Quigley and I. Goldie, *Housing and Slum Clearance in London* (London, 1934), 64.

124 See LCC, Annual Report of the Council for 1912, Vol III, Appendix D, lxviii.

125   Gibbon and Bell, 374–5.

126   Bermondsey Borough Council, *Minutes* (November 1904), 418.

127   Hammersmith Borough Council, *Annual Reports* (1904), 57. City of Westminster, *The City of Westminster Dwellings* (London, 1904).

128   See, for example, Hammersmith Borough Council, *Annual Reports* (1904), 57.

129   Public Records Office, *Housing and Local Government*, I, 14, 676, 31/03.

130   *Ibid*, I, 14, Part I, 676, 31/04.

131   LCC, *Housing*, Gen/2/33/Miscellaneous, 28.

132   Fulham Borough Council, *Annual Reports* (1900–01), 49.

CHAPTER II

WORKING-CLASS HOUSING
IN GLASGOW, 1851-1914

John Butt

THE elegance of the eighteenth-century city of Glasgow, the subject of comments by travellers so diverse as Daniel Defoe[1] (1727), Thomas Pennant[2] (1772) and Dr Samuel Johnson[3] (1773), was ravished by the Industrial Revolution. Property speculation by small contractors to provide for an ever-increasing population from the 1780s produced the 'backjams' and 'backlands', tenement properties added piecemeal to existing buildings or built in the gardens of formerly wealthy burgher residences.[4] Around the old regality of Glasgow, villages grew substantially into suburbs. Highlanders and Irish, pulled by the prospect of employment and pushed by the reality of rural poverty, poured into the city and its environs, especially in the 1820s and 1830s, creating irremedial stresses on the social capital of Glasgow.[5] The pride of earlier historians of the city, like John Gibson,[6] Andrew Brown[7] and James Denholm,[8] gave way at first to the troubled enumerations of social statisticians like James Cleland,[9] Robert Cowan[10] and William Logan[11] and finally to the didactic strictures about housing and public health by medical men like William Gairdner,[12] James Burn Russell,[13] and Andrew Chalmers[14] and to the rumbling protests and polemical outbursts of W. C. Spens,[15] John Honeyman,[16] G. W. Barras,[17] Robert Bremner,[18] William Smart,[19] and Joseph Burgess.[20]

Asa Briggs has rightly emphasised the need for a combination of the quantitative and qualitative approaches to urban history.[21] So far modern writers on the history of Glasgow's housing, with the notable exception of J. B. Cullingworth, whose concern is primarily with relatively recent history, have concentrated more on the latter than the former. Indeed, there is a temptation because of the volume of secondary sources to concentrate on the untypical, like the City of Glasgow Improvement Trust,[22] or the comparative and circumstantial.[23] Most of this essay is unashamedly quantitative in its methodology, since comparative impressionistic assessments have few universally acceptable tests of validity and the untypical, though interesting—perhaps as a foretaste of future developments—*per se* has obvious limitations.

By 1851 Glasgow's municipal authorities—and those of adjacent suburbs—had already recognized the existence of a housing problem in the old centre of the city. Through the operation of the Dean of Guild Court, the powers of which had been extended by the sixth Police Act (1843), dangerous slum property was already being demolished.[24] The coming of the railways from 1830 onwards had begun the alteration of the city centre without lowering its population density.[25] The movement westward of Glasgow's 'respectable' population left room for the influx of Highlanders and Irish, and where there was no room, they still managed to find it. They were attracted by cheap rents in decaying property near the markets, slaughterhouses, docks, stations, foundries, gasworks, chemical works, tanneries and mills where casual and unskilled labour was able effectively to compete with the indigenous population and to form close-knit defensive communities. In the city centre by 1851 there was, therefore, created an unhealthy overcrowded ghetto, subject to seasonal flooding from the Molendinar and Camlachie burns, two streams which had long lost their pristine purity through industrial effluent and sewage pollution, with levels of population density varying from 500 to 1,000 persons per acre.[26] Provision for water supply, street cleansing, refuse and sewage disposal varied from the non-existent to the primitive.[27] Contaminated water, adulterated food, insecure employment, irregular wages were the lot of many; submersion in an over-supply of drink was the refuge of more than a few. Destitution, poverty, criminality, prostitution, child-beating, pawnbroking, drunkenness, shebeens, illicit distillation, all inter-related phenomena, flourished in so luxuriant a fashion that private individuals, voluntary associations and municipal authorities, through conscience or necessity, had to intervene.

Inspired by past cholera disasters and the growing fear of typhus, the provision of a better water supply and the creation of a sanitary inspectorate were slowly achieved. A private company supplied the Gorbals with water by February 1848 and the Corporation Water Works Act (1855) was an essential prelude to the Loch Katrine scheme which came to fruition in October 1859.[28] From the appointment of an inspector of cleansing in 1843 there was a long trail of miscellaneous, small-scale improvements, institutionalised in the Committee on Nuisances (1857) and its successor, the Sanitary Committee (1862). The first Medical Officer of Health, William T. Gairdner, took up office in January 1863, and almost immediately, the suppression of overcrowding by ticketing houses to limit occupancy began.[29] The City of Glasgow Improvements Act (1866) and the Glasgow Ninth Police Act (1866) formalised and codified the intentions of the municipal authorities to intervene in the building development of the city.

However, the most significant feature of the period 1851–1901, as may be seen from Table 2.1,[30] was the great increase in the net housing stock of the city, to which the City Improvement Trust contributed an aggregate of a mere 1,697 houses under the Act of 1866—473 one-apartment houses, 1,033 two-apartment, 180 three-apartment, and 11 larger than three-apartment—and a further 257 houses by 1902 under the Improvements and General Powers Act of 1897 which supplemented, but did not supersede, the earlier Act.[31]

The City Improvement Trust was originally intended to last for fifteen years and given power under the Act of 1866 to spend £1,250,000 in purchasing and demolishing 88 acres of congested slum property. This sum was increased to £1,500,000 by Section 2 of the Glasgow Improvements Amendment Act of 1880. Thirty-nine new streets were to be formed; twelve existing ones were to be improved.[32] Yet the Trust faced great problems. Compelled by legal precedents to limit its activities to localities specified in the Act of 1866,[33] though other areas were equally subject to rapid deterioration, it could not, in practice, build working-class houses at any great rate but merely provided, at public auctions without jobbery, additional stocks of land at prices intended to stimulate alike the land market and local entrepreneurship in the building industry. In the central area specified in the Act of 1866, normal market forces had ceased to operate efficiently. Albeit infrequently, the Trust was obstructed by litigious, and occasionally rapacious, property-owners in search of compensation;[34] in general, few cases went to arbitration, since compensation bordered on the generous, being equal to eleven to twenty years gross rental, depending on the condition of the property.[35]

No revolutionary displacement of population was planned by the Trust, though it was anticipated that ultimately, 50,000 working people would have to move. The Trustees could only displace a maximum of 500 people every six months, unless they could prove in the Sheriff Court of Lanarkshire that provision for alternative housing had been made. Technically, the Act of 1866 allowed them to build 'dwelling houses for mechanics, labourers and other persons of the working and poorer classes' to offset the effects of their demolition programme.[36] More objectionable to the municipal electorate

Table 2.1

POPULATION, LAND AREA AND HOUSING IN GLASGOW, 1851–1911

Census Year	Total Population	City Acreage	Population Density per acre	Total Houses			Total Houses available for occupancy	Total Families	Percentage of Families above Inhabited houses
				Inhabited	Uninhabited	Building			
1851	329,096	5,063	63	63,153	1,547	1,032	64,700	64,854	2·62
1861	395,503	5,063	78	82,609	4,002	962	86,611	83,588	1·17
1871	477,732	5,063	94	100,876	2,134	1,025	103,010	106,861	5·60
1881*	511,415	6,111	93 84	106,238	12,264	377	118,502	112,710	5·74
1891†	565,714	11,861	56	134,339	6,491	768	140,830	144,828	7·24
1901	741,124	12,687	58	155,526	7,225	1,535	162,751	163,548	4·9
1911‡	784,496	12,975	62	163,057	20,903	487	183,960	167,896	2·9

* Boundary changes by Municipal Extension Acts of 1872 and 1878.
† Extensive boundary changes in 1891, Population density given before and after changes.
‡ Boundary changes in 1905.

were the financial provisions of the Act. Section 32 empowered the Trustees to levy, during the first five years of the operation of the Act, an annual assessment not exceeding 6d in the £1 of rental or annual value and, for the following ten years, not more than 3d in the £1. As a consequence of the Glasgow Improvements Amendment Act of 1880, a maximum assessment of 2d in the £1 was imposed—but with no time limit. Fear of censure from the electorate on the part of councillors, firmly imprinted *ab initio* by the startlingly vindictive but successful campaign against Lord Provost John Blackie in 1867,[37] vitiated any prospect of greater financial support for slum clearance and vitrified the original zeal of the Trustees.

Much slum property was bought: by 1869 £565,016 had been spent by the Trust. But there was a considerable delay before its purchases were put to use. By 1884–5 30,000 people had been displaced, but half of these were made homeless by three railway companies who had made extensive purchases of land in the areas scheduled for demolition and improvement. Unfortunately, neither the Trust nor the railway companies provided new houses for those displaced.[38] Thus, working people were shunted out of slums into the nearest, next-worst property.[39] Private builders in the early 1870s bought land cleared by the Trust at a minimum of £2 per sq yd, when they were estimating that the maximum they could afford to pay for land for working-class housing was 25s to 30s per sq yd. Of the 134,000 Glasgow people housed by private builders in the period 1866–74 few came from families displaced by the actions of the Trust or from those earning less than 25s per week.[40] Yet the Improvement Trust benefited, since the general demand for houses was so great—and capital existed especially in the early 1870s to provide for their building—that the high prices paid to slum landlords were more than recouped.

By the autumn of 1876 there was a marked slackening in the city's property market, and in 1877 the sale of Improvement Trust land to private builders gradually ceased. The failure of the City of Glasgow Bank in 1878 did not begin, but completed, the crisis in confidence; interest rates soared, business failures among Glasgow builders multiplied, and the profitability of house-building was greatly reduced. Despite a reduction of 20 per cent in its land prices in 1879, the Trust could still not find customers; in 1880 land prices in a few cases were reduced by as much as 60 per cent. However, chronic slackness in demand persisted; private building remained at a low level throughout the 1880s; moreover, from 1878 to 1884 there were few new houses built for renting. This can be partly explained by reference to Table 2.1 which shows that 12,264 houses were uninhabited and available for rent in 1881, much the highest total and proportion in the period 1851–1901. Piece-meal conversion of property, sub-division of old middle-class property for working-class occupancy, these were the expedients of many small builders. Even by 1885 demand for building land was so ineffective that vacant ground owned by the City Improvement Trust was responsible for an annual loss of about £10,000, borne by the rates.[41]

This was not the sole financial cause of the opprobrium which the Trust elicited from some ratepayers. One of the reasons for the Corporation's seeking the Glasgow Improvements Amendment Act (1880) was that the Trust had exceeded its borrowing powers by £57,304 because of the shortfall in income from land sales while stocks had to be maintained. An interesting empirical response on the part of the Trust was to repair and relet houses previously purchased for demolition. Paradoxically, this produced the situation reported to the Royal Commissioners in 1885, when 'the Improvement Trust still owned some of the worst property in the town'.[42] Not until 1888 was the remainder of the property, scheduled in 1866, demolished.

Paralysis in the land market in the 1880s encouraged the development of municipal house-building. In the Saltmarket, a small tenement was built in 1890, and this was followed by further house-building in Townhead, Calton, Cumbernauld Street, and Stobcross. The 1897 Act empowered the Corporation to acquire compulsorily congested areas totalling 5½ acres in High Street, George Street, Nelson Street, King Street, Jail Square, Bridgegate, Fish Market, and Gorbals and to obtain a further 25 acres either within the city or within half a mile of the city boundary as land space for dwellings 'for the poorer classes'. Borrowing powers up to £560,000 were granted for these purposes.[43] By 1902 the proposed demolition programme of 1897 had been largely accomplished, but only 257 houses had been built, providing accommodation for between 700 and 800 people. Land, originally costing the Cleansing Department 4s to 5s per yd in Baltic Street and 7s in Haghill—both in the East end— had been used to provide 112 one-apartment and 145 two-apartment houses.[44]

Under the terms of the 1897 Act the Corporation also purchased 72,963sq yd of ground at Kennyhill and a small area in Springburn. In October 1901 an architectural competition was announced for Kennyhill, where working-class housing was projected; 30 per cent were to be one-apartment, 40 per cent two-apartment and 30 per cent three-apartment dwellings.[45] Considerable delay then occurred, but by October 1906 tenements had been built in Kennyhill, Howard Street (Bridgeton), in St Ninian Street and Muirhead Street (South Side), and in Stockwell Street and Bridgegate.[46] By 1914, however only 245 further houses had been built since 1902, and the total added to the housing stock of the city by its Improvement Trust from 1866 onwards was 2,199 : 592 one-apartment houses, 1,334 two-apartment, 257 three-apartment, and 16 larger than three-apartment houses.[47] Thus, the Corporation, through its Improvement Trust, probably housed about 10,000 people, one per cent of a total population of over one million and fewer in total than were housed in any one year by private builders in the periods 1867–78 or 1893–1902.

There was, as we have seen, a marked tendency for Corporation house-building to slow its pace in the decade before World War I. Partly this was a consequence of higher and higher land prices, especially in central districts, which precluded purchases by the City Improvement Department.[48] The capital cost of buildings erected on cleared sites, 1866–1912, was £593,442 16s 5d, and the annual loss for 1901–13 on houses built under the 1897 Act was less than 3 per cent of rental. Interest charges were another deterrent to increasing the pace of building : whereas the average rate paid in 1902 was £2 15s 10½d per cent, by 1913 it was £3 5s 9d.[49] Significantly, nearly 68,000sq yd of the Kennyhill purchase still remained unused in 1914, though on 20 October 1913 the Corporation decided to build eight tenements of three storeys (72 houses in all) there.[50]

The lodging houses of the city provided residence for more people than the City Improvement Trust. The character of Glasgow's lodging houses began to change from 1843 when James Lumsden of Yoker Lodge became Lord Provost. Together with John Blackie and James Watson, both later Lord Provosts, Lumsden established three 'model' lodging houses, situated in Carrick Street, McAlpine Street and Greendyke Street at a cost of £17,000.[51] These were later taken over by the City Improvement Trust. Yet, in 1878,

despair about the common lodging houses of the city and their
denizens was commonplace :[52]

> the state of the lodging houses, and the cellars especially, beggars descrip-
> tion, the floors thereof being packed at night with human beings—men,
> women and children like so many bundles of rags, and the walls and roof
> black with vermin.

Such conditions were primarily a consequence of severe overcrowding, which placed all the market advantages with lodging-house
keepers, of inadequate inspection and of personal indifference, which
led the city as a whole to tolerate a situation where at the Census
of 1871 23 per cent of all Glasgow's families contained lodgers; 20
per cent of these families lived in one room with their lodger and 48
per cent in two rooms. J. B. Russell, for obvious reasons, regarded
'the tendency to keep lodgers as a serious social disease'.[53]

For moral and other reasons, the City Improvement Trust,
between 1871 and 1879, created seven model lodging houses at a
cost of £87,000 with 1,922 beds.[54] They varied in size from Greendyke Street Model, the smallest, with 240 beds to Portugal Street
Model, the largest, with 438 beds. Accommodation varied in price
from 3d. to 4½d per night. Morality, sobriety, cleanliness, order and
discipline were important themes in the organisation of Corporation
lodging houses. The superintendents were usually well qualified to
enforce discipline. High wages and perquisites—about £100 per
annum and all found—attracted men like a Drill Sergeant of the
Third Argyll Rifles, appointed in 1878 from over 100 applicants to
be Superintendent at Portugal Street. In case ejecting rowdies presented undue problems, the police, by arrangement with the Chief
Constable, visited the lodging houses on Saturday nights to show
an awe-inspiring presence. Free Bibles and regular Sunday religious
services added a tinge of religion to this panoply of para-military
power. 'Saturday Night Entertainments'—readings, music recitals,
talks and lectures—'for the amusement and improvement of the
residents' were a central feature of the campaign to keep lodgers
away from drink; inevitably, limited success attended these efforts.
Free baths for residents were instituted in 1891, and in 1884 and
1897, during smallpox epidemics, a week's free lodging was given
to inmates who agreed to be vaccinated.[55]

Expansion of the model lodging houses was continued in the
1890s, as the City Improvement Trust became more energetic.
Drygate Model, opened in 1871 with 274 beds was extended in 1892

Page 65   Old Vennel, Glasgow in 1868

Page 66   Hospital St, Gorbals, Glasgow

so that 102 new beds costing £2,400 were added. Portugal Street Model extensions provided 110 new beds, costing £4,000. Additions were also made to the East Russel Street Model, but the most important development was the decision, in 1894, to build, a 'Family Home' in St Andrew's Street. Opened in 1896, at a cost of £12,000, it catered for widowers with young children. There were 160 rooms, each isolated, centrally heated by a hot-water system, lit by electricity, and capable of accommodating a man and up to three children. Additional children slept in the dormitory, and communal rooms existed for other services, including a dining-room and a nursery where staff were employed to care for children under school age. Charges were 8d–9d per night per room, and children were looked after and fed for 1s 4d–1s 6d per week.[56] Tenants were carefully selected, and in 1902, well-to-do artisans, earning 30s to £2 per week in secure employment, were the Family Home's chief occupants.[57]

John Stirling Duncan, superintendent of the Portugal Street Model, gave the Municipal Commision in 1903 some account of conditions in the more typical male establishment. He had charge of 468 beds let at $3\frac{1}{2}$d, 4d and $4\frac{1}{2}$d. The men did their own cooking, and about half of them bought provisions from the store in the lodging house. A sample survey, when the house was full on the night of 22 January 1903, showed 113 skilled men in residence and 355 unskilled. The latter, in good times, could earn, on average, 22s to 25s per week, but, taking into account broken time and irregular employment, the average wage was about 18s per week. But Duncan estimated that inmates could live on 7s per week and their rent. He thought, though this is even more difficult to believe, that his residents preferred the relative freedom and modernity of model lodging houses to private lodgings. Most of them, he declared, were single men, addicted to drink, who would have married and had houses of their own, were it not for their moral weaknesses.[58]

Throughout the 1870s and 1880s the lodging-house account was in surplus, showing about 5 per cent return on capital invested.[59] Total capital expenditure by 1914 was nearly £113,000, of which, by the operation of a Sinking Fund, established in 1890, £78,442 17s 7d was still outstanding. Relatively full capacity working (97 per cent of beds) ensured profitability throughout the 1890s and indeed, up to 1908. Commercial depression reduced the demand for beds: in 1909 28 per cent of the beds were empty but there was a gradual improvement to 1913/14 when 10 per cent of the beds were unoccupied. For the first time, the lodging-house account moved into deficit, and this, of course, discouraged greater provision of model lodging-house places.[60]

The presence of Glasgow's model lodging houses greatly stimulated improvement in the private sector. J. B. Russell noticed the increase in quality and size of common lodging houses and diminution in numbers apparent by 1889,[61] and newspaper reporters were similarly impressed. In 1887 101 private lodging houses were registered with the Corporation, and these provided accommodation for 6,273 people. There were sixty-seven such lodging houses in 1902, providing accommodation for 9,705 men in fifty-one and 577 women in the remaining sixteen. At that date the Corporation provided 2,430 beds. Together all the lodging houses housed just over one per cent of the city's population.[62]

If registered lodging houses were one response to obvious over-crowding, more significant was the system of ticketing houses, for which the Corporation received powers under the City Improvements Act of 1866. Houses of three rooms or less, not exceeding 2,000cu ft were measured, and their capacity inscribed on a metal ticket, fixed to the door or lintel, together with the number of occupants allowed by law, at the rate of 300cu ft for every person over eight years old.[63] By the 1880s Glasgow possessed 23,228 ticketed houses, 16,413 of which were one-apartment and the remaining 6,815 two-apartment. About 75,000 people, one-seventh of the total population of the city in 1881, occupied these houses. However, less than half of Glasgow's one-roomed houses were ticketed. Indeed, only 35 per cent of those living in one room occupied ticketed houses and only 14 per cent of those living in two rooms.[64]

Most ticketed houses were 'made-down', ie they were sub-divisions of existing property, the plans for the alteration of which before 1900 required no approval from the Dean of Guild Court. Many 'made-down' houses escaped ticketing, since the ceiling heights in dwellings once owned by the departed wealthy were such that their cubic capacity was beyond the prescribed limit. Occasionally, the sanitary inspectors, responsible for operating the ticketing procedure and for night inspections, waived their legal rights to avoid the humilation of decent and respectable working people living in well-kept but substandard accommodation. Two pairs of inspectors constantly inspected ticketed houses at night, and in the course of any year in the early 1880s, they made about 40,000 visits.[65]

The propensity to overcrowd in ticketed houses persisted throughout the period before World War I. Fines of 1s and admonitions for first offenders up the scale to 5s for the regularly guilty did little to reduce the number of offences.[66] Blame seems to have been taken as a communal obligation and therefore passed around. This explains the very large proportion of first offenders—which civic health authorities complacently found comforting—in the total number of cases, shown in Table 2.2.

The extent of working-class solidarity in this ticketed community can be gauged from the fact that of 1,637 transgressions, 1,400 were first offences. Further, in these overcrowded houses, 999 offences could be explained by the presence of lodgers. There was both a willingness to accommodate friends and relatives, even with the prospect of a fine, and a temptation to sublet, thereby raising the family income. Alexander McCallum, assistant sanitary inspector in the Eastern Police District, which in 1902 contained 6,244 ticketed houses, had found people concealed in every conceivable corner of these houses—in cupboards, under beds and even on the housetops. In the worst case of overcrowding found in the city he took seven people from an adjoining roof and eleven other adults from a house which contained only 880cu ft or 80ft per adult. He had, on occasion, found two tiers of people in one bed, one on the boards or on the mattress, the bed then flung over, and another tier on top of that.[67]

The number of ticketed houses remained relatively constant between 1881 and 1914 : in March 1902 there were said to be less than 21,000 occupied and in 1913–14 Peter Fyfe, the sanitary inspector responsible for their supervision, estimated there were 22,000.[68] Similarly, the volume of people living in them remained unchanged at about 75,000, but as the city's population increased, the proportion in ticketed houses fell. Overcrowding of ticketed houses fluctuated substantially from 8 per cent in 1866, to 5 per cent in 1885, to 12·74 per cent in 1901, to 6–8 per cent in the decade before 1914. At that date there were six inspectors, operating from 11.30 pm to 5 am in a frustrating attempt to prevent overcrowding.[69]

From Table 2.1 and Table 2.3 some indication of the rate of development in the aggregate housing stock of the city can be ascertained. The total of houses available for occupancy increased by

TABLE 2.2

OVERCROWDING IN GLASGOW'S TICKETED HOUSES, 1882–3

| | POLICE DISTRICTS | | | | | | |
---	Central	Eastern	Northern	Southern	Western	Whole City
Total Night Inspections	8,356	8,667	12,577	7,006	3,678	40,284
Houses found overcrowded:						
once	234	389	366	280	131	1,400
twice	14	54	20	51	20	159
three times	7	11	4	20	6	48
more than-three times	5	5	4	13	3	30
Total offences	260	459	394	364	160	1,637
Cases pending at 1 May 1883			11		20	31
Householders admonished	157	352	334	271	137	1,251
Householder fined/imprisoned	52	65	27	57	36	237
Non-apprehensions	33	22	44	36	7	142
Cases pending	18	20				38
Cases of lodgers found in overcrowded houses	172	290	198	236	103	999

Source: Royal Commission on Housing of Working Classes, *PP* (1884–5), XXXI, Appendix C.

11,411 in the decade 1851–61, by 16,899 in the decade 1861–71, by 15,492 in the decade 1871–81, and by 22,228 in the decade 1881–91. Boundary changes substantially increased the city's acreage, housing resources and population in 1891 (when the burghs of Crosshill, Govanhill, Hillhead, Maryhill, Pollokshields East and West and the districts of Kelvinside, Langside, Mount Florida and Shawlands were absorbed), in 1905 (when Kinning Park joined Glasgow) and in 1912 (when the burghs of Govan, Partick and Pollokshaws and several small suburban districts were acquired[70]). This extension of Glasgow makes nugatory any generalisations about housing stock in and after 1891—except the obvious comment that the number of houses available for occupancy in the greater Glasgow increased at a faster rate than the growth of population.

Since demolition and closing of houses were features of municipal policy, such housing gains were net not gross. The two decades 1851–71 were less significantly affected in this way than the next four. An increasing scale of municipal intervention was based on stricter building regulations and more carefully defined Public Health requirements. 1,269 houses were demolished between 1891 and 1901 under the two Improvement Acts of 1866 and 1897, making a total of nearly 11,000 house demolitions since 1866. Section 32 of the

TABLE 2.3

HOUSES AUTHORISED BY GLASGOW'S DEAN OF GUILD COURT, 1862–1901

Period	1 *Apartment*	2 *Apartment*	3 *Apartment*	*Aggregate*
1.9.1862–31.12.1866	602	1,816	462	2,880
1.1.1867–31.12.1871	3,192	6,889	2,663	12,744
1.1.1872–31. 8.1876	5,331	11,202	4,519	21,052
1.9.1877– 1881	1,286	3,344	1,128	5,758
1882– 1886	443	1,789	1,053	3,285
1887– 1891	1,153	3,550	1,414	6,117
1892– 1896	2,262	7,078	3,557	12,897
1897– 1901	3,403	10,277	3,388	17,068
Total	17,672	45,945	18,184	81,801
Representing percentage of all authorisations	18	48	19	85

Source: GCA, Municipal Commission Minutes, 81, contains an annual statement of authorisations, upon which this table is based.

Glasgow Police (Amendment) Act and Section 30 of the housing of the Working Classes Act of 1890 gave the Corporation additional powers to close uninhabitable houses. Under the terms of the first Act, 916 houses were closed by 1909; by the authority of the second, 3,092 houses were condemned and closed, mainly in the period 1902–7. The Housing, Town Planning Act of 1909 (sections 17–18) was operated from 1910 to the end of 1913, when a further 853 houses were closed. Thus, at least 16,000 houses were demolished in Glasgow from 1866 to 1914, and this number had to be replaced, mainly by private builders operating under free market forces, before any gain in the housing stock would show.[71]

Private builders built working-class housing on a great scale from 1868 to 1877 and from 1893 to 1904 but the 1880s, despite the apparent increase shown in the census of 1891, saw a great hiatus, and after 1904 there was a cataclysmic fall. From Table 2.3, covering the period 1862 to 1901, it should be obvious that private enterprise dominated the supply of new and 'made-down' housing. The latter, for most of the period, required no authority from the Dean of Guild Court and, therefore, cannot be quantified except from city assessor's data.

In considering Table 2.3, which refers to 85 per cent of all houses authorised between 1862 and 1901, it should be remembered that authority gained from the Dean of Guild Court in a particular year did not necessarily mean that houses were built that year. Yet the procedure was sufficiently serious—and cumbersome—that the figures in Table 2.3 may be taken as a reliable guide of builders' intentions in particular periods. Other reliable evidence suggests that in the decade 1866–76 about 40,000 new and 'made-down' houses, or 25 per cent of the inhabited houses of 1901, were built by private speculation. Of those built in the period 1866–70, 22 per cent were one-apartment, 50 per cent two-apartment and 19 per cent three-apartment dwellings. This heavy emphasis on small houses continued consistently from 1871 to 1875, during which time 25 per cent of those built were one-apartment, 49 per cent two-apartment, and 19 per cent three-apartment.[72] Over the period 1862–1901, 18 per cent of all houses authorised were one-apartment, 48 per cent two-apartment, and 19 per cent three-apartment. The proportion of newly authorised one-apartment houses—but not the volume—clearly fell, while that of other small houses remained fairly constant.

From 1878 to 1892 high domestic interest rates, coupled with mounting returns on capital in the international economy, militated against a continuation of the boom in house-building. So did the market for houses. In the winter of 1878–9 there were 14,000 applications for poor relief, and taking dependants into account, this involved over 40,000 people. Economic activity in 1878–9 and 1879–80 had to be stimulated by a municipal works programme costing over £26,000 in the first of these winters.[73] Little wonder that nearly 11 per cent of the total houses available for occupancy in 1881 were empty. From Table 2.1 the figures for uninhabited houses in 1881 and 1891 illustrate a general slackness in demand for houses. Rent movements reflected the same trend. Over the period 1861–1901, for which good data on rents exist, there was an average rise of nearly 27 per cent in rents; from 1870 to 1902 the rise was just under 17·5 per cent, most of this occurring in the 1890s. But it should be noticed first, that rents did not increase at the same rate as most real wages for those who retained employment (and, more particularly, real wages in the Glasgow building industry, which showed an average increase of 81 per cent) and secondly, rents did not increase as fast as family formation figures, the only reasonable indicator as to the level of likely demand. Rents rose most rapidly in the 1860s and 1890s, and they faltered after 1879, especially for two or more rooms, as some families trying to economise, sought cheaper one-apartment accommodation to match wage-cuts and irregular employment.[74]

It should not surprise anyone that rent-rises should encourage private speculation in house-building. But in the 1890s, such rises were often an indication of increased costs. Property taxes were rising and after 1908 rose further as a result of Lloyd George's budgets. House improvements were enforced on builders by stricter municipal byelaws and these forced up costs. Maintenance costs rose also, as higher wages were paid to the building trades. A reputable Glasgow builder, Thomas Binnie, who had considerable experience in valuing property from 1857–8 as well as in building working-class housing in Glasgow, believed that by 1902 the cost of building tenements had risen 50 to 60 per cent. He was also convinced that it was far less profitable to own houses for rent in 1902 than in the 1850s.[75] Robert Bremner thought that building costs for tenements had risen at least 20 per cent since the mid-1880s.[76]

Since building costs were rising from the 1890s, and the profitability of building working-class housing, especially, was less certain, it is not surprising that further upturns in costs, provoked mainly from 1904 by higher interest rates, should be accompanied by a dramatic fall in authorisations for new building. In the decade 1901–11 plans for 2,901 one-apartment, 4,459 two-apartment and 5,516 three-apartment houses were approved by the Dean of Guild Court, but about a third of these were granted in 1902 alone.[77] This marked decline in the provision of cheaper housing later caused the Royal Commission on Scottish Housing (1918) to comment on 'the failure of private enterprise to provide and maintain the necessary houses sufficient in quantity and quality'.[78] From Table 2.1 it can be seen that the number of families exceeded the number of inhabited houses throughout the period, though this tendency was most definite from 1871 to 1891.

But the more enterprising builders could be expected to seek alternative opportunities in building other forms of public, commercial and private property—municipal buildings, shops, offices, public utilities, suburban development in the West End for the middle classes. The less resourceful builders relied on penny orders for houses from the 'shopocracy', who were the main speculators in working-class housing from 1851 to 1914;[79] subject to credit restrictions, they were also less capable of achieving productivity gains to peg rising costs. Many of these smaller building firms concentrated on the conversion of substantial middle-class property into 'single-ends'. This subdivision of buildings which had outlived their use by their original owners provoked wry comment from Thomas Binnie in 1902 : 'The one great fault in our ordinary tenement building has been that the buildings are made to last too long.' His view that buildings which outlive their day degenerate into slums has a certain universal applicability in Glasgow's history, but his idea of planned obsolescence after seventy years perhaps represented a partial view.[80] The oldest and worst houses in the city throughout the period 1851–1914 were usually managed by factors for trustees who did not always bother to familiarise themselves with the poor quality of the property for which trust deeds made them responsible.[81]

Although the conversion of middle-class tenements into madedown houses proceeded steadily after 1901, private enterprise had virtually ceased to provide new houses for the working-classes after 1907. Private builders, like MacTaggart, increasingly concentrated upon meeting the needs of the 'salariat'. From 1900 to 1917 his firm built 2,330 houses. Yet only 55 were of one-apartment and 1,075

of two-apartments, the latter being expensive and beyond the rents
which most working-class people could afford, since they usually
had a bathroom with hot and cold water and a separate water
closet.[82] Various explanations, set out in the Minority Report of the
Royal Commission (1918), were made for the failure of private
builders to provide houses for the working classes. High feus, byelaws relating to access roads, legal expenses, capital charges, increased building costs, rates, new heritable land taxes and uncer-
tainty about local authority plans for building houses, all were
cited.[83] Sufficient to say that the private builder found it less profitable to erect houses at rent levels suited to the incomes and expectations of the majority of the working classes.

Apart from company housing, which was provided in Glasgow
and its suburbs mainly by railway companies like the North British
Railway at Springburn and the Glasgow & South Western at
Corkerhill, and housing provided by co-operative societies, the main
institutional ventures in financing house-building for the working
classes were artisans' building societies. Some were very shortlived
and organised almost like clothing credit clubs, with low subscription
shares, by directors recruited mainly from the petty bourgeoisie, and
they were intended to serve those in good steady employment. For
instance, the shortlived Glasgow First Model Building Society,
registered under the Building Societies Acts of 1874, 1875 and 1879
on 23 May 1891, recruited Thomas Cameron, a wood-turner who
took four shares on which he paid 6d per share per week. A ballot
gave him an interest-free advance of £400 which he repaid at
£2 5s 0d per calendar month as well as continuing his 2s per week
on his shares. He, however, lost his money and his advance when
the society was dissolved on 5 July 1897.[84]

Far more beneficial were the activities of the Glasgow Workmen's
Dwellings Company, established in 1890 with a capital of £40,000.
By 1903, this company had spent over £54,000 on 669 houses and
provided accommodation for over 2,000 people, whom the directors
believed to be most deserving. This company made a small but
worthwhile contribution to housing the working classes and yet it
averaged 4 per cent on capital. Following plans originally pro-
pounded by the Glasgow Social Union, a voluntary society intent on
ameliorating social conditions in the city, the Glasgow Workmen's
Dwelling Company built their six new tenements with balconies, and
every house was fitted with bed-frames, kitchen range, grate, dresser,

coalbox, gas fittings and water supply, with use of a water closet on the balcony shared with one other tenant. Twenty-seven other tenements were acquired by the company for repair and improvement.[85] William Smart, one of its directors, first mooted the idea of a municipal commission on the housing of the working classes, modelled on the procedure of Royal Commissions.[86] Thus, this company was influential, beyond the number of houses it provided, in formulating municipal attitudes towards the housing problem of the city.

'House-farmers' also provided furnished accommodation of a rudimentary kind, usually in poor property in the older parts of the city, for which the owners received a fixed rent and yet avoided responsibility. This type of activity increased in the 1890s, and by 1902 'house-farmers' controlled 617 single-apartment and 322 two-apartment houses, accommodating 2,695 occupants. Sub-tenants, on average, lived for just under six months in 'farmed' accommodation, and, no doubt, this system of furnished sub-tenancies met a real demand from transients in a period of urban expansion.[87]

It was certainly very profitable to the house-farmers. Some indication of the capital costs of furnishing these houses can be gathered from the evidence given to the Municipal Commission of 1902 by Philip Macauley, who began as a 'house-farmer' in 1899; he spent £3 per room on furniture.[88] Mrs Margaret Cruikshank, who had 'farmed' houses for over twenty years by 1902, leased her houses from the owners at about £6 each annually, and collected from her sub-tenants at the rate of at least £20 per house *per annum*.[89]

The widely differing patterns within the general supply of cheaper housing in Glasgow were imperfect representations of the social structure of its working class, of incomes and expectations. 'Farmed' houses were occupied by people 'with no furniture, and . . . practically bankrupt in estate'.[90] They usually paid their rent nightly—in 1902 8d for old customers and 10d for new. This covered the cost for a couple; cots were provided for children at the nightly rate of 4d for old customers and 6d for new. Many sub-tenants could earn reasonable wages when in employment, but drink was the main reason for their downfall, according to the house-farmers. Some certainly could earn up to £2 per week in 1902, but it is significant that many of the listed occupations of sub-tenants in a sample of 909 (see Table 2.4) involved seasonal unemployment.[91] At the census, taken in 1902, of occupants of 'farmed' houses,

TABLE 2.4

OCCUPATIONS OF SUB-TENANTS IN 'FARMED' HOUSES 1902

Males	No	Females	No
Dock labourers	186	Charwomen	22
Other labourers	279	Caretakers	5
Unskilled Trades	79	Hawkers	5
Carters, Vanmen	66	Laundry workers	2
Artisans	156	Seamstresses	2
Street musicians and vendors	35	Machinists	2
Unclassified	48	Miscellaneous unskilled	7
		Nil	15
	849		60

Source: GCA, Municipal Commission Minutes, 44.

TABLE 2.5

REASONS GIVEN FOR LIVING IN 'FARMED' HOUSES 1902

Drink	558 or 59·1 per cent
Want of a factor's line or reference	169 or 17·9
Unemployment	110 or 11·6
Illness	54 or 5·7
No assigned reason	53 or 5·6

the reasons given by sub-tenants themselves for living in these places support the views of the 'house-farmers'. See Table 2.5.[92]

A mixture of the feckless and the luckless, the householders in this group had an average income of £1 0s 11d per week in 1902, but in about a third of the families, this wage was supplemented by an average of 8s 11d per week by the wife and/or the family. The average rent paid by sub-tenants was 4s 6½d per week or about 22 per cent of the average income of householders alone. Over 84 per cent worked in the city, over 13 per cent were employed elsewhere and slightly over 2 per cent were unemployed. Travelling costs to work must have been a substantial problem, even allowing for the development of suburban transport services and cheap workmen's fares. Some in this group averaged as little as 18s per week, because they could get neither steady nor well paid work. Apart from the enormous obstacle presented by inadequate earnings, there was the general difficulty which inhabitants of ticketed and 'farmed' houses commonly shared. Factors in charge of better accommodation were reluctant to take people from either type of house because they lacked references and were notorious for bad habits. It was easier for them to evict their existing tenants, to lease the property to 'house-farmers' and to collect a steady income from one reliable source than to be bothered with a host of tenants, some of whom were bad financial risks if nothing worse. The necessity that any working man wanting to move house in Glasgow had to be able to provide an adequate reference for the factor before he could hope to get a house cannot be overemphasised. Some factors also charged key-money and then demanded a month's rent in advance. These practices demanded more capital than sub-tenants commonly possessed.[93]

In 1902, the social structure of the tenantry of ticketed houses was also dominated by unskilled labourers and other poorly paid workers (see Table 2.6). The social investigators of 1902 described

TABLE 2.6

OCCUPATIONS OF TENANTS OF TICKETED HOUSES

	One apartment Percentage	Two apartments Percentage
Unskilled labourers	40	47
Other poorly paid workers	28	26·75
Skilled labourers	24·5	21·75
Unemployed	7·5	5

Source: GCA Municipal Commission Minutes, 43.

64 per cent of the tenants, in a sample survey of 3,970 houses (about 20 per cent of all ticketed houses), as respectable, 24 per cent as addicted to drink but not criminal, and 12 per cent as either loafers or 'vicious criminals'. Without considering supplementary income from wives or families, these tenants earned from 16s to 29s per week, a strikingly wide range of primary incomes, with the average at about 23s. Tenants paid an average of 2s per week for one-apartment houses and 2s 9d for two apartments, nine per cent and twelve per cent of average income respectively.[94] These proportions made

little or no advance from the 1870s to 1902, but there was a marked upward trend in rent levels for most property, including ticketed houses, from 1902 to 1914.[95]

There was a very close affinity between those who lived in lodging houses and those who lived in 'farmed' houses, though the cost of lodging-house accommodation in 1902, since it was communal, was only about half the average rent of the 'farmed' house. The inhabitants of both kinds of accommodation were essentially the same type, unskilled labourers with an average income of 18s per week from insecure, irregular employment and a substantial leavening of skilled men earning better wages but unwilling or unable to allocate sufficient to paying for better housing. The cost of accommodation represented 10 to 14 per cent of the unskilled man's weekly earnings and did not increase from the 1880s to 1914.[96]

The Glasgow Workmen's Dwellings Company, according to John Mann junior, its secretary, had an annual rent roll in 1902 of £4,600, collected weekly, rather than nightly or monthly, every Monday. Its tenants were respectable working people. Those who occupied one-apartment houses earned on average 19s 5d per week and those in two apartments earned 25s per week. Mann believed that these tenants were representative of the 'industrious poor'—mainly unskilled—as opposed to the 'dirty, destructive, depraved' who were all too common, he thought, in ticketed houses. The rents of the company's houses were very cheap for the accommodation provided : 1s 10d to 2s 8d per week for one-apartment houses and 3s 2d to 4s 3d for two apartments in new tenements; 1s 9d to 2s 3d per week for a single apartment and 3s 1d to 3s 4d for two apartments in converted or repaired property. These rents represented a range from 9 to 14 per cent of earnings for a single apartment and from 12 to 17 per cent of earnings for two apartments.

The company intended to educate its tenants in the advantages of social improvement. Each of its tenements had a resident caretaker to 'supervise the people generally and press steadily upon the habits of filth and disorder'. A policy of selective tenancies was also followed; would-be tenants were tested as to both character and income. No one would be considered by the company unless he had a month's rent already saved. Since rents had to be paid a week in advance, a tenant had to have at least ten shillings saved before he could hope to be selected for a one-apartment house. If tenants followed the company's rules, they lived rent-free during 'Glasgow

Fair' and at the New Year. Club rooms were provided by the company and administered by a committee elected by the tenants, assisted by the lady volunteers of the Housing Committee of the Kyrle Society, which also provided a family advisory service to the tenants.[97]

The City Improvement Trust also followed the policy of selecting its tenants carefully. It also from 1902 fixed a wage maximum for some of its houses built after 1897 of 22s per week for tenants of single apartments and 26s for those occupying two apartments 'to secure [its houses] to the poorest classes'. Rents varied according to the type and quality of the property as did incomes. £5 was an average annual rent for a single apartment and £8 for two apartments. Incomes of those living in two apartments, in practice, averaged over £60 per annum and those living in a single apartment earned an average of £58 per annum. Thus, the 'honest poor', on average, paid 9 to 13 per cent of their income in rent. The rents of these houses rose only very slightly by 1914.[98] But, like the Glasgow Workmen's Dwelling Company, the City Improvement Trust could only provide for a select few of the city's large unskilled population.

The displacement of population by the demolitions of the City Improvement Trust was carefully studied by J. B. Russell.[99] In the 1860s and 1870s—and indeed, much later—the view that 'the deserving poor will provide themselves with homes' was prevalent.[100] Russell found that, in general, those displaced, 40 per cent of whom were labourers, moved to bigger houses and paid higher rents. Overcrowding was lessened although people did not move far from the houses they had lost.[101] Since in the period 1866 to 1914, the Trust demolished many more houses than it built, the net economic effect of its operations was to raise rents by accentuating the demand for housing. Rents for single apartments in 1902 ranged from £4 per annum in the East End to £7 per annum for better property in more desirable surroundings.[102] Thomas Binnie thought the lowest economic rent for new single apartments was about £6 10s 0d per annum,[103] and many private builders and landlords in 1902 had relatively good single apartments to let at £7 to £9 5s 0d per annum; two-apartment houses were available at rents of between £9 10s 0d and £14.[104] For the Northern Police District, one of the more crowded areas, rent movements in the period 1866–1901 are given in Table 2.7.

TABLE 2.7

ANNUAL AVERAGE RENTS IN THE NORTHERN DISTRICT OF GLASGOW,
1866–1901

Year	Rent for 1 apartment	Rent for 2 apartments
1866	£3 17s 6d	£6 9s 9d
1876	£4 13s 1d	£7 15s 0d
1891	£5 5s 0d	£8 10s 0d
1901	£6 0s 0d	£9 0s 0d

Source: G.C.A. Municipal Commission Minutes, 144.

Over the period as a whole, rents in this district rose for single
apartments by 55 per cent and by 38 per cent for two apartments.
The rents of larger houses rose by progressively smaller amounts.
This trend was representative of the city as a whole.[105] Since there
was a shift away from the single apartment to larger houses, as
indicated in Table 2.8, it is difficult to generalise about the proportions that these rent increases represent in relation to family incomes
of differing socio-economic groups.

TABLE 2.8

GLASGOW'S POPULATION DISTRIBUTION AND OCCUPANCY RATES BY
HOUSING CATEGORIES (1861–1911)

	1861	*1911*
*Number of people		
living in 1 room	105,752	103,815
2 rooms	160,363	367,341
3 rooms	52,372	160,083
Percentage of families living		
in 1 room	34·1	20·0
2 rooms	39·3	46.3
3 rooms	12·6	18.9
Persons per 100 rooms	204	185

Sources: Census of Scotland 1861–1911.
　　　　　Third Statistical Account Glasgow, Tables 69,71 and 73.
　* Bathrooms, sculleries, closets and landings were not counted as 'rooms'.

However, a good sample of unskilled labourers' conditions in 1902 was provided by the superintendent of Glasgow Corporation Employment Bureau, John W. Warrington. From 1896, when the Bureau opened, to 1902, an annual average of 3,500 men and 1,500 women used it, and to avail themselves of its services, they had to give details about their wages. From the male sample in 1902, Warrington found that 1,680 labourers had wages averaging 19s per week, but the range varied from 16s to 26s. Basing calculations on the average labourer's wage and the annual average rent for one apartment in 1901, his rent was 12 per cent of his income. 720 porters earned 17s 9d on average per week, but their wages varied from 15s to 25s. Rent, calculated on the same basis for this group, was 13 per cent of income. 720 carters and vanmen earned on average 21s 2d per week, and their wages ranged from 16s to 30s per week. Rent for the average in this group was 11 per cent of income.[106] Salvation Army representations to the Municipal Commission of 1902 declared that rents were high in relation to the wages earned by many of the unskilled, and this led to overcrowding.[107] Wage data from a variety of other sources[108] suggests that insecurity of employment and casual, irregular earnings were probably more significant problems than low hourly rates. But the basic difficulty for many labourers trying to house their families was essentially a wage problem. Glasgow's municipal authorities and its charitable organisations, as might be expected, found the same problems that Charles Booth encountered in London and Seebohm Rowntree found in York. It was not the low percentage of income allocated to rent by this group which was the cause of their poor living conditions; it was that the income level for labourers in a wide range of Glasgow's industries was too low to allow a man to keep his wife and children in decent accommodation.

Yet there was a marked unwillingness in Scotland, and particularly in Glasgow, to divert the same proportion of income to rent as in England or in America. The obvious shift away from single-apartment houses, apparent from Table 2.8, would have proceeded faster, had house-building and renting been more profitable. Nor should we neglect the evidence that 11 per cent of Glasgow's houses were unoccupied in 1911 (see Table 2.1). There was some improvement in the rate of occupancy of rooms by 1911; there had been a considerable increase in the supply of houses over the previous sixty years. But there were no grounds for complacency. The reduction in

Page 83 (above) Back
view of City Improve-
ment Trust Housing, Glas-
gow; (below) street view

Page 84 (above) Riley's Court, Leeds: a street of seven pairs of back-to-backs on either side, (c 1800) entered by a tunnel arch at each end; one of these frames the photograph. In 1869 the railway viaduct made it even more like a human warren; *(below)* Cannon Street, Leeds: a cul-de-sac halted by a property boundary. Nos 1, 3, 5 and 7 were built back-to-back with the south side of Byron St (Leylands) in 1827, and a tunnel connected the two streets: see LCD no 6472

overcrowding as a gross problem did not maintain its momentum in the decade before 1914. Whereas in 1901 54·7 per cent of the city's population lived more than two to a room, in 1911 the corresponding figure was 55·7 per cent. Yet it is true that the proportions of those who lived three and four to a room fell slightly between 1901 and 1911.[109]

What other possibilities could be considered for Glasgow by 1914? Higher rents would have provided incentives for private enterprise to build more houses and for landlords to maintain their property. But this was an impossible alternative for the bottom stratum of the working population without a substantial increase in wages. The alternative of subsidised housing for this particular group was supported by an uninfluential minority in what has been rather superficially called 'an era of municipal socialism'. Outworn slogans like self-help still dominated the minds of most of those who had concerned themselves with housing reform in the city. Even the most concerned professional administrators, like the surveyor of police and municipal assessments, the medical officer of health or the sanitary inspector, were limited in their vision and inhumane in their remedies. For some, personal cleanliness was 'the first step in the right direction', or whitewashing internal walls twice a year.[110] The childless in 'farmed' houses, A. K. Chalmers advocated, should be put into model lodging houses. Those with children, more reasonably, he thought, should be given a 'second chance' in Corporation houses, 'suitably supervised'.[111] The one-apartment house was still good enough for the old and the single, thought James Henry, the city assessor.[112] Although the City Improvement Trust had functioned since 1866, it was a generation later before these professional administrators came round to the idea that the Corporation should rehouse those whom its policy of demolition displaced.[113] Even Dr J. B. Russell, despite his admirable and sympathetic surveys of the 1870s and 1880s, like 'Life in One Room' and 'Uninhabitable Houses', stood firm for the operation of normal market forces.[114] His successor, A. K. Chalmers, feared that if too much help was given to the unskilled labourer, earning 16s to 18s per week in 1901, the mass of untrained labour in the city would increase.[115]

Some believed that the Corporation should act as a rescuer and guardian for the feckless, the vicious and the criminal. Even the private landlords and builders could accept that element of 'municipal socialism'. Thomas Binnie expressed the common view that the

F

rest of the market should be left to private enterprise. He openly feared that the Corporation would create houses for a large army of its own employees and, perhaps with more percipience, believed that a large number of electors would be committed by their residence in Corporation houses to a policy of cheap rents.[116]

The philosophy motivating the Glasgow Workmen's Dwellings Company was little better. As Professor William Smart commented : 'Cheap rents are as desirable as cheap food', but rate support for Corporation housing 'is nothing more nor less than the municipality offering a bounty to come and dwell in Glasgow'.[117] Temperance for working men—and a reduction in the £15,000 'drawn at Police Courts in Glasgow in fines mostly for drunkenness'—was advocated by John Mann.[118] Meanwhile, they continued to disseminate the thoughts of Octavia Hill and opposed subsidised housing for even the bottom layer of Glasgow's working classes.

As might be expected, both opponents of the Corporation's increasing intervention in the property market and sympathisers relapsed into hyperbole. The lawyers, in particular, were alarmed by the collectivist aspect of Glasgow's municipal policies and the expansion of its boundaries. For the *Scottish Law Review* (1905) Glasgow was the 'oppressor of the West'.[119] Robert Bremner, writing in 1902, clearly hoped for the millenium :[120]

> I am told that slum landlords are decerned worthy to enter the membership of, and hold office in, the Christian Church. The day, I believe, is coming nearer when the man who deliberately invests in slum property will be decerned less worthy to enter decent society than the drunkard or the harlot whom his greed helps to manufacture.

The reality for 75,000 people living in ticketed and 'farmed' houses was 'the lowest depths of wretchedness and poverty'.[121] Despite urban renewal, which led Dr Chalmers to speak of the 'depopulation' of the centre of the city,[122] the reports of groups of councillors on night inspections at the time of the Municipal Commission provide consistent support for this general impression of squalor and degradation.[123] Glasgow's 'municipal socialism' had done little to affect the general proportions of its housing problems before 1914, but no city had done more.[124]

NOTES

1 Daniel Defoe, *A Tour thro' the whole Island of Great Britain*, ed G. D. H. Cole (1927), II, 746 ff.

2   Thomas Pennant, *A Tour in Scotland and Voyage to the Hebrides*, 5th edition (1790), II, 145 ff.

3   J. Boswell, *Journal of a Tour to the Hebrides with Samuel Johnson, 1773*, ed F. A. Ottle and C. H. Bennett (1963), 364.

4   J. R. Kellett, 'Property Speculators and the Building of Glasgow, 1780–1830', *Scottish Journal of Political Economy*, VIII (1961), 211–32; cf also his *Glasgow, A concise history* (1967), 10 ff.

5   J. E. Handley, *The Irish in Scotland 1798–1845*, Cork University Press (1943), *passim; First Report for inquiring into the condition of the poorer classes in Ireland.* Appendix G. Report on the state of the Irish Poor in Great Britain, *PP* (1836) XXXIV; M. W. Flinn (ed), *Edwin Chadwick's Report on the Sanitary Conditions of the Labouring Population of Great Britain* (Edinburgh, 1965), 9–10 and 97–9; M. Gray, *The Highland Economy 1750–1850* (Edinburgh, 1957), 223 ff; R. H. Campbell, *Scotland since 1707: The Rise of an Industrial Society* (Oxford, 1965), 194 ff.

6   John Gibson, *The History of Glasgow from the earliest accounts to the Present Time* (Glasgow, 1777).

7   Andrew Brown, *History of Glasgow* (Glasgow, 1795–7), 2 vols.

8   James Denholm, *The History of the City of Glasgow and Suburbs to Which is added a Sketch of a Tour to the Principal Scotch and English Lakes*, 3rd edition (Glasgow, 1804).

9   James Cleland, *Abridgment of the Annals of Glasgow* (Glasgow, 1817); *Enumeration of the inhabitants of the City of Glasgow and its connected suburbs, together with population and statistical tables relative to Scotland and England* (Glasgow, 1820); *The Rise and Progress of the city of Glasgow, comprising an account of its public buildings, charities and other concerns* (Glasgow, 1820); *Statistical Paper relative to the criminal business at the Circuit Courts in Glasgow* (Glasgow, 1830); *Statistical Facts descriptive of the former and present state of Glasgow* (Glasgow, 1837).

10   Robert Cowan, *The Vital Statistics of Glasgow* (Glasgow, 1838); *Vital Statistics of Glasgow, illustrating the sanitary condition of the population* (Glasgow, 1840).

11   William Logan, *The Moral Statistics of Glasgow* (Glasgow, 1849); A Sabbath School Teacher [William Logan], *The Moral Statistics of Glasgow in 1863, practically applied* (Glasgow, 1864).

12   W. T. Gairdner, 'Defects of House Construction in Glasgow', *Proc Roy Phil Soc Glasgow*, VII (1870–1), 245 ff.

13   Russell's papers appear in A. K. Chalmers (ed), *Public Health Administration in Glasgow* (Glasgow, 1905).

14   A. K. Chalmers, 'The Death-Rate in one-apartment houses: an enquiry based on the census returns of 1901', *Proc Roy Phil Soc Glasgow* (1903) and *The Health of Glasgow* (Glasgow, 1930).

15   W. C. Spens (Sheriff-Substitute of Lanarkshire), 'On the Necessity of a General Measure of Legislation for Scotland with regard to Public Health', *Proc Roy Phil Soc Glasgow*, XI (1877–9), 129–43.

16   John Honeyman, 'Social and Sanitary Problems', *Proc Roy Phil Soc Glasgow*, XX (1888–9), 25–39.

17   G. W. Barras, 'The Glasgow Buildings Regulations Act (1892)', *Proc Roy Phil Soc Glasgow*, XXX (1893–4), 155–69.

18   R. L. Bremner, *The Housing Problem in Glasgow* (Glasgow, 1902).

19   William Smart (Adam Smith Professor of Political Economy in the University of Glasgow) was associated with the Glasgow Workmen's Dwellings Company; cf his *The Housing Problem and the Municipality*, Glasgow University Free Lectures (1902).

20   Councillor Joseph Burgess, a founder member of the Independent Labour Party, and of the West of Scotland Housing Reform Council (1900) was clearly influenced by Ebenezer Howard in his demand for working-class garden suburbs for Glasgow. Glasgow City Archives, (GCA) C3/2/18, Minutes of Evidence taken before Glasgow Municipal Commission on Housing (1902–3), 254 ff.

21   Asa Briggs, 'The Victorian City: Quantity and Quality', *Victorian Studies*, XI (1967–8), 711–30.

22   Cf C. M. Allan, 'The Genesis of British Urban Redevelopment with special reference to Glasgow', *Economic History Review*, Second Series, XVIII (1965), 598–613.

23   Cf Geoffrey Best, 'The Scottish Victorian City', *Victorian Studies*, XI (1967–8), 329–58.

24   Cf Senex, *Glasgow, Past and Present*, Glasgow (1884), i, xv–lx and especially, lxi-lxxiii.

25   Cf J. R. Kellett, *The Impact of Railways on Victorian Cities*, (1969), 229 ff.

26   Allan, 603.

27   Cf Sir J. D. Marwick, *Glasgow—The Water Supply and various developments of the city till the close of 1900* (Glasgow, 1901).

28   A. K. Chalmers (ed), *Public Health Administration in Glasgow* (Glasgow, 1905), 18–19.

29   W. T. Gairdner's preface to J. B. Russell's papers in Chalmers, v; cf also 27 and 160.

30   Sources for Table 1: Total population is derived from *The Census of Scotland* 1851–1911; Statistics for City acreage, families and housing from 1851–1891 from William West Watson, *Vital, Social and Economic Statistics of Glasgow* (Glasgow, 1880), J. A. Nicol, *Vital, Social and Economic Statistics of Glasgow* (Glasgow, 1891), GCA, Municipal Commission Minutes *passim*, and *Municipal Glasgow* 1914. Census data for 1851, 1861 and 1871 are inadequate and misleading on housing statistics, since a house was considered to be the external walls of a building. This method of enumeration was clearly unsuitable for Scottish tenements. The Census of Scotland in 1881 was amended to count every separate residential part of a building: (a) with an outside door or entrance, (b) with a door opening on to a common staircase.

31   GCA, C3/2/18 Municipal Commission, 133 ff. The statistical problem, which Professor Best observantly notes (*op cit* 341n), is a result of an error by J. F. J. Sykes, 'Results of State, Municipal and Organised

Private Action on the Housing of the Working Classes in London
and other Large Cities in the United Kingdom', *Journal of the Royal
Statistical Society*, LXIV (1901), 189–251. His figure of 1,184 houses
is certainly too low. C. M. Allan's total for Corporation-owned (*not*
City Improvement Trust built) houses of 2,488 in 1902 seems to me
eminently reasonable, since it would certainly include tied houses for
supervisory and other Corporation staff employed in cemeteries, gasworks, parks and other Corporation-owned public utilities.

32   GCA, C3/2/17, Note of evidence to be given on behalf of the Cor-
     poration of Glasgow by the Honourable Samuel Chisholm, Lord
     Provost, 1902.

33   Cf W. Ashworth, *The Genesis of Modern British Town Planning*,
     (1954), 95.

34   Eg Scottish Record Office, Court of Session Papers, CS 248/3330/1,
     Thomas Lockerby *v* James Watson and magistrates of the Glasgow
     City Improvement Trust, 1872.

35   Allan, 604–5; this level of compensation and the process of arbitration
     was fixed by the Land Clauses Consolidation (Scotland) Act 1845 and
     amended in 1860.

36   GCA, Acts of Parliament relating to the City of Glasgow, i (1855–
     73): The City of Glasgow Improvements Act, 1866, Sections 23 and
     28.

37   Anon, *The Lord Provosts of Glasgow 1833–83* (Glasgow, 1883), 237 ff.

38   Royal Commission on Housing of the Working Classes (Dilke Com-
     mission), *PP* (1884–5) XXXI, C 4409–1, 60.

39   J. B. Russell, 'On the Immediate results of the Operations of the
     Glasgow Improvement Trust . . .' in Chalmers, 96 ff.

40   Dilke Commission, 46–8.

41   Allan, 605–7; cf also *City of Glasgow Bank Publications* (Edinburgh,
     1879), *passim*; *Municipal Glasgow, its evolution and enterprises*
     (Glasgow, 1914), 31.

42   Dilke Commission, 49.

43   GCA, C3/2/17, Note of evidence to be given on behalf of the Cor-
     poration of Glasgow by the Honourable Samuel Chisholm, Lord
     Provost, 1902.

44   GCA, Municipal Commission Minutes, 133 ff.

45   GCA D-TC 7/12/4 Corporation of Glasgow (City Improvements
     Department), Report on the work of the past year, 1902, by William
     Crawford Menzies, 7.

46   GCA D-TC 7/12/4, Notes on the operation of the City Improvements
     Department by William Crawford Menzies, October 1906.

47   *Municipal Glasgow, its evolution and enterprise* (Glasgow, 1914), 69.

48   *Ibid.*

49   *Ibid*, 65–8.

50   *Ibid*, 66.

51   *The Lord Provosts of Glasgow 1833–83*, 87, 237 and 297–8; A. K.
     Chalmers, ed, *Public Health Administration in Glasgow*, 14–15.

52   *Sanitary Journal*, 1877.

53   J. B. Russell, 'Common Lodging Houses' in Chalmers, 243–9.

54   *Ibid*, 246.

55   *Municipal Glasgow 1914,* 50 ff.

56   *Municipal Glasgow 1914,* 54–6. By 1914 the rent was 5s 6d; additional
     children beyond three cost 8d each per week, and children were boarded
     at 1s 10d per week.

57   R. L. Bremner, 20.

58   GCA Municipal Commission Minutes, 126–8.

59   J. Nicol, *Vital, Social and Economic Statistics of Glasgow* (Glasgow,
     1891), 134–5; Chalmers, 247.

60   *Municipal Glasgow 1914,* 53–4; GCA Municipal Commission Minutes,
     104.

61   Chalmers, 247–8.

62   GCA Municipal Commission Minutes, 104 ff.

63   GCA Miscellaneous Prints, vol 36, 368. Space requirements were in-
     creased to 400cu ft for adults and 200cu ft for children by the Glasgow
     Police Act of 1890.

64   J. B. Russell, 'On the Ticketed Houses of Glasgow' in Chalmers, 206–
     28.

65   Dilke Commission, 49.

66   *Ibid*, 50.

67   GCA Municipal Commission Minutes, 122.

68   *Ibid*, 40–1; *Municipal Glasgow 1914*, 240.

69   GCA Municipal Commission Minutes, 42; *Municipal Glasgow 1914*,
     240.

70   J. Cunnison and J. B. S. Gilfillan, ed, *Third Statistical Account of
     Scotland: Glasgow* (Glasgow, 1958), 421–2.

71   GCA, Municipal Commission Minutes, 100 ff; *Municipal Glasgow
     1914*, 259–60; Chalmers, 95 ff.

72   J. B. Russell, *The Decennial Census of 1881* (Glasgow, 1881), 20; GCA
     Municipal Commission Minutes, 30.

73   A. K. Cairncross, *Home and Foreign Investment*, 1870–1913 (1953),
     12–36; J. B. Russell, *Census of 1881*, 26.

74   GCA, Municipal Commission Minutes, 102–3, 303, and 502.

75   *Ibid*, 304–10.

76   R. Bremner, 24.

77   GCA, Municipal Commission, Minutes, 81; cf Third Statistical
     Account: Glasgow, 454.

78   Report of the Royal Commission on the Housing of the Industrial
     Population of Scotland (Rural and Urban), *PP* (1917–18), XIV para
     1,937.

79   Cf GCA, Municipal Commission Minutes, 339, evidence of George
     Eadie, a speculative builder who had lived in Glasgow since 1851 and
     built 200 tenements of 12 houses each by 1902, mainly for shop-
     keepers.

80   *Ibid*, 304.

81   Cf especially J. B. Russell, 'Uninhabitable Houses', in Chalmers, 240.

82   Royal Commission on the Housing of the Industrial Population of
     Scotland Rural and Urban, *PP* (1917–18) XVIII, Cd 8731, 59.

83   *Ibid*, 77; A. Stalker, ed, *Summary of the Report by the Royal Com-
     mission on Housing in Scotland* (1918), 74.

84   The Co-operative Building Society, backed by the SCWS, issued a
     prospectus in May 1869. W. Maxwell, *History of Co-operation in Scot-
     land* (Glasgow, 1910), 248 and *The Co-operator*, ix, (3 July 1869),
     487. I am grateful to James Kinloch for this reference. Scottish Record
     Office, Court of Session Papers, Unextracted Process, CS 250/1355/1,
     Thomas Cameron *v* The Glasgow First Model Building Society and
     Others (2 June 1898).

85   GCA, Municipal Commission Minutes, 368 ff; C3/2/29(5) Glasgow
     Workmen's Dwellings Company Ltd, *Some Experiments in Housing*
     (Glasgow, 1901); John Mann, *Better Houses for the Poor; Will they
     Pay?* a paper read to the Royal Philosophical Society of Glasgow on
     14 December 1898 and separately published in 1902 [GCA C3/2/29
     and 30]; R. L. Bremner, 11 ff; Wm Smart, *The Housing Problem and
     the Municipality* (Glasgow, 1902), *passim*.

86   Smart, 19 ff.

87   GCA, Municipal Commission Minutes, 17–18, 32–3, and 44.

88   *Ibid*, 544.

89   *Ibid*, 85–9.

90   *Ibid*, 44.

91   *Ibid*, 85–9, Evidence of Margaret Cruikshank; 90, Evidence of Jane
     MacDannoch; 93–6, Evidence of James Doherty. All three were 'house-
     farmers'.

92   *Ibid*, 44.

93   *Ibid*, 44 and 93–6.

94   *Ibid*, 19 and 43–4.

95   J. B. Russell, 'Ticketed Houses' in Chalmers, 218–20.

96   GCA, Municipal Commission Minutes, 126–8; J. B. Russell, 'Common
     Lodging Houses' in Chalmers, 247; *Municipal Glasgow 1914*, 52 ff.

97   GCA, Municipal Commission Minutes, 368 ff; Glasgow Workmen's
     Dwellings Company Ltd, *Some Experiments in Housing* (Glasgow,
     1901), 26–9; British Association for the Advancement of Science,
     Handbook (Glasgow, 1901), 230; R. L. Bremner, 11; John Mann,
     4 ff.

98   GCA, C3/2/17, Note of evidence to be given on behalf of the Corpora-
     tion of Glasgow by the Honourable Samuel Chisholm, Lord Provost,
     1902; Municipal Commission Minutes, 133 ff; D–TC 7/12/4 Corpora-
     tion of Glasgow (City Improvements Department), Report on the work
     of the past year, 1902, by William Crawford Menzies; Notes on opera-
     tion by W. C. Menzies, October 1906; *Municipal Glasgow 1914*, 48–69.

99   Chalmers, 95–146.

100 Cf John Mann's evidence to the Municipal Commission in 1902
     (Minutes, 409) repeated exactly the sentiments of William Logan, *The
     Moral Statistics of Glasgow in 1863* (Glasgow, 1864), 25.

101   'On the Immediate results of the Glasgow Improvement Trust', in Chalmers, 96–146; cf also GCA, Municipal Commission Minutes, 40.

102   GCA, Municipal Commission Minutes, 5.

103   *Ibid*, 311.

104   *Ibid*, 144.

105   *Ibid*, 3–4.

106   *Ibid*, 580–4.

107   *Ibid*, 539.

108   For instance, Carswell, Secretary of Glasgow Trades Council, reported in 1903 that labourers in heavy engineering and building earned only 17s 4d per week over the year. Most were married, often with two or more children (R. L. Bremner, 22n); Royal Commission on Labour 1892–4, *PP* (1892) XXXIV; (1892) XXXVI; (1893–4) XXXIV; (1893–4) XXXIX.

109   Census 1911, 48–9.

110   GCA, Municipal Commission Minutes, 1.

111   *Ibid*, 32.

112   *Ibid*, 1.

113   *Ibid*, 6–8, and 52.

114   Cf Chalmers, 222–3 and 227.

115   GCA, Municipal Commission Minutes, 38.

116   *Ibid*, 319–20.

117   William Smart, *The Housing Problem and the Municipality* (Glasgow, 1902), 19.

118   GCA, Municipal Commission, 409–11.

119   Cf Geoffrey Best, 338 ff.

120   R. L. Bremner, 8.

121   *The Glasgow Herald* (16 March 1903).

122   GCA, Municipal Commission Minutes, 11–12 and 28.

123   GCA, C3/2/27 Reports by groups of Commissioners on night inspections to ticketed houses, 1903.

124   I would like to thank the following for their help in the preparation of this essay: Richard Dell and the staff of Glasgow City Archives, John Robertson, my colleagues C. M. Allan, J. R. Hume, and J. Pickett and Mrs C. M. Thomson who helped in the collection of material.

CHAPTER III

THE BACK-TO-BACK HOUSE IN LEEDS, 1787-1937

M. W. Beresford

Although condemned as a town in its entire locality at the first glance, [Leeds] may really have only peculiar points of local influence from whence the gross results are derived. Robert Baker, *On the State and Condition of the Town of Leeds* (*PP*, xxvii [HL] of 1842), 23.

Back-to-back houses were run up in defiance of the universal condemnation of all persons, without the slightest regard to the health and comfort of the inhabitants. Editorial, *Leeds Mercury* (14 October, 1862).

The characteristic feature of working-class housing in Leeds is the prevalence of the 'back-to-back' type of dwelling. Small 'through' houses are being built at the present time in considerable numbers but even in the case of new dwellings in the more outlying parts of the city, the back-to-back plan has by no means been superceded. The continued erection of this type of house forms a marked exception to the general rule followed by the large towns of the country. A. W. Fox, *Report of an Inquiry into Working Class Rents, Housing and Retail Prices* (*PP*, cvii of 1908), 258.

I

THIS essay is wholly concerned with working-class housing of a type that reformers condemned, though, like Robert Baker, I am aware that the provision of houses for the growing population of industrial Leeds did not result in a town that was one continuous slum. Any detailed local study of reformist critics and their targets might seem to be heading straight for the platitudinous, a reiteration of generalised complaint familiar both to the audiences of the sanitary reformers and to historians of the sanitary movement. Fortunately, the Leeds critical tradition took its tone from Baker, the town's first social statistician.[1] As the quotation at the head of this study indicates, he was well aware that the proper study of housing was a micro-study, an intensely local scrutiny. Baker's house-to-house enquiry, organised for the Statistical Committee of the reformed Corporation in 1837-9, gave him both chapter and verse with which to confound the sceptical and the complacent.[2] In his later writing, especially in the influential *Local Report* submitted to the Lords Committee of 1842, he continued to set the housing problem in terms of particular streets and particular houses. Indeed, Baker's need to convince his readers, as well as his scientific interest in objectivity, made it necessary for him to stress the difference between the good and the bad streets. The ratepayers in the good streets had to be reminded that the improvement rates were spent largely on improving *their* environment; while the localisation of bad and good housing conditions was an important part of his argument, based on the cholera map[3] of 1833. In his sanitary map of 1842 he showed that the Angel of Death had left whole streets in the 'first class' areas untouched, concentrating on certain areas of the town, almost solidly covered with the red and blue spots that indicated cholera and contagious diseases of 1834–9. These blocks of spots were in the areas of worst quality housing, and Baker wanted the correlation to be driven into his readers' minds.[4] Death, disease, moral squalor, poverty, high poor relief, and high crime rates were found under the same group of roofs, making up what increasingly began to be known as the East End.

II

Alongside the reiterated criticism of particular streets the critical literature of Leeds housing in the nineteenth century has another preoccupation, with which this essay will be concerned. Critic after critic, decade after decade, national as well as local, fastened on a distinctive form of housing, to condemn the 'back-to-back'. Leeds was not alone among industrial towns in having back-to-backs but no other town continued to build them for so long nor fought so tenaciously to retain them.

No one has yet made a study of their regional distribution but they were few even in the meanest parts of London, and there were many northern towns without them. Manchester had 10,000 of them by the 1890s,[5] and they were to be found in many West Riding factory towns. Bradford had them : in 1854, the first year of its municipal building byelaws, 1,079 of the 1,601 plans sanctioned were for back-to-back houses.[6] Yet when Bradford and Manchester began to forbid further back-to-backs, Leeds continued to permit them. Despite the general ban on this type of house in the Housing Act of 1909, they continued to be built in Leeds until 1937. Abolition was slow, and demolition was slow, so that the back-to-back was at the centre of the postwar housing problem in Leeds. In the last few years the clearance programme has demolished virtually every back-to-back that appears on the Ordnance Survey plan of 1850 but the field-worker in housing archaeology can still (1969) find back-to-backs built in the 1850s and 1860s.

TABLE 3.1

STOCK OF HOUSES, AND PROPORTION OF BACK-TO-BACKS,
LEEDS BOROUGH, 1801–1920

		Back-to-backs	
	All houses	*number*	*percentage*
1801	11,500	less than 1,000	less than 10
1886	61,000	49,000	71
1920	108,000	78,000	71

Sources: 1801 houses, Census; back-to-backs, Rimmer *art cit* in note 8 (p 122), 187 for total of all types of working-class cottages, 1790–1800. 1886: houses, total of 1921 Census less building as in Table 3.3; back-to-backs, Table 3.3 1920: houses, 1921 Census; back-to-backs, G. W. Rhodes, *Housing Developments in Leeds, 1919–39*, (unpublished Leeds MA thesis, 1954), 11.

But even those who have never seen a back-to-back house[7] will not find it difficult to grasp and appreciate its distinctive feature : the lack of a back door; of a back window; and, indeed, of any through ventilation, since these houses were built so closely and economically together that houses in adjoining streets had their back walls abutting (or shared). You enjoyed a neighbour not only on both side walls of your room but also on the third, the back wall. The symmetry of identical houses set along a street frontage, which had reached its most civilised form in the Georgian squares and terraces, was rapidly degraded into the meanness of 'rows'.

The back-to-back house was small, and initially it had only one ground-floor room and one bedroom above, the 'one-up, one-down'. It was thus part of high-density building development and the search for the maximum rent or the maximum number of saleable houses per acre. Each house, even in the 1850s, was no more than 5yd by 5. The back-to-back thus came to the attention of the sanitary reformers in consequence of the physical and social defects of closely packed living. But it was not just the small size of the Leeds back-to-back that made it a target for critics : as Professor Rimmer has shown, in size the urban 'cottage' (as the back-to-back was so often called) was no smaller than many rural cottages.[8] The new town houses for the working classes that, from the 1750s, were crowded into the innyards, burgage plots, and gardens of the older houses at the centre of the town were of this size also. Nor was the back-to-back unique for its day in the paucity of its provision of water, its drains, and its sanitation. The unique defect of the back-to-back was the absence of through ventilation and the extreme restriction of light, since only one of the four walls of any room was able to have a window. Poor ventilation was more than the inconvenience of unmoving smells. Medical knowledge was becoming increasingly aware of the risk of airborne infection, and of the diseases and deformities that arose from scarcity of light and air.

If the eighteenth-century cottage labourer lived in a small room with poor water and poor sanitation, yet he had his back door : historians of vernacular architecture are coy about back doors, but post-medieval cottages of all sizes seem to have had them, even if they gave access only to a mean yard, a small garden, or a fold yard. Whatever else he gained on coming to live in a back-to-back street, the town labourer lost his back door.

How did the back-to-back come to be accepted as a tolerable way of housing for the urban working classes, when it was part of the tradition neither of mean rural cottages nor of early town development? The early importation of an alternative, rurally-derived, house type into the industrial districts of Leeds is plainly shown in the fold-yard type of development illustrated in Fig 3.1. This was the type of new housing that Tuke's map of 1781 shows spreading in quasi-ribbon development along the main roads from Leeds to the south, south-east, east and north-east. These 'Folds' stand out on contemporary plans, particularly the first large-scale plan of Leeds (1815), since they gave no straight-line edge to successive frontages, such as the upper-class terraces or the sides of fashionable squares had given. Instead, even such a main road as Marsh Lane varied in width since the groups of houses were stepped back at different distances.

This *Folds* development, which may be approximately dated to the period 1750–80, was accompanied by a second type of urban cottage building, the occupation of whatever vacant space was still left in innyards, gardens and orchards lying behind the houses that lined the streets of the old core of the town, especially Briggate, Kirkgate, Vicar Lane, and the Headrow.[9] Indeed, here, it may be hazarded, lay the unintended transition to the back-to-back in the form of a single cottage with no through ventilation, no back windows and no back door. How? The new housing was obtained by lining the interior walls of an innyard or a garden with cottages : but

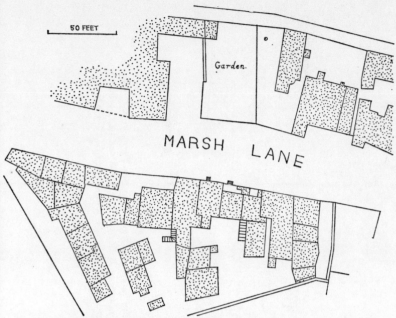

Fig 3.1. Leeds working-class cottages before the back-to-back: infill of two *Folds* on the south-east side of Marsh Lane, from survey of 1793, Leeds City Archives, DB 204/8.

there was usually room for no more than one line along each wall, thus the front—and only—door faced inwards to the yard, the remnants of which made up the yard of a court. Here from the mid-eighteenth century at least, incomers to Leeds were living in houses without back- or side-windows or doors.[10] (See Fig 3.2).

As it happened, all the principal streets of inner Leeds were lined with houses, shops and inns that gave available spaces for development in the long, narrow crofts behind them. In Kirkgate there were the crofts of the original village, in Briggate the burgage plots laid out in 1207, and in the Headrow the new extensions of the early seventeenth century. The town plan of 1815 shows these former open spaces virtually solid with infilled cottages, warehouses, and finishing shops.

Until at least 1781 the spread of roadside Folds and burgage infill was sufficient to meet the demands for working-class housing as population rose, without creating any new streets; and development

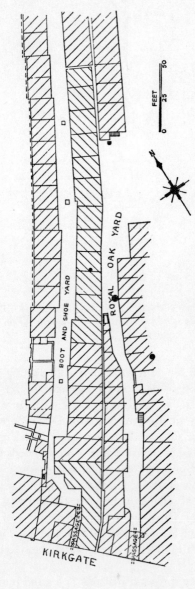

Fig. 3.2. Leeds working-class cottages before the back-to-back: infill of two *Yards* in Kirkgate, with cottages abutting on the Yard walls; the notorious Boot and Shoe Yard and its neighbour were cleared in 1844 under the Improvement Act of 1842: plan from LCD No 69.

in Park Row, Park Place and Park Square was catering for the much smaller number who could afford elegant housing. Tuke's plan of 1781 is a fortunate piece of evidence; for it shows Leeds replete with Folds and central infill, and just initiating its West End, but quite devoid of any new *cottage-streets* north of the river. The West End terraces apart, there was still no straight-line street outside the old burghal core in 1781. A long block of houses on the east side of Mabgate might seem to be such a street but on close examination it turns out to be *Near and Middle Fold*, a ribbon of cottages 200yd long.[11] Despite the name, which suggests a cluster of the Marsh Lane type, these two Folds in Mabgate were made up of two parallel rows of cottages, some with cellar dwellings, side by side for a length of over 200yd; the detail on the 1850 OS plan makes it clear that these were not back-to-backs; for even where the two parallel ribbons were set closest to each other there was a distinct space between the buildings. The ground on which these two Folds were built was not an innyard, for it lay in open country, but it had plainly once been a small, narrow, but long, field.

The techniques of developing such a field, end-on to a thoroughfare, would soon have to be applied more widely, for the main-road frontages within a reasonable distance of the town were becoming continuously built up by 1781, and if the open spaces nearer the town were to be taken over for building it would have to be by the creation of brand new streets opening up their interior and breaking through at some point into the existing thoroughfares.

The first place where such a block of streets was laid out for working-class cottages lay just north of the Kirkgate crofts, east of Vicar Lane but west of Sheepscar Beck, thus adjoining that part of the old town where infill development had already created a working-class area. This development, begun in 1787, created Union Street, Ebenezer Street, George (or George's) Street, and Nelson Street, with the short Sidney Street to join them to Vicar Lane on the west. On the east they abutted on the beck, where the street called Mill Garth formalised a trackway to the mill and the waterside meadows.

The houses which lined these pioneer streets were undoubtedly back-to-back cottages, many of them having separate cellar dwellings underneath. The large-scale OS plan of 1850 clearly marks them as back-to-back,[12] and the shape and position of the houses in 1850 is exactly as on the first medium-scale plan of the town,

G

drawn in 1815, and the dimensions of the building plots and the houses on these two plans are exactly those of the original deeds of 1787–8.

If it is true that these were the first back-to-backs in Leeds, the manner of their creation is the more interesting. They were not a speculative investment by the owner of the field, nor the speculation of some commercial or industrial capitalist; the latter type of investor is exemplified by Richard Kendall's 65 cottages and Paley's 175 cottages (1800–05) in the East Ward.[13] The Union Street back-to-backs were erected by a building club, one of those terminating building societies of the type described by Mr Seymour Price but not actually known to him. Its articles of agreement were drawn up on 3 November 1787, providing for the division of the *Crackenthorpe Garden* into fifty-two building lots. A number of the original conveyances from the building club to the first owners have survived among the deeds that have come to the town clerk in the process of compulsory purchase for clearances. With the deeds of the pair of back-to-backs later known as nos 22 and 26, Union Street, is the will of Sarah Brown, made 11 February 1794 and devising

> two cottages or dwelling houses being the front and back house site in Union Street, Leeds, then occupied by Robert Anderson and William Waddington, next adjoining the tenements of William Brown.

Six other pairs of back-to-backs in Ebenezer Street had five cellar dwellings under the back part of the range, entered from Union Court. Three other pairs, built in Union Street near Sarah Brown's, also had cellar dwellings opening into the other side of Union Court; these originated in the sale of Lots 11 and 12 by the Crackenthorpe Garden Building Club.[14] (See Fig 3.3, top line.)

The Union Street development of back-to-backs was only a few months ahead of another building club, already known to the historian of building societies,[15] though not hitherto dated. On 27 February 1788 an agreement was signed for the Hill House Building Club to purchase *Chamfor Close*, between the Aire and the slopes of the Bank, and divide it into forty-two lots. On these lots back-to-backs were also built, making King Street and Queen Street.[16] It is a curious coincidence that these two areas—the Crackenthorpe group of streets and the Hill House streets—were the first where the Corporation used its powers in the 1870 Improvement Act for the purchase and clearance of insanitary buildings.[17] Piecemeal and slowly the back-to-backs of 1787–8 began to come down,

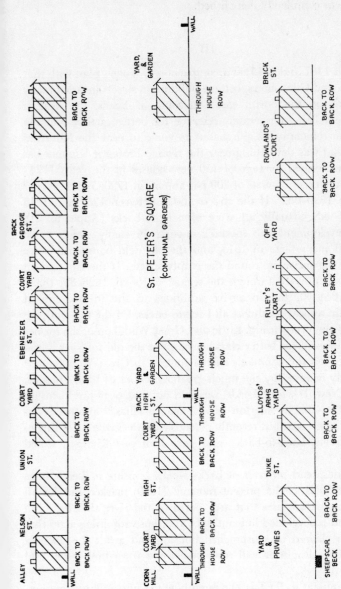

Fig 3.3. Back-to-back streets and courts: spacing illustrated by early examples. (*Upper*) back-to-backs, probably the first in Leeds, Crackenthorpe Gardens Building Club, 1787; (*middle*) the back-to-backs of the Lesser Building Society, and the through houses of the Greater Building Society in St Peter's Square adjoining, 1787–9; (*lower*) back-to-backs and courts developed on Richard Paley's land, 1795–1803. Scale 1in=25ft. (See also Fig 3.4 and plate page 84).

a century old. It was to be 170 years before this first group of back-to-backs was completely demolished.

III

Between 1787 and 1815, as a comparison of Tuke's plan with that of Netlam and Giles shows, cottage building in streets invaded many more fields on the north, east and south of Leeds, the western development being desperately reserved for better quality building despite the reluctance of purchasers to come so near the industrial precinct that was developing near the river.[18] Professor Rimmer has counted an annual average of 150 new houses in the years 1774–1815, with energetic bursts of 200 per annum in 1790–5 and 900 per annum in 1800–05.[19] If the streets added between 1787 and 1815 are examined, virtually all were of back-to-backs (Appendix II), though development was sporadic enough for many streets to be shown still incomplete in 1815, and the old field boundaries were shown by the surveyors round the empty spaces. If the comparison of maps is continued through the series[20] 1815–26, 1826–33, 1833–44 and 1844–50, the successive additions to the in-township of Leeds again appear as almost all back-to-backs. Of the two outlying hamlets of the in-township, Little and Great Woodhouse, the former was still reserved for better class housing but the old fold-yards and the cottages on the commons encroachments in Great Woodhouse[21] were slowly eclipsed by the much greater number of back-to-backs. While a 'New Town of Leeds' was laid out just over the township boundary in Chapel Allerton as well spaced villas,[22] another *Newtown*[23] (at Sheepscar but recently demolished) was made up of single-cottage streets, back-to-backs, and *pace* Professor Rimmer, closed courts.[24]

The widespread progress of back-to-back housing in Leeds from 1787 to 1850 is at the present moment (1969) marked out for all to see : for it comprises that area north of the river that has been cleared and redeveloped in giant flats, and those adjoining acres that have been cleared of substandard housing and await the phoenix that the City Engineer will some day rouse from their ashes and rubble.

The argument so far has suggested how the unventilated, one-up-one-down, cottage spread from the innyards into independent streets, where the rows of cottages were thrust so close together that no space remained between each row, and the back walls of adjoining rows were built to touch each other. If the transition was as smooth as this, it is not surprising that there was no contemporary comment on the birth of the back-to-backs, and no outcry on behalf of their inhabitants.

If the cottages were to be occupied by the working classes, then rents had to be low, and if rents were to be low, then the capital costs per house had to be kept low. This economic pressure towards high-density housing is understandable in the early developments such as Union Street and Paley's York Street estate, taking up land of high value near the town centre : but the back-to-back development continued, as we have seen, far away from the town centre into isolated fields neighboured only by cow pastures and tenter grounds; into the quite remote hamlet of Great Woodhouse; and in the isolated field on Carlton Hill that gave birth to Little London.[25] High land values could not have been the coercion here.

No doubt the spread of back-to-backs was facilitated if people came to accept in outlying areas what they already knew in the inner town;[26] and no doubt, as Baker often argued, the zeal for maximising rents per square yard was infectious among landowners.[27] But the economical beauty of back-to-backs in a property developer's eye was not only their density, yielding maximum rents per square yard, but the neat way into which they fitted into the shape of the vacant spaces available in Leeds as 'building ground' : fields on the eastern edge of the town are designated in this way in printed maps of the town from 1821 onwards but 'eligible building ground' was a commonplace in the advertisement columns of the local press[28] from the 1780s.

The size and shape of the fields comprising these 'building grounds' were important determinants of the type of housing development that took place on them. The open fields of Leeds had been enclosed at an unknown date, probably in the later Middle Ages. Their enclosure produced the characteristic long, rather narrow, fields which can still be seen outside the built-up area in the town plan of 1815 or in earlier manuscript plans of particular holdings. Fields of this size and shape had not been inconvenient for pasture or hay-ground around a developing town, and they were not unsuited to market gardening, while many of the grass fields were also used for rows of tenters. But their small width, in proportion to length,

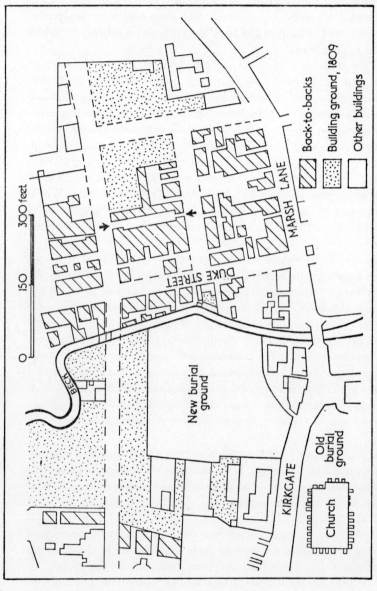

Fig 3.4. Estate development of back-to-back streets and courts in Leeds sold off in small plots by Richard Paley, 1795–1803: from plan following his bankruptcy, Leeds City Archives DB Map 119. The arrows mark Riley's Court (plate page 84).

Back-to-backs

Building ground, 1809

Other buildings

300 feet

150

BECK

DUKE STREET

MARSH LANE

New burial ground

Old burial ground

KIRKGATE

Church

posed particular problems when it came to laying out houses and streets within such fields.

The typical working-man's cottage of the late eighteenth and early nineteenth centuries was about 15ft square, and the minor streets of Leeds were usually 30 or 40ft wide. Thus a street of single cottages needed a ribbon of land with a minimum width of 60ft (ie 15 + 30 +15). It will be noticed that in such a ribbon, 30/60ths, or half the surface area was unproductive of house rents : dead ground as far as a developer was concerned.[29] But if, instead of a row of single cottages, a row of back-to-backs was set on either side of such a street, then the 30ft of dead ground would be matched by 60ft of housing, a reduction in 'dead ground' from 50 per cent to 33 per cent. A further economy could be made by not having streets of full width between the back-to-back rows, merely separating them by a courtyard; if access to such a courtyard was given by a tunnel it enabled all the four sides of the court to be built upon, and the use of a tunnel rather than an alley permitted an extra room (which meant extra rent) over the tunnel passage.

The typical field available as 'building ground' in Leeds after 1750 was from 120 to 200 ft wide, and about 600ft long, an area of from 1 5/6 to 2¾ acres.[30] In these long narrow fields there was room for more than one parallel unit of back-to-back + street + back-to-back. Some actual distributions will be seen in Fig 3.3. Fields of this size and shape, undoubtedly the parcelled-out furlongs of former open arable fields, can be seen in the 1815 plan on either side of the road—significantly known as Long Balk Lane, later Camp Road— that gave access to the level plateau north of the town, and on either side of the Harrogate turnpike, the principal northward artery. It was on the east side of the latter that the fields known as the *Leylands* became covered with what were to become notorious back-to-backs; the fact that all these fields had their long axis at right-angles to the thoroughfare gave them an additional advantage, for the streets could be led straight in.

The tyranny of the pre-existing narrow fields as the dominating units of building development was accentuated by another inheritance from pre-industrial Leeds. Not only were fields small and narrow but the pattern of landownership was dominated by the smallholder. There were very few large estates,[31] and the largest and most compact, the former manorial demesne of the *Parks*, had already been taken up for the West End developments of the 1780s and 1790s. The land which earliest came on to the market for building development was usually simply a single field, the whole of a man's patrimony, and so the problem of optimising the layout of new streets was the problem of utilising a single field. Had developers several adjacent fields to work in, they could have made cross streets, or the long streets of one field could have been connected to the long streets of the next field. But nothing is more characteristic of the early piecemeal back-to-back streets of Leeds than to find their ends blocked by a wall, by a change in level, or by the sides of other houses in another unconnected street. The line of blockage is simply the old field boundary. On one side a developer has set out his streets : and on the other side a different developer at a different time has set out his; and never the twain should meet.

The extreme of subservience to an existing field—and property— boundary is demonstrated in the 'half-backs'—lines of cottages only one room deep but so pressed against the edge of a field that no room was left for a back alley. The builder, therefore, put up half a back-to-back house as far as the peak of the roof and then dropped vertically down what would otherwise have been the partition wall between back-to-backs.[32] Doubtless in some cases there was the hope that at a later date the next field might be developed, and the lonely singles matched off. Certainly the piecemeal progress of lot purchases and house erection must also have left singles temporarily in mid-air within normal back-to-back streets. Where a half-back was never matched off, its vertical wall formed a grim cliff face to a court, or became the closed end of some alley, court, allotment, cemetery or factory yard. They were beloved of bill-posters. It was a forbidding aspect when the only doors of back-to-backs were thrust against one of these half-back cliffs (see plate page 84).

Short disconnected streets not only accentuated the airlessness of the back-to-back environment but were inimical to the development of through drainage, water and sewerage systems. This is why sanitary reformers took piecemeal building development as a main target for criticism.

> The land has been disposed of in so many small lots to petty proprietors who have subsequently built at pleasure, both as to inward form and outward ideas.[33]

In 1844 the sewerage engineer, Vetch, wrote :

> It is to be regretted that, on so great an extent of low ground destined so soon to be covered with population, some general plan of new streets

should not be adopted in conformity with good drainage and ventilation.[34]

The piecemeal disconnected streets, leading nowhere in particular and often at right-angles to thoroughfares, were also of little use as highways, and the highway authority was reluctant to adopt them. Fifteen years after Vetch's regrets the Privy Council's Medical Officer wrote of Leeds :

> The principal streets are fewer than is common in other great towns and the interspaces between the principal roads are occupied by dense and often complicated congeries of ill-kept streets and courts, which have but seldom been adopted as highways by the municipal authority, and are in a very foul state.[35]

One of the reasons why the Leeds back-to-backs of the 1870s and 1880s are more pleasing than those of the earlier period is not only the wider spacing laid down in the byelaws after 1866, but also the fact that streets became very much longer, and linked with each other, some of them being sufficiently arterial to have early tram and bus routes along them. Their length was made possible by an important change in the size of the characteristic development unit. By the early 1860s, particularly in the north and north-east, very little undeveloped land lay within the actual township (or 'in-township') of Leeds, and the building grounds were now moving into the fields of rural townships (such as Roundhay, Potter Newton, Headingley, and Chapel Allerton) where there were both larger fields, and (more important) larger estates to be developed as planned entities. Closed-in courts and narrow alleys, like cellar dwellings, are not considered in this short essay, though, as the last quotation shows, they were often linked with back-to-backs in reformers' criticisms. So far, back-to-backs have been considered as the components of 'streets', that is, spaces left between facing doorways that were of the width accepted elsewhere in Leeds as a street; for the pavements, roadsurfaces, drainage and scavenging of these 'streets' was often of the lowest quality, as the last quotation also indicates. But even less attractive were the back-to-backs crowded so closely that there was less than a street's width between facing rows, and made up into so short a cul-de-sac that there was no through ventilation, and the building blocking the cul-de-sac (a factory or a wall of half-backs) also blocked out light and sun. If the development was set behind old-established properties, access to it would be through a narrow passage or by a tunnel, further restricting air, sun and ventilation. Courts and alleys were commonplace in all towns, and in essence they were little different from the infill of the old innyards and burgage plots, but back-to-backs facing into courts of this type in Leeds gave an additional ill-savour not found everywhere.[36]

IV

It can hardly be said that back-to-backs crept in through the back door since that was the very feature that they lacked, but no contemporary comment on their arrival has yet been noted in the Press. Explicit criticism of back-to-backs by sanitary reformers also came later, though the streets cited by Baker in his criticisms of 1833, 1839 and 1842 included many that were made up of back-to-backs.

The notion that it might be necessary to regulate the builder's activity through laws and byelaws was a natural accompaniment of proposals for laws to determine standards of water supply, drainage and sewerage. In his evidence to a Select Committee in 1833 John Marshall, MP for Leeds, put building regulation in such a context :

> It is advisable to have some improvement made in sewerage and regulation of buildings and small tenements . . . for the health of the inhabitants, and for the comfort of the humbler classes, combined with the saving in the poor rate.[37]

In the same year, Baker's report to the Leeds Board of Health devoted seven pages of close print to a list of streets in which there had been cholera deaths. As one would expect, the leaders in disrepute—'most wretched', 'very very dirty', 'wretchedly filthy', 'most confined'—were the crowded courts and yards of the innermost town, such as the Boot and Shoe inn yard; and the decaying agricultural cottages of the Folds : indeed the cholera had begun in Leeds in Blue Bell Fold,[38] 'small and dirty containing about 20 houses inhabited by poor families many of whom are Irish'. But back-to-back streets were also among the leaders : there were eight deaths in Bath Street, eight in Orange Street, eighteen in Quarry Hill, eleven in Richmond Road and eight in York Street (see Appendix 3.2, below).

In the 1839 *Report* of the Council's Statistical Committee nine places were named as 'proverbial' for their squalor : two were innyards (the Boot and Shoe, and the Wellington) and the other seven were back-to-backs, including the pioneers, Union Street, George Street and Ebenezer Street.[39] The five streets named by the Streets Committee in 1842 as 'the worst for typhus' were all back-to-backs, as were three of the four named as 'outstandingly unhealthy' in Vetch's sewerage report of 1844.[40] Similarly the cholera deaths of 1849 and the diarrhoeal mortalities of 1854–8 were severest in the back-to-backs of Camp Field, Mill Street and Quarry Hill;[41] and the prize for squalor awarded by the Privy Council's MOH in 1865 was again Ebenezer Street, unequalled in age and disrepute : 'filthiest street of all'.[42] From 1870 the borough MOH's reports regularly listed the fever streets, and they were generally made up of back-to-backs.[43]

The reports cited so far took as their target the conditions of specific streets but did not condemn the back-to-backs as such, though in his report to the House of Lords Committee in 1842 Baker had used the term *back-to-back* and came near to a general condemnation, both for their size and lack of ventilation.

> The building of houses back-to-back occasions this in great measure. It is in fact part of the economy of buildings that are to pay a good percentage.[44]

Baker did, however, set out figures of costs, rents and working-class budgets to show how a labourer would not be able to afford the rent if house-builders had built houses any larger.[45]

It is a curious irony that, in the very months when Chadwick's *Report on the Sanitary Condition of the Labouring Population* was being printed, a direct attack on the back-to-back by legislation was being defeated. Following on a recommendation of the Select Committee of 1840 on the Health of Towns,[46] a 'Bill for Regulating Buildings in Large Towns' was introduced into the Commons on 7 May 1841 and only minutely amended in Committee on 24 May. The bill did not go to the Lords until the following February, and on its return it still contained its original clause outlawing back-to-backs :

> it shall not be lawful to build any house, except corner houses, on any new foundation unless there shall be a clear space of at least Twenty Feet wide between the back wall of such house and the back wall of any opposite house;

and the marginal rubric was even more explicit : 'Houses Not To Be Built Back-to-Back'.[47] However, the building interests were aroused, and at this late stage the Commons sent the Bill to a Select Committee which met between March and mid-June 1842.

The witnesses heard by the committee ranged from reforming

interventionists to classical advocates of laisser faire. The 1840 committee's report had tried to assuage fears about regulations:

> the regulations would be framed so as to interfere no further with everyone's right to manage his own property than was necessary to protect the health of the community; nor would they extend beyond what that urgent duty of government justified;[48]

but the majority of witnesses heard in 1842 were horrified at the idea of limiting a builder's freedom. It was this idea of a 'duty of government' that had moved Dr James Williamson of Leeds to say to the 1840 Committee,

> the working classes are now exposed to the evils arising from cupidity and defective arrangements of many of their landlords, and they seem to me to require the protection of some such general enactment.[49]

The witnesses from Leeds in 1842 were of a different mind. Mr Beckett of Kirkstall Grange, who admitted that no other house except his own porter's lodge lay within half a mile of his own, told the committee that the Bill's proposals had 'created a very strong sensation throughout the country', and clearly not a sensation of approval. The town clerk of Leeds also gave evidence against the ban on back-to-backs 'which would drive the lower classes into lodgings' by putting up rents. He advocated a compromise solution: to permit back-to-backs to be built in blocks of eight (ie four front and four back) with spaces between each block in which a privy could be sited. His council had been advised by builders that to follow the bill and give a back yard and privy to each house would have entailed a rise of about 30 per cent in the cost of each house of back-to-back size.[50] (Thomas Cubitt was to say much the same in his evidence of 1844 to the Royal Commission on the State of Large Towns:[51] 'it is a much cheaper mode, and if we prevent it we prevent houses for the accommodation of poor people'.)

After this and similar evidence the Select Committee deleted the clause on back-to-backs from the bill, and the whole bill was dropped after the end of June 1842, ostensibly to await the Poor Law Commissioners' (that is, Chadwick's) *Report*, which was available on 9 July, 1842. In the event, the Public Health Act of 1848 contained no reference to back-to-backs.[52]

In the absence of national legislation to ban the building of back-to-backs it was necessary for urban councils to take powers by specific clauses in local improvement acts that they were promoting, or to pass byelaws under other statutory authority, such as the Public Health Act of 1858. Leeds was decidedly not of this mind. In Manchester, said its town clerk in 1869, 'since 1844 the building of back-to-back houses has been illegal' through the requirement that every new house should have a privy and ashpit behind it (Manchester Police Act, 1844).[53] The town clerk of Liverpool, who had been town clerk at Bradford 1861–6, also gave evidence to the same Royal Commission. Liverpool had used its powers under an act of 1861 to pass a byelaw 'that prevents back-to-back houses'; the town clerk of Halifax also said, 'I think back-to-back houses are exceedingly injurious.'[54]

The former town clerk of Bradford's evidence included his ring-side view of the local turmoil at Bradford after the building bye-laws of 1860.

> Their effect was to prevent a class of house that had been built until that time, that is to say, back-to-back houses in long rows . . . the effect was to prevent any houses being built of that sort.[55]

The method of the byelaw was to prescribe an open space at the rear and side of each house, so that a block of two pairs of back-to-backs would have been the maximum permitted. There had been considerable local agitation following 1860, based on statements that builders had been deterred, and housing consequently scarcer and dearer.

> I do not think that was the cause of the scarcity, but the agitation led to certain concessions in 1866 that were to a great extent temporary, (for example back-to-backs built on land already laid out as building ground).[56]

James Hole's prize essay of January 1865, which had a public reading before the mayor in Leeds Town Hall, setting off a long debate in the local press, praised the Bradford byelaw of 1860 and bemoaned Leeds'

> want of municipal regulations, especially including one to prohibit the erection of back-to-back houses which have now unfortunately become almost the universal plan for the dwellings of the working class of Leeds, and even for some as high as £20 annual rental.

He was, naturally, even more critical of the old existing back-to-backs. He recalled Baker's criticisms of 1839 and 1842, and added : 'a large proportion of these homes still exists, made worse for twenty years' additional wear and tear'. Hole was driven to conclude that the council needed powers to regulate the type of new buildings erected :

> the utter powerlessness of the working man over the construction and condition of his dwelling justified municipal interference, and the municipal power had as much right to prevent these as to insist on their proper sewerage.[57]

The best that the mayor could do in reply was to adduce the alleged scarcity that regulation had brought to Bradford (a junction of cause and effect that, it will be recalled, the town clerk of Bradford had denied), and certainly to exaggerate :

> in Bradford where this class of houses could not be built, the effect had been so much to increase the rentals that three or four families were driven into one house.[58]

While Manchester, Liverpool and Bradford had been formulating byelaws Leeds had done nothing. There had been improvement acts in 1842, 1848, 1856 but no mention of back-to-backs in them. It was true, Hole admitted, that section 190 of the 1842 Leeds Improvement Act had given the council power to compel a proper privy for each newly erected house, but

> if the cottage speculator chooses to disregard such regulations he may do so with impunity. No summons has been issued for many years for any breach of building regulations. The back-to-back system of house-building has rendered this (clause) all but impracticable.[59]

The tolerance of back-to-backs did not make all property owners in Leeds enthusiastic for them on their own doorsteps. For example, the deeds for the sale of the plot of land on which no 8 Cavendish Road (now part of the School of Economic Studies) was to be built prescribed in 1864 that 'no house of the description known as back-to-back shall be erected on the said plot', nor for the next twenty years was it to bear a public house.[60]

The only effective—and still partial—restriction of back-to-backs in Leeds came in 1866 with the byelaw that took up the proposal made by the town clerk in 1842 : new houses of this type could not be built in blocks of more than eight (four front and four back), and yard privies had to be placed between each block.[61] It is the serried ranks of these blocks, regularly broken by the privy yard space, that still catch the eye of the visitors from the south or from the northern towns that never had back-to-backs.

The continuance of back-to-back building, even in blocks of eight, remained the target for sanitary critics. Articles in *The Builder* in 1869, 1891 and 1897 cited Leeds as an incorrigible friend of the back-to-backs,[62] and a standard textbook on building development, published in 1883 observed sadly : 'I understand that back-to-back houses are still being erected in some northern towns'.[63] In Leeds the Council[64] and builders were unabashed at such comments. In 1888 an official inquiry by Barry and Smith showed that in each of the years between 1875 and 1887 (when 16,070 new houses were built in Leeds) two-thirds of all new houses were back-to-backs. Table 3.3 shows these proportions continuing until 1903, and Leeds was not yet alone in its affection for the back-to-back.

> In all the large manufacturing towns of Yorkshire back-to-back dwellings have been and are still being built to a considerable extent. In Lancashire, the Potteries and the Black Country it has been almost discontinued.[65]

Their report examined cases in Halifax, Morley, Stainland, Todmorden and Keighley : they were able to show, contrary to the arguments of mayors and master builders, that the difference in cost of a through house and a pair of back-to-backs of the same floor area was negligible, but the division enabled two separate tenancies to be created, and the return from the back-to-backs was made about some 20 per cent higher.

At about this time the secretary of the Leeds Permanent Building Society, Fatkin, was giving evidence to another royal commission. About one-seventh of his 9,348 members owned two adjoining pairs of back-to-backs which they had erected on a single building lot 10yd square, living in one of the four and drawing an income from the rents of the other three, out of which they were paying off their mortgage. The fashion in back-to-backs was changing, he said : instead of a kitchen in the cellar, more and more of his members were putting up houses that had a small kitchen alongside the parlour on the ground floor.[66]

These 'superior' back-to-backs were the £20 pa rentals mentioned by Hole in 1865, and described in 1906 by Lupton :

> modern scullery houses which contain a living room on one side of the door, and a scullery on the other, a bedroom over each, and usually a third attic bedroom with dormer windows built in blocks of eight, with rentals of from 3s 9d to 5s 6d.[67]

(Through houses at that time were rented for 5s 3d to 6s, and older, one-up one-down, back-to-backs were then 2s to 3s).[68]

It is significant that in 1898, when the corporation were planning the houses that they would rebuild in the York Street area after their first major slum-clearance programme, they wished to put up back-to-backs, and sent a deputation to the Local Government Board in Whitehall to argue their case. They failed to convince London.[69] Indeed official opinion was now so firmly set against back-to-backs that the Housing, Town Planning Act of 1909, section 43, laid down the countrywide ban that the Bill of 1841 had attempted.

> Notwithstanding anything in any Local Act or byelaw in force in any borough or district, it shall not be lawful to erect any back-to-back houses intended to be used as dwellings for the working classes.[70]

The official views of the medical officers of health were undoubtedly coloured by the evidence of disease differentials. A good deal of such local evidence was brought together in Darra Moir's report of 1910 :

> even relatively good types of back-to-back, when compared with through, have a death rate 15 to 20 per cent in excess, although this is not evident when they are in blocks of four only, possessing some degree of ventilation.[71]

The excessive mortality was found in all types of fatal illness as well as chronic diseases of the chest and in defective growth.

In 1909 the Leeds Master Builders Association petitioned against legislative ban on back-to-backs, as might have been expected.[72] Their arguments were the old ones, that through houses would put rents beyond the reach of working-class incomes. Darra Moir's report believed that the rise in rent for a through house of equivalent size would have to be about 20 per cent if a landlord were to have the same return on his capital. Rents in Leeds were not in fact high : the Board of Trade's survey of wages and prices in 1908 had showed that Leeds ranked as low as thirty-second of the seventy-three largest towns in England and Wales in respect of its rent index, and other local prices were also low; Leeds ranked fifteenth among the seventy-three local price indexes. In absolute terms a two-room back-to-back could then be rented at 3s to 3s 6d, a three-room from 3s 6d to 4s 6d, a four-room from 4s 6d to 6s, and a superior five-room from 5s to 6s 6d.[73]

In the event, 1909 did not see the end of back-to-back building in Leeds : the escape route for builders lay through a provision that the Act should not apply to streets where the plans had been

TABLE 3.2

LEEDS BUILDING PLANS APPROVED, 1886–1914

	Total house-plans	Villas	Semi-Detached	Through houses	Back-to-back	per cent
1886	1,596	13	10	441	1,132	71
7	1,847	18	16	693	1,120	61
8	2,058	14	8	620	1,416	69
9	2,010	13	12	605	1,380	69
90	1,990	18	26	689	1,257	63
1	1,845		na			—
2	2,097	15	35	664	1,383	66
3	1,923		na			—
4	2,017	9	30	586	1,392	69
5	1,794	21	28	391	1,354	75
6	2,242	12	42	518	1,670	74
7	2,350	21	54	747	1,528	65
8	3,318	21	84	1,033	2,180	66
9	4,596	21	132	1,124	3,319	72
1900	3,549	19	133	1,097	2,300	65
1	2,947	19	88	812	2,028	69
2	2,635	18	140	728	1,749	66
3	3,529	38	177	912	2,402	68
4	3,144	54	134	1,291	1,665	53
5	2,559	21	133	1,403	1,002	39
6	1,553	30	105	735	683	44
7	1,290	33	102	580	575	45
8	1,074	22	87	439	526	49
9	724	19	67	332	306	42
10	903	28	87	411	377	42
1	441	25	78	264	74	17
2	363	37	43	221	62	17
3	276	22	56	134	64	23
4	359	35	71	196	57	16
TOTALS	57,029	616	1,978	17,666	33,001	58

Source: *Annual Reports* of Building Clauses Committee, Leeds Corporation.

H

TABLE 3.3

LEEDS HOUSES COMPLETED, 1886–1914

	Total	Back-to-backs	Back-to-backs per cent
1886	1,103	719	65
7	1,208	783	65
8	1,723	1,084	63
9	1,571	1,179	75
1890	1,728	1,194	69
1	812	552	68
2	1,876	1,212	65
3	1,915	1,258	66
4	1,949	1,308	67
5	1,707	1,134	66
6	1,681	1,229	73
7	1,832	1,396	76
8	2,399	1,633	68
9	2,903	2,034	70
1900	3,059	2,143	70
1	3,030	2,035	67
2	2,201	1,358	62
3	2,572	1,563	61
4	2,923	1,751	60
5	2,442	1,170	48
6	1,748	765	44
7	1,135	504	44
8	919	410	45
9	836	411	49
1910	584	226	39
1	505	122	24
2	350	110	31
3	220	32	15
4	287	26	9
TOTALS	47,218	29,341	62

Source: *Annual Reports*, Building Clauses Committee (1886–98); Building Plans Sub-Committee of Improvements Committee (1899–1914).

approved by the council before 1 May 1909 : the slow completion of streets had long been a regular feature of Leeds housing history, even streets begun in boom years. (I have shown elsewhere how Prosperity Street, a street of back-to-backs, took from 1874 to 1901 to complete, although only made up of sixty-four pairs.[74]) In 1910–14, when 1,946 houses were built in Leeds, a quarter were back-to-back.[75] Then all building virtually ceased for six years and it was 1937 before the last street was completed, so that back-to-backs were still being built in the years when the 150-year old back-to-backs on Quarry Hill were being slum-cleared. (See plate page 197.)

The strength of the back-to-back tradition in Leeds is a part, perhaps the most extreme part, of that 'local influence' in building styles, with which this essay began. The surprise of southern visitors, first seeing the northern hillsides and their regimented streets, is one indication that we are not dealing with a nationwide style of working-class housing. Cubitt declared that he had never built one himself, and they do not seem to have been a feature of the London industrial districts. It has been seen above that Liverpool, Manchester and Bradford had their back-to-backs, but fell out of love with them. Darra Moir's study of 1910, which is concerned with the whole country, cites examples in a very limited number of towns, all northern. Besides Manchester and Bradford, he refers to Shipley, Morley, Huddersfield, Batley, Bradford, Halifax, Keighley, Cleckheaton, Brighouse, Dewsbury, Linthwaite, Heckmondwike, Pudsey (Yorks), and Chester le Street (Co Durham). Barry and Smith's study of 1888 refers to 'discontinuance' of back-to-back building in Lancashire, the Potteries, and the Black Country. The actual examples they cite lay in Halifax, Morley, Stainland, Todmorden and Keighley.

Such an uneven local distribution is difficult to explain. The back-to-back seems to have lingered longest in the wool textile towns but there was no functional role for the back-to-back in the industrial process : the back-to-backs were not built as weavers' chambers, though some in their middle age lived on to be part of clothing sweatshops. Anyway, they existed outside the textile towns. If they seem to be built to match the low purchasing power of their working-class tenants (as the protagonists of back-to-back always claimed), there were many industrial areas with equally low wages and yet not a back-to-back in sight. Nor can they be satisfactorily claimed as the consequence of high land values; in Leeds they were

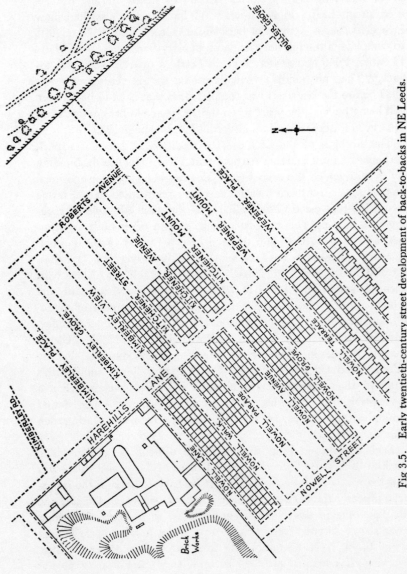

Fig 3.5. Early twentieth-century street development of back-to-backs in NE Leeds.
Scale: 1in = 20ft

found on the dear land and on the cheap land; and there is no evidence that land values were systematically higher in those industrial towns that made the most of every square foot of their building grounds by packing in the back-to-backs.[76] Baker characterised back-to-backs as 'part of the economy of buildings that are to pay a good percentage',[77] but, again, there is no reason to think that cupidity or philanthropy among English landowners was distributed in the same way that we find the presence and absence of back-to-backs in industrial towns of the nineteenth century.

Using historical evidence, it has been suggested when and how the back-to-back working-class cottage came to Leeds; and it has been argued that it matched the particular size and position of fields, and the size of ownership units. It will need studies in other towns where back-to-backs proliferated to determine whether the Leeds chronology and typology are universal. But all periods of English vernacular architecture—and working-class housing is a part of the vernacular—have displayed such local and regional differences. In general, the observed differences discussed by architectural historians relate either to function or to the local availability of different building materials. Neither of these can apply to the back-to-back. It had no industrial function peculiar to it; and, while the majority were made of cheap bricks, there were Pennine back-to-backs that used local quarry stone. Driven from a simple economic explanation and deprived of arguments from use and materials, there is nothing left except a rather desperate refuge in 'cultural' factors,[78] of the sort that have produced local differentiation in the demand for fish-and-chips, Yorkshire pudding, Rugby League, and Lancashire hot-pot. Differences of taste, they lie beyond the quantifiables of price, income, density, costs, rents, returns, and land values.[79]

NOTES

1   Robert Baker was medical officer to the Poor Law Guardians, then a councillor, and later a factory inspector. His reports [hereafter cited as *Baker, 1833*; *Baker, 1839*; and *Baker, 1842*] were: *Report of the Leeds Board of Health* (1833); 'Report upon the Condition of the Town of Leeds and of Its Inhabitants, by a Statistical Committee of the Town Council, October 1839', *Journ (Royal) Stat Soc,* ii (1840), 397–422; 'On the State and Condition of the Town of Leeds', *Sanitary Condition of the Labouring Population, Local Reports,* Parliamentary Papers [hereafter *PP*], xxvii, Lords (1842).

2   Leeds Civic Hall, Committee Strong Room, shelf 36: Minute Book of the Statistical Committee; unprinted Council Minutes, iv, ff 525–9.

3   This map, more crudely constructed than that of 1842, was printed in *Baker, 1833* and is reproduced in K. J. Bonser and H. Nicholls, *Printed Maps and Plans of Leeds, 1711–1900, Thoresby Soc,* xlvii (1960), no 72.

4   The map was printed in *Baker, 1842,* in colours. In the more salubrious north-west suburb it is significant that the only streets with spots were the two blocks of back-to-backs: St James St and Little London (Carlton St and Reuben St). The environmental factor was further emphasised by Baker's use of smoking chimneys to locate the factories of Leeds.

5   A. Redford, *The History of Local Government in Manchester,* i (1939), 418.

6   Asa Briggs, *Victorian Cities* (1963), 155.

7   Baker employed the term 'back-to-back' in 1842 (*Baker, 1842,* 5) but it cannot be traced further since the absence of early references from the *Oxford English Dictionary* suggests a narrow experience of the world among Oxford lexicographers.

8   W. G. Rimmer, 'Working Men's Cottages in Leeds, 1770–1840', *Thoresby Soc,* xlvi (1961), 165–99; although it is not plain, the 'cottages' of 1787–1800 were mainly back-to-backs. See note 16, below.

9   Ventilating flues were incorporated by some later builders (*Leeds Mercury,* 20 October 1862). The 1866 building byelaws envisaged pipe or shaft ventilators, but the 1869 bye-laws were less specific: 'means as shall be satisfactory to the Council'.

10 Rimmer, *art cit* in note 8, discussed the infill development, using material from the 1792–4 survey of the Pious Uses (sc Charities) Estates, now Leeds City Archives, DB204/8; the *Fold* pattern can be seen in the plan of a Marsh Lane estate in the same survey.

11 An old-established animal-fold use for the crofts enclosed behind house-frontages of any shape is suggested, not only by the long narrow *Folds* of Mabgate, but also by *Fold* as an alternative name for the Yards of Kirkgate inns: the Wellington Inn Yard deeds (Leeds Civic Hall, Deeds Strong Room [hereafter cited as LCD], no 300) refer to 'eight tenements in the Fold', and call the Yard 'Kay Fold' or 'Peckers-gill Fold'. Kay was the owner c 1632, and Peckersgill c 1704.

12 Shown by dotted partition lines within the firm outline of the whole building block. The almost standard size of a back-to-back, 5yd square, is also prominent on the plan. Directories also reveal back-to-back streets by having twice as many house-numbers than there are house-frontages on the plan; courts in back-to-back streets are usually named but their inhabitants not listed.

13 Rimmer, *art cit* in note 8, 187, based in the Rate Books, Leeds City Archives. Paley's development lay between York Road and Marsh Lane (Fig 3.4); and LCD no 1128, twenty-three cottages built in Watkinson's Yard with deeds going back to Paley's sale to William Watkinson, joiner, in 1792).

14 LCD nos 320, 334, 423 and 435. This land had been released for building development by the Anne Wilson Settled Estates Act of 1765.

15 S. J. Price, *Building Societies* (1958), 19–31.

16 LCD nos 604 and 607. In 1789 the St James St Building Club began to operate (LCD no 5706, ii) but its land purchases also date back to 1787. In 1789 the more elaborate 'Greater' and 'Lesser' Building Societies were beginning St Peter's Square and High St on Boggard Closes, Quarry Hill, which they had bought in 1787, the year after their foundation. The former was a quite elegant square but the latter was mainly back-to-backs (LCD nos 945, 1787 and 8433). In July 1786 the Union Row Building Association also bought its plot on Quarry Hill: building on its twenty-two lots was complete by 1796 (LCD nos 1999 and 1893C); these houses were of 'cottage' size but a single row only.

17 In 1869 a sub-committee of the council, considering a clause in the next improvement bill, cited 200 houses and 46 cellar dwellings in Back George St, Nelson St and Mill Garth, ie the town's veteran back-to-backs (Civic Hall, Committee Strong Room, Sub-scavenging and Nuisances [Cellar Dwellings] Committee, minutes, August 1869). When the Social Science Congress met in Leeds in 1871 the editor of *The Builder* (xxix [1871], 778, 817 and 929) took the Ebenezer St courts as the worst example of housing in the host town.

18 The frustrated development of the Wilson (Park) Estate at the West End of Leeds is illustrated in M. W. Beresford, 'Prosperity Street', in M. W. Beresford and G. R. J. Jones, ed, *Leeds and its Region* (1967), 186–97, and figs 42–3. In the course of the smoke-abatement action heard against Gott's mill in 1824 it was stated that 'many houses have been built . . . as cheaply as possible for labouring people. Two or three of them were partly blown down during the winter': *Report of the Trial and Indictment* (1824), 8–9. The status of the intended West End was not enhanced by the building of a gasworks there in 1826.

19 Rimmer, *art cit* in note 8, 187. The *Leeds Intelligencer,* 27 March 1787, reported 'near 400 houses erected' in 1786 and the same number anticipated for 1787.

20 Printed town plans are calendared in Bonser and Nicholls, *op cit* in note 3.

21 This development can be traced in the Denison Mss (Univ of Nottingham, Dept of Mss), eg DeH 20 and 38.

22 The New Town project on land belonging to Earl Cowper was mooted in 1825 as 'this Utopia . . . without manufacturing smoke' (*Leeds Mercury*, 30 July 1825), delayed by a bankruptcy of leading partners, abortively put up in lots in 1828 and offered again in 1839; the earliest sales so far noted in the deeds are of 1848 (LCD no 9172).

23 The more humble New Town project was developed on Griffith Wright's land from 1823 (LCD nos 4564, 4613 and 4954).

24 Rimmer *art cit* in note 8, 186: Mushroom Court, between Cambridge St and Grey St was wholly enclosed, and entered only through tunnels,

with steps to allow for the slope of the hill on which the estate lay (OS five-foot plan, 1850).

25   LCD no 6477, with plan; 10040, and 12543.

26   It could be argued that experience of cottages in innyards that were entered through archways would accustom people to living in closed courts entered through tunnel passages.

27   *Baker, 1842*, 5. 'Cottage property in Leeds realizes about 7 or 7%, and in many cases a much greater percentage . . . It is very well known that property of that description realizes a better rate of interest than property of a higher description': evidence of Matthew Johnson of Leeds, *Sel Comm on Rating of Tenements,* (*PP*, xxi of 1837–8), Q 2325. Similar returns were assumed by correspondents of the *Leeds Mercury*, 16 October 1862, a quarter-century later.

28   'Land in the skirts of the town frequently sells for £300 an acre, and there are instances of ground well adapted to building selling for £1,000 an acre. Of the prosperity of Leeds . . ₃ the many new streets in the town and the manufactories and villas in the neighbourhood erected and being erected are very convincing proof.' Sir F. Eden, *The State of the Poor* (1797), 847–8; also Rimmer *art cit* in note 8, 189–91 for other evidence of land values.

29   Minimum street widths of 36ft appear in the Building Regulations of 1866; alleys were to be at least 12ft wide.

30   The average size of fifty-four fields designated as *Building Ground* in the Tithe Award of 1847 (Leeds City Archives) was just over $1\frac{1}{4}$ acres; streets laid out in the grounds of large houses of the 1790s were similarly confined.

31   Only four landowners had more than 60 acres of field-land in 1847 (Tithe Award); three lay on the eastern edge of the township and the fourth on the western edge.

32   A line of these is illustrated in Beresford, *Time and Place* (1961) plate ii. The influence of a boundary on street lengths is shown by the irregular group near Henrietta St, determined by the jagged township boundary at that point.

33   Baker, 1842, 4.

34   *RC on the State of Large Towns and Populous Districts, PP*, xvii of 1844), 9.

35   *2nd Rep of the MOH to the Privy Council, for 1859* (*PP*, xxix of 1860), 134.

36   Among the nastiest, although not publicised like the Boot and Shoe Yard, must have been the inward-facing houses of the *Rows* that filled up the 456sq yd of Camp Field, south of the river and eventually surrounded by mills. Development of these back-to-backs began in 1805–6.

37   *Sel Comm on Public Walks* (*PP*, xv of 1833), Q 607.

38   Blue Bell Fold lay behind 46 East St at the Bank.

39   *Baker, 1839*, 400.

40   *RC on the State of Large Towns and Populous Districts* (*PP*, xvii of 1844), Qq 5761 and 5766.

41 *PP, xxix of 1860,* 133–9 (see note 35).

42 *8th Rep of the MOH to the Privy Council, for 1865* (*PP*, xxxiii of 1866), 226–45.

43 The MOH's *Report of the Sanitary Condition of Leeds for 1867* (1868) has a dot distribution map for fever cases, and subsequent *Reports* from the Leeds MOH followed suit.

44 *Baker, 1842,* 5.

45 *Ibid,* 11–13. Baker was not unsympathetic to the economic realities of landlordism, and he particularly praised Croisdale's cottage property management on the Bank, and Holdforth's in Mill St (*Baker, 1839,* 401; *Leeds Mercury,* 2 November 1839; Rimmer *art cit* in note 8, 183).

46 *Rep of Sel Comm on the Health of Towns* (*PP*, xi of 1840).

47 The original Bill is bound in *PP, i of 1840* as 93–124; the amended Bills as *Ibid,* 125–56 and *PP, i of 1842* 287, 319, 351 and 367. The clause quoted was originally no 17 and later no 20.

48 *PP, xi of 1840,* xv.

49 *Ibid,* Qq 1667–1807: Dr Williamson had been a member of the Council's Statistical Committee of 1839.

50 *Rep of Sel Comm on Building Regulations Bill and Improvement of Boroughs Bill* (*PP*, x of 1842), 143–9, 160–1 and 306. Eddison himself had shares in a philanthropic company for London tenement building (*Leeds Mercury,* 22 July 1848).

51 *PP, xvii of 1844,* Q 174.

52 The Royal Commission on the State of Large Towns which reported in 1844 and 1845 had also rejected building regulations as a remedy for urban discontents (*PP, xvii of 1845,* 63), and twenty years later, when proposals for building controls in a Leeds Improvement Bill were put forward, an alderman made it clear that local magistrates might have the same ideas on the sanctity of private property that had inspired the Commission of 1845: 'it would be difficult to obtain the sanction of Quarter Sessions to any byelaws interfering with property' (*Leeds Mercury,* 3 February 1865). See also note 61, below.

53 *1st Rep of the Sanitary Comm* (*PP*, xxxii of 1868–9), 129–30 and 144.

54 The Liverpool byelaw of 1864 made back-to-backs illegal *in courts.*

55 *Ibid,* Q 990.

56 *Ibid,* Qq 2213 et seq.

57 James Hole, 'The Working Classes of Leeds', prize essay of January 1865, reprinted as appendix to his *Homes of the Working Classes* (1866), 125.

58 *Leeds Mercury,* 3 February 1865.

59 Hole, *op cit* in note 57, 128.

60 Univ of Leeds, Bursary deed no 27, seen by permission of the Bursar.

61 'In no case shall dwelling houses be erected in blocks so that any block contain more than eight dwelling houses': Building byelaw no 11 of 1866; byelaw 8 of 1869 reiterated this provision, and banned blocks of more than four half-backs. No printed copy of these early byelaws

has been found but they were enrolled at Quarter Sessions despite fears voiced in 1865 (note 52 above): Leeds City Archives, QS Minute Books, November 1866 and April 1869. See 35–6 Vict ch xcvii, S.23 (1872).

62 *The Builder*, xxvii (1869), 26; lxi (1891), 172 and 326; lxxiii (1897), 22 and 237.

63 F. Maitland, *Building Estates, a Rudimentary Treatise* (1883), 28.

64 But the Leeds MOH, it may be noted, 'objected on sanitary grounds to the erection of back-to-back houses' (Leeds Civic Hall, Committee Strong Room, shelf 11: Building Clauses Committee Minutes, 27 October 1871). The eight-in-a-block byelaw was being enforced at this time (eg plans disallowed, 5 February and 25 March 1870; demolition of an offending building, 14 May 1875).

65 F. W. Barry and P. G. Smith, *Joint Report on Back-to-back Houses to the Local Government Board* (1888), 2.

66 *RC on the Housing of the Working Classes, Minutes of Evidence* (*PP*, xxx of 1884–5), ii, 371–9.

67 F. M. Lupton, *Housing Improvement: a Summary of Ten Years' Work in Leeds* (1906), 2.

68 The Leeds Industrial Dwellings Co, which owned many blocks of working-class property in Leeds, had a revaluation of its houses in 1889 (LCD no 1988), and its back-to-backs were then letting at from 2s to 3s 8d a week.

69 *The Builder*, lxxv (1898), 567 and lxxvi (1899), 99.

70 9 Edward VII, cap 44.

71 L. W. Darra Moir, *Report on Back-to-back Houses* (*PP*, xxxviii of 1910), 1.

72 *The Builder*, xcvii (1909), 103.

73 A. W. Fox, *Report of an Inquiry by the Board of Trade into Working-Class Rents, Housing and Retail Prices* (*PP*, cvii of 1908), 256–61.

74 M. W. Beresford, *op cit* in note 32, 4-9.

75 Table 3.3, p. 118.

76 There seems to have been no shortage of building ground in the in-township of Leeds before the 1880s. There was no building upwards, except Paley's Galleries, a sort of vertical back-to-back, described in the *Leeds Mercury* of 22 July 1848 as being as bad as the new tenement flats in the Metropolis, 'completely airless'.

77 *Baker, 1842*, 5.

78 It was, after all, a Leeds MOH who stated publicly that local people actually preferred to live in back-to-backs (*PP*, vii of 1885, 325–7).

79 This essay has grown from work in progress on a total building history of Leeds. Work during 1966–8 was assisted by a grant from the Social Science Research Council, and by the help of Mary Forster and Richard Peppard, research assistants. The minute books of committees and the property deeds in the Civic Hall strong rooms have been consulted by kind permission of the Town Clerk, and with much help from two of his staff, Mr Blair and Mr Senior. The figures have been drawn for me by Mr P. D. Reardon.

Appendix 3.1

STREETS FREQUENTLY CASTIGATED BY CRITICS AND CONTAINING
BACK-TO-BACKS

Brighton Court	4 back-to-backs on either side
Camp Field	3 rows of back-to-backs
Cavalier Street	all back-to-backs
Clarkson's Yard	8 back-to-backs, entered through a tunnel
Cross Lisbon Street	some back-to-backs
Dufton's Yard	12 back-to-backs, 6 through
Ebenezer Street	38 back-to-backs, 11 through
Goulden's Buildings	24 back-to-backs in interior court; adjoining graveyard
Harper Street	33 back-to-backs, 11 through; adjoining markets
Howarth Court	14 back-to-backs, entered through tunnel
Mill Street	31 back-to-backs
Nelson Street	41 back-to-backs, 9 through
Noah's Ark	10 back-to-backs in totally enclosed court but one of the few developments south of the river that came to the attention of reformers
Off Street	53 back-to-backs
Orange Street	40 back-to-backs, 3 through
Paley's Galleries	back-to-backs of several stories, unique in Leeds
Phillip's Yard	11 back-to-backs
Quarry Hill	26 back-to-backs, many through
Riley Court	7 back-to-backs
Somerset Street	29 back-to-backs, 2 through
Spring Street	23 back-to-backs, 4 through
Sykes Yard	14 back-to-backs
Templar Street	49 back-to-backs, 36 through
Union Street	53 back-to-backs, 3 through
Walker's Yard	18 back-to-backs
Wellington Place	12 back to-backs (at least)
Wellington Yard	38 back-to-backs and 15 single cottages (at least)

Appendix 3.2

THE FIRST GENERATION: THE 43 STREETS MADE UP WHOLLY OR PARTLY
OF BACK-TO-BACKS BUILT BETWEEN 1781 AND 1815

Bow Street (6)
  Back Bow Street (1)
Brick Street (4)
Bridge Sreet (3)
  Little Bridge Street (1)
*Burmantofts (Street) (4)

Camp Field (10)
  Front Row, Middle Row,
  Back Row
Cankerwell Lane (2)
Cavalier Street (21)
Charles Street (17)

*Chatham Street
Copper Street (2)
Copenhagen Street
Duke Street (15)
*Ebenezer Street (11)
Ellerby Road
  Ellerby Lane (27)
  Back Ellerby Road
Flax Street (4)
*George's Street (10)
  Back George's Street (6)
Goulden Square
  *Goulden's Buildings (11)
*Harper Street (5)
High Street (7)
  Back High Street
*Hope Street (2)
John Street (1)
Kendall's Buildings
Kendall Street
  Kendall Row (9)
(East) King Street (4)
Leighton Lane
Line Street
  Little Line Street
Lisbon Street
  Lisbon Court
Marsh Lane (55)

*Nelson Street (9)
New Park Street (3)
New Row (3)
Nile Street (2)
  Back Nile Street
*Off Street (10)
Park Court
(East) Queen Street (2)
Randerson's Yard
Richmond Road (25)
St Anne's Lane (5)
*St James' Street (9)
Steander Row (7)
Sykes Street
  *Sykes Yard (3)
Templar Street
Union Street (8)
  Union Row (6)
Walker's Place
  Walker's Row
Walker's Yard
*York Street (30)
  Back York Street
Zion Street (4)
  Back Zion Street (2)
  Zion Square
*Little London—Reuben Street (2)

NOTES TO APPENDIX 3.2

The numbers in brackets after each name are the cholera cases in 1832 (Robert Baker, *Report of the Leeds Board of Health* [1833], 21–7). The 372 cases in these 43 streets made up 28 per cent of the total (1,448) for the in-township.

The list consists of streets, etc, that (a) appear on Netlam and Giles' plan of 1815 and also (b) have back-to-backs indicated on the large-scale (five-foot = one mile) OS plan of 1850. It also includes Reuben Street, Little London, which lay within the in-township but just beyond the bounds of the 1815 plan; Great Woodhouse hamlet, also part of the in-township, lay beyond the area of the 1815 plan but Thorpe's plan of 1821 shows no streets laid out beyond the courts and folds except possibly Pickard Street (which was back-to-back).

Streets marked by asterisks * also had cellar dwellings.

Appendix 3.3

THE SECOND GENERATION: 360 OTHER STREETS WITH BACK-TO-BACKS, BUILT
1815–1850
(Back-to-back houses on OS 'Five-foot' plan of Leeds, 1850)

Sheet 1
Smith's Bdgs
Clarkson's Row
Pleasant Green
Pleasant Court
King's Row
King's Court
Graveley Tce
Graveley Row

Sheet 2
Moseley St
Albert St
Chancellor St
Rhodes Sq
Buslingthorpe Row
Scott Hall St

Sheet 3
Hobson's Bdgs
Close St
Mark St
Spenceley St
St Mark's St
Cross Mark St
Asquith St
Cemetery St
Cross Cemetery St
Scotts Tce
Holborn Tce
Charing Cross St
Huddersfield St
Bateson St
Toulson Row

Sheet 4
Lapish St
Pickard St
Pickard Green
Horrock St
Tolson St
Daisy St
Hobson St

Walsh Row
Oaklands Row
Oaklands St
Beckett St
Alfred Tce
Camp St
Meanwood St
Reuben St
Bk Reuben St
Primrose St
Sheepscar Bdgs
Victoria Place
Barrack St
Buslingthorpe St
Buslingthorpe Lane
Buslingthorpe Tce
Chapletown Rd
Wild's Court
Roundhay Rd
Wingham St
Wingham Place
Wingham Tce
White St
Roundhay St
Queen's Tce
Sheepscar Row
Sheepscar Green
Sheepscar Vale
Chapeltown St

Sheet 6
Fenton St
Sunny Bank Tce
Toulson Place
Cankerwell Lane
St James' St
Portland Crescent
Bk Portland Cres

Sheet 7
Carr St
Elmwood Vale
Elmwood St

Cobourg St
Queen's Pl
Barclay St
Whitelock St
Stamford St
Darley St
Lilac Tce
Concord St
Imperial St
Myrtle St
Busfield St
Vandyke St
Byron St
Cannon St
Mason St
Cloth St

Sheet 8
Winnflower Place
Lincolnfield Tce
Lincolnfield Row
Lincolnfield Place
Lincoln St
Hay Mount Place
Hay Mount Bdgs
New Cleveland St
Cherry St
Cherry Row
Pilot St
Rushworth St
Haigh St
Cambridge St
Grey St
Lion St
Tiger St
Violet St
Low Close Bdgs
Providence Bdgs
St Luke's Tce
Upper Cherry St
Green St
Pollard St
Lilac Tce

Concord St
Accommodation Place
Accommodation Tce
Harrison's Bdgs
Farrar St
Boston St
Selby St
Whitehall St
Anglesea St
Beckett St

Sheet 9
Hollis St
Grattan St
Florist St
England St
Dover St
Corporation St
Baker St
Angel St
North Hall St
North Hall Tce
Pimlico St
Burley Rd
Caroline Place
Park Lane
Newcastle St
Durham St
Darlington St
Wortley St
Wellington Tce
Abbey St
Denton St
Thackray St

Sheet 10
Harcourt Place
Marlborough St
Chatham St
Hanover St
Bk Hanover St
Howard St
New Park St
Bk Park St
Park Court
Fountain St
Caroline St
Parliament St

Government St
Somers St
Bedford Place
Chorley Lane
Leighton Lane
Oxford St
Bentick St
Portland St
Portland Cres
West St
Henrey St
Charley St
Forest St
Mercy St
Wellington St
Well St
Bk Well St
Skinner St
Grove St
Lisbon St
School St
Eldon St
Cropper Gate
Wellington Place
Calder St
Airedale Pl
Westminster Pl
Cross Lisbon St
Castle St
Saville St
Little Queen St

Sheet 11
Russell Pl
Merrion St
Belgrave St
Bk Nile St
Nile St
Copenhagen St
Hope St
Templar St
Lower Templar St
Cross Templar St
Bridge St
Livery St
Malt St
Templar's Court
Moscow St

Noble St
Sun St
Star St
Gower St
Brewery St
Bell St
Poland St
Saint St
Time St
Pendulum St
Tulip St
Pink St
Rose St
Little Bridge St
Lydia St
Nelson St
Union St
Ebenezer St
George's St
Bk George's St
East Lane
Harper St
Sykes' Yard
Sykes St
Goulden's Bdgs
Goulden's Square
Dyers St
Somerset St
Upper Somerset St
Little Somerset St
Cross Somerset St
Duke St
Quarry Hill
St Anns Lane
Charles St
Clarkson's Yd
St Mary's Row
Church St
Little Line St
Billett St
Cross Billett St
Shear St
High St
Bk High St
Upper Corn Hill
Little Albion St
York St
Brick St

Off St
 Brussels St
 Lee's Square

Sheet 12
Linsley Row
Union Row
Boynton St
Hound St
Fox St
Cross High St
Prospect Row
Lemon St
Orange St
Mason's Bdgs
Stone St
Plane St
Stainburn Sq
Vienna St
Vienna Court
Cross Vienna St
Purdy St
Giles St
Chapel St
Carver St
Cross Ebenezer St
Helen Court
York Court
Crispin St
Cato St
Railway St
Grantham St
Madras St
East Field St
Clay St
Glue St
Cross Shannon St
Steel St
Flint St
Forester's Arms Court
Cleveland St
Plaid Row
Cable Row
Shannon Row
Vincent St
Rodney St
Sloe St
Hatfield St

Shaw St
Elm St
Oak St
Upper Accommodation
 Rd
Keeton St
Sugden St
Blackburn's Cres
Cottage St
Woodman St
Bath St
Beckett St
East Beckett St
East Grove St
Rock St
Burmantofts
Upper Burmantofts St
Cross Burmantofts St
Barker's Row
Barker's Bdgs
Waterloo St
Pea St
Anchor St
Bean St
Acorn St
Upper Acorn St
Mulberry St
Wheat St
Bread St
Apple St
Windsor St
Edgar St
Plato St
Railway Tce
Accommodation Row
Pleasant Place

Sheet 14
Front Row (Camp
 Field)
Middle Row
Back Row
Stone Row

Sheet 15
Pool Row
Pitt Row

Short Row
Williams Court
Walker's Row
Walker's Yard
Steander Row
New Lane
New Lane Place
Hinchcliffe's Court
Land's Court
Kendall St
Kendall Row
Waterloo St

Sheet 16
Foundry St
Milk St
Brook St
Lower Cross St
Upper Cross St
Upper Cross Yard
Spring St
Spring Yard
Giles' Bdgs
Ball's Bdgs
Lumb St
Brighton Yard
Brighton Court
Wheeler St
Mill St
Worsted St
Spinner St
Richmond Rd
East Field St
Clay St
Edmund St
Catherine St
Providence St
Cross St
Little Providence St
Dolphin St
Little Dolphin St
Short Dolphin St
Cross Dolphin St
Dufton St
Wrigglesworth St
Copper St
Brass St
Brown's Bdgs

Upper Wrigglesworth St

New Row

Flax St

Kendall's Bdgs

Back Ellerby Rd

East King St

East Queen St

Zion St

Back Zion St

Zion Square

Cavalier St

Upton's Court

Willis St

Morpeth St

Upper Cavalier St

High Markland St

Fawcett St

Cookson St

Sussex Court

Sussex St

Surrey St

Leicester St

Kent St

Elam St

Sheffield St

Bachelor's St

Bachelor's Bdgs

Lower Bachelor St

Ellerby Lane

Walker's Place

Carnation St

Dahlia St

Sheet 19

John St

Orfeur St

Barstow St

Douglas St

Banner St

Sheet 20

Bridgefield Bdgs

NB No back-to-back
houses on Sheet 5.
Sheets 13, 17, 18, 21–
25 cover land outside
in-township.

CHAPTER IV

WORKING-CLASS HOUSING
IN NOTTINGHAM DURING
THE INDUSTRIAL REVOLUTION

S. D. Chapman

THERE are three reasons for selecting Nottingham for a study of working-class housing. Though the town enjoyed a reputation as an attractive centre for county gentry for much of the seventeenth and eighteenth centuries,[1] the Second Report of the Health of Towns Commission maintained in 1845 that slums and overcrowding were worse than those of any other industrial town,[2] and the grounds for this complaint must be examined. The two staple trades of nineteenth-century Nottingham were hosiery and lace, but in the first half of the nineteenth century their prosperity showed a remarkable contrast, the framework knitters being a depressed class of workers and lacemakers, for the most part, a well paid and prospering class.[3] The quality of housing must clearly reflect the income and security of the tenants or owners, and Nottingham presents an unusual opportunity of identifying the social gains and losses of the Industrial Revolution in terms of diverging standards of domestic comfort. Thirdly, Nottingham was one of the most religious towns of the Victorian age, and the reforming aspirations of its evangelical leadership at mid-century are worth some attention.[4] The long-delayed enclosure of the common fields of the town gave them a unique opportunity for regulating new housing and planning the layout of the new town, and their response to this challenge, resulting as it did, in the layout of modern Nottingham, can be traced in some detail.

I

Although there is no survey of Nottingham housing until 1832, sufficient evidence exists to identify four categories of working-class dwelling common in and about the town on the eve of rapid industrial growth. The year 1784 is a suitable point of departure for this analysis, since it coincides with the beginning of a cotton boom, population explosion and rapid building development in Nottingham.

In the middle decades of the eighteenth century, the staple industry of Nottingham and the surrounding area was the domestic hosiery manufacture. Up to the beginning of the French Wars, the framework knitters were not the depressed class that they subsequently became. Knitters earned 10s–12s for a full week, a few earning substantially more in the 'lace' branches. According to one memoir, a young journeyman might save 5s–7s a week out of a wage of 12s if he restricted his spending to board and lodging.[5] Under the domestic system, he could quite conveniently live up to a dozen miles from the hosier's warehouse.

In such favourable circumstances, it is no surprise to read in the same memoir that a few industrious artisans were still to be found building their own cottages as late as 1785. William Felkin (1745–1838), a Bramcote knitter, was allotted a roadside plot, 60yd by 10yd by the squire of the village. Having previously shared a cottage, he began at the age of 38 to build his own with the aid of his son. It was built in brick, stone, timber and thatch, and according to the grandson was similar to others erected in the village :

> The dwelling house, consisting of house place and weaving shop, scullery, pantry, and with two bedrooms above, was 32 feet long and 16 feet in width, and height of the roof tree was 26 feet, the roof thatched or tiled. Adjoining was a building open to the roof, furnished with large bread oven, copper and space for coal and firewood. Another lean-to was for a piggery and hen roost . . . The garden space was 450 square yards . . .

Cottage rows and single cottages on this pattern are still fairly common in the countryside, but it is, of course, quite another matter to ascertain the number of knitters who lived in similar cottages. Almost certainly very few artisans could rise to this standard of accommodation at the period; significantly William Felkin was nearly 40 years old before he could afford to build his own cottage, and he is known to have been an abstemious and industrious artisan, engaged on the best work.

This kind of cottage dwelling must have been even less common in Nottingham itself, though contemporary prints and Stretton's Map (1799–1800) show numbers of scattered cottages round the margins of the town, a few of which might possibly have been built by artisans for their own benefit. The same sources suggest that most of the housing was larger and more substantial than these cottages, but it is difficult to imagine even the most prosperous knitters or mechanics being able to afford one of these. The solution is suggested by analogy with what is known of conditions in other towns. Mrs M. D. George, writing of eighteenth-century London, notes that 'the standard dwelling of the artisan, even in a "genteel trade", seems to have been a single room . . . while in many trades this was workshop as well as living and sleeping place'.[6] In Manchester, according to

Scholes's *Directory* (1794), 'of the houses occupied by working people . . . , many have two, three and sometimes more families in each'.[7] It seems likely that it was quite usual for families to share houses in Nottingham throughout our period, but there are only a few supporting fragments of evidence. The earliest evidence of shared accommodation comes from advertisements in the *Nottingham Journal*, for instance :

> To Be Sold, a new and well-built house, situate in . . . Nottingham . . . The premises might suit a hosier; and are convenient to be occupied by one or two families . . .[8]

At the beginning of the nineteenth century we read of the town's two biggest mansions—Nottingham 'Castle' and Plumptre House—being divided into tenements for middle-class people,[9] so there is no reason to suppose that a lower social class abjured the idea. The upper rooms of the buildings in the streets round the market place were occupied by prosperous silk framework-knitters at the beginning of the century, and by the domestic lace-makers in the 1820s and early 1830s, and it seems likely that the practice was much older.[10] The statistical evidence of census returns shows that there were more families than inhabited houses throughout our period; in 1779, the only local census in the second half of the eighteenth century, Sutton enumerated 3,556 families and 3,191 inhabited houses.[11]

In addition to these two principal types of dwellings, there were two other common types which had survived the material progress of the earlier decades of the eighteenth century. The more primitive were the rock dwellings to the north-east of the town, in and around Sneinton Hermitage. Throsby's edition of Thoroton's *History of Nottinghamshire* (1797) has an engraving of these dwellings, showing that they were a series of caves, walled up at the mouth with bricks or turf. Throsby refers to the rock-dwellers as living 'in dens and caves of the earth, called the Hermitage'. Farey, writing about 1807, refers to the 'subterranean abodes' found in 'the gravel rock at the north end of Nottingham town', and refers to similar ones in Mansfield and near Buxton, where there were still 200 or more at the beginning of the nineteenth century.[12]

Finally, there were probably still a number of very small cottages along the margins of the town, inferior in size and structure to those already described and inhabited by the poorest classes. Deering (1751) has a few etchings of charity dwellings, the like of which probably survived another generation into our period. Deering's illustrations show a row of small one-storey dwellings roofed with thatch and with only one room, or possibly two. They were frequently patched and tumbledown, and were strung along lanes which (to judge from Corporate records) were typically unpaved, undrained and unswept. A few had a little garden space attached.[13]

In 1784 several concentrations of working-class housing had already appeared on the map. Easily the most congested was that to the north of the market square, between Long Row and Back Side (now Parliament Street). This area (later known as 'the Rookeries') was so packed with cottage terraces that (if Henson's account is to be trusted) a fugitive from the law could hide there in a few minutes. The peripheral Narrow Marsh and Broad Marsh were only beginning to emerge as distinct working-class districts, and even at the end of the century still contained gardens. Even so, Deering's enumeration of housing suggests that the area contained at least 17 per cent of the houses in the town.[14]

II

A general improvement in the structure of housing is discernible through the seventeenth and eighteenth centuries. The shortage of local timber and increasing supplies of brick were favourable to building in the superior materials. Brickmaking began on the outskirts of Nottingham at the beginning of the seventeenth century,[15] but according to Mr M. W. Barley, 'field work shows that the adoption of bricks as the normal building material in the East Midlands did not begin until after 1660'.[16] By the time that Deering wrote, the one-time prolific supplies of oak from Sherwood Forest were all but used up, and considerable quantities of foreign timber were imported through Hull.[17] The Restoration and early decades of the eighteenth century in fact saw a campaign of rebuilding in brick and tile, beginning with the resident nobility and gentry and gradually permeating down the social hierarchy to wealthy merchants and tradesmen.[18] This process of rebuilding seems to have reached the artisan classes in the last two decades of the eighteenth century. This is not to infer that the operative classes were all segregated in small wattle and daub cottages until these two decades, but rather—to chance a generalisation—to suggest that up to this time they generally benefited from improving standards in the town by taking rooms in larger houses.

It has been supposed that the population explosion of the later eighteenth century was the cause of considerable housing congestion, particularly in industrial towns.[19] This is misleading if it is taken to imply that Nottingham's open spaces were overrun by long rows of dark terraces, cheek by jowl with the dark satanic mills, in the eighteenth century. The fields, gardens, orchards and paddocks were not swallowed up until the bobbin-net boom of 1812–25. In the last decade of the eighteenth century Arkwright's Hockley mill still adjoined a garden and fields, and the nearby James's mill (formerly Hargreaves and James) had a clear vista to the Mapperley Hills. Alderman Green's cotton mill adjoined gardens in Broad Marsh, while Morley's pottery and mill at Beck Barns (St Ann's Well Road) and Denison's new factory at Penny Foot Stile still stood out in open country. In 1785, rumour of a proposal to erect a Savery steam engine in Coalpit-lane resulted in a petition to the mayor, complaining of the pollution of the air which would surely follow.[20]

The last two decades of the eighteenth century saw a boom in Nottingham's cotton-spinning industry, following the legal termination of Arkwright's patents. The same period also coincides with the heyday of the domestic hosiery manufacture, after the reverses suffered during the American War of Independence. The ingenuity of Nottingham workmen resulted in the production of new meshes, fabrics and garments on the stocking-frame. These two manufactures generated the income which enabled housing standards to be improved during a period when population was growing at an unprecedented rate.[21]

The years after 1784 also witnessed a housing boom.[22] Most of the houses were erected on a similar pattern. They consisted of three 'boxes' placed on top of each other, used respectively for living, sleeping and working. There was very often a cellar underneath, and the second floor invariably had the familiar long workshop windows. Blackner, writing before 1815, describes the type in some detail :

> The houses of the working-class, at the present time, generally consist of a cellar, a room to dwell in, called the house-place, a chamber [ie bedroom], a shop over it to work in, a room in the roof, called a cockloft, and a small pantry, though in the manner of building there are many exceptions, some for better, some for worse; and they are generally composed of plaster floors for the upper rooms, lightly timbered with deal; brick walls, some 4½ and some 9 inches thick; and cast-iron grates

for the fireplaces, frequently with ovens and boilers of the same material[23]

The 'plaster' floors were in fact made of gypsum-concrete, a mixture of gypsum (mined locally near Gotham) with sand and other aggregate, laid on the top of beams and thick layers of rushes. The floors were connected by a staircase, which was typically steep, dark, narrow and winding.

Though Blackner does not say as much, it is clear that the kind of habitation he describes was invariably built 'blind-back' (ie without windows or doors at the back), or back-to-back. The blind-back house very likely originated with the practice of infilling innyards and the interior length of crofts and gardens with cottages. Badder and Peat's map shows that this practice was already well established in the Rookeries in 1744, and Stretton's map (1799–1800) names fourteen infilled yards in the area, several of them—Crown Yard, Wheatsheaf Yard, Greyhound Yard, Blackboy Yard, and Maypole Yard—named after local hostelries. In 1800 the congested area of Broad Marsh and Narrow Marsh was still being built by a process of erecting a jumble of little terraces and blocks on the gardens stretching down to the Leen, while the area between Glasshouse Street and St Ann's Street (subsequently so congested that a plan of the site was condemned in the Health of Towns Report in 1844) had recently been built but was still known as Spring Gardens and Rick's Garden. At this time there were only three areas of Nottingham, all on the north-east side, in which back-to-backs were being built as part of a regular pattern of development of new sites. Sherwin's Cherry Orchard, next to James's cotton mill, was sold for building in 1783, and Sherwin then sold off closes in Millstone Lane (1785) and Plat Street (1791), all to small speculative builders. Development plans of these sites (Fig 4.2) suggest that open-ended courts were built one at a time, so that the first full row of back-to-backs was not created until the second phase of building. The notorious Nottingham practice of blocking the mouth of the court with another 'front house', and granting access only by a tunnel between the houses, seems to have appeared somewhat later, probably in the second housing boom in the early 1820s.[24] Professor Beresford shows, in his contribution to this book, that the earliest back-to-backs in Leeds were built by artisans' terminating building societies, but the surviving deeds and legal papers in Nottingham offer no clear evidence on this aspect of investment in housing.

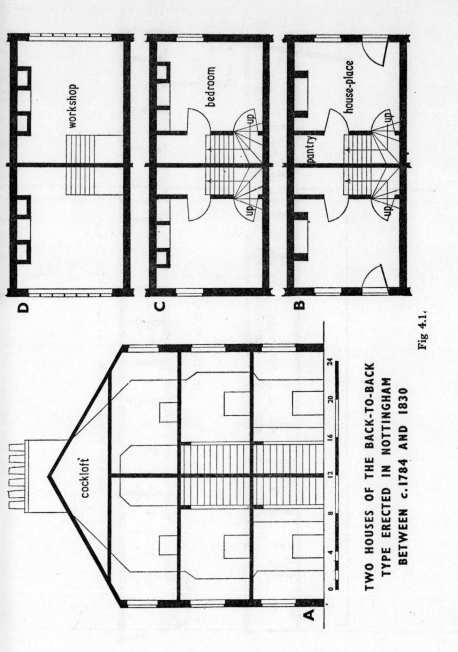

A

cockloft

0 4 8 12 16 20 24

D

workshop

C

bedroom

up up

B

pantry

house-place

up up

TWO HOUSES OF THE BACK-TO-BACK
TYPE ERECTED IN NOTTINGHAM
BETWEEN c.1784 AND 1830

Fig 4.1.

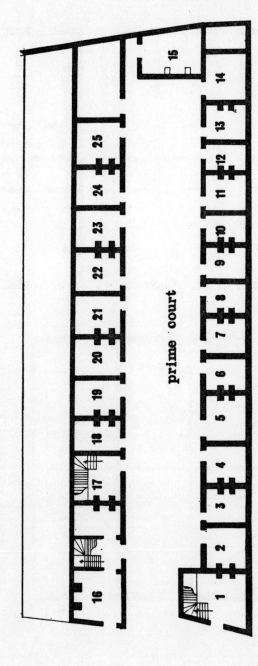

prime · court

Fig 4.2. Prime Court, Millstone Lane, Nottingham, built in 1783

This is not to say that the working classes did not make a financial contribution to the building boom of the 1790s. Some years later it was claimed that a great number of small houses in Nottingham were erected by builders assisted by working-class 'money clubs', partly, it may be supposed, as a fruitful investment for the clubs' funds, but also as a measure of self-help. Thomas and Charles Osborne, the speculative builders who built Prime Court, Crown Court, and the adjacent properties in Millstone Lane, borrowed £2,350 on mortgage between 1785 and 1791 from a variety of unspecified sources, and their practice appears to have been widespread. Borrowing from 'money clubs' seems to represent a transitional stage between the friendly society and terminating building society.[25]

During the last decade of the century, a few rather more substantial artisan houses began to be built in Nottingham and the villages. They may well have been bought by independent knitters, or by 'bag hosiers', who operated a number of frames on their own account. The earliest advertisement for this type of house appears in the *Nottingham Journal*, 2 February 1793 :

> To Be Let. Several new brick homes, with slated roofs, three storeys high, two rooms on a floor, and a small garden before each house; particularly adapted to stocking-makers, having room for eight or ten frames; and situate near Cross Lane . . . Arnold . . .

Several examples of this kind of house have survived around Nottingham; their unusual height, together with the workshop windows on the second floor enables them to be identified easily.

The occupation of the third floor by stocking-frames was more common in Nottingham than elsewhere, probably as land was more expensive. In Leicester and its county, the adjoining or garden workshop was the more usual situation of the domestic manufacture. Even so, there are occasional newspaper reports of outside workshops, rented by other tradesmen, and containing perhaps eight or a dozen frames. Moreover, most hosiers' warehouses had what was called a 'home department', where a few frames were worked to provide special and express orders. Not all framework knitters lived with their work.

Inevitably the population explosion which took place within the medieval boundaries of Nottingham gave rise to a rapid inflation in land values. Thus in 1808, when the first plots of land in 'the Park' were sold for building, 9,000sq yd of land on Standard Hill were sold for £7,000—or 15s 6d per sq yd, a phenomenal price in those days.[26] Middle-class housing also began to be erected outside the town, at Sneinton (Notintone Place) and on Sion Hill (Canning Circus). Speculators tried to take advantage of the land shortage by buying up plots of land on the edge of the open fields and building on them in open defiance of the grazing rights of the burgesses. As the lawyer Samuel Turner explained to Daniel Parker Coke, MP for the town, in 1789 :

> . . . within these few years last past, entire land about this place being very scarce and difficult to obtain, and the general increase of inhabitants holding forth a prospect of advantage . . . to builders . . . , some of the closes immediately contiguous to the town have been bought at a very high price, and the purchasers . . . have taken the opportunity of building several houses thereupon . . .[27]

A subscription was raised to prosecute property-owners making encroachments on the Lammas fields. The offenders were brought to court, and the committee for the 'vindication of burgess rights' won its case.[28] This success, together with several succeeding legal victories, had the unfortunate consequence, however, of so strengthening the hand of the burgesses that complete enclosure of the common fields did not begin until 1845.[29] The result of the failure to enclose, in the nineteenth century, was a degree of congestion of housing worse than any other town in the country.

Right at the end of the eighteenth century, the first trickle of workers began to take houses built for them beyond the Sand Field, at New Radford. The Lenton Enclosure Act of 1796 allowed most of the land beyond the town's open fields to be built upon, and, quite naturally, the first overspill of population found its way to the nearest part of the enclosed land, in the parish of Radford. Building began in 1796, when Benjamin Darker, a needle-maker, built a row of thirteen back-to-back houses on land covered with gardens and orchards at Sion Hill (now Canning Circus).[30]

III

The appearance of cotton spinning in Nottingham benefited Nottingham artisans only indirectly, as the mills mostly employed women and children. The main consequence to Nottingham of the shift to factory spinning was to reduce the price of cotton and worsted yarns and so accelerate the growth of domestic framework knitting; between 1782 and 1812 the number of stocking-frames in

Britain increased by 50 per cent. A few framework knitters in the fashion branches earned 30s or even 50s a week, but the growth of the lace manufacture (following Heathcote's patent of 1809) created the main period of opportunity for working-class enterprise and high wages. The early bobbin-net machines were very complicated and difficult to work, requiring constant attention to every moving part and every thread, and workmen who could operate them earned very high wages. Felkin maintained that the best workmen could earn from £5 to £10 a week, but other writers record more modest sums. It seems more likely that, while Heathcote and his partners paid their workmen 30s to 60s a week, according to their strength and skill, most artisans in the trade earned from 15s to 20s, with a few highly skilled earning rather more.[31] This was still a sufficiently large income to allow a provident workman to save, and an unusual combination of circumstances allowed many to become machine-owners.

In Nottingham, as Blackner remarked, 'patentees and other inventors mutually laugh at and invade each others schemes'. Heathcote tried to insist on his patent rights, but for three years (1813–16) he was held up by legal difficulties. The initiative was finally taken by a rival manufacturer, and it was July 1817 before a special jury gave the verdict to Heathcote's assignee. The cost of the lawsuit amounted to nearly £20,000 and, though Heathcote's patent was fully established, he felt that he could not prevent further infringements without being continually involved in a series of cases that might exhaust his resources. To simplify administration of the patent, and to reimburse his legal costs, he sold licences freely to machine-builders. It was not until 1819 that he began to be more restrictive and license machine-owners, but even then the rates were not high—£5 per 'quarter' (9in width of lace) pa, or up to £30 a machine.[32]

The new Nottingham lace manufacture thus enjoyed unrestricted expansion for seven years. At the end of the period (1819) some eighty-two small owners were known to the patentees, mostly in the town, and this number grew very rapidly during the boom which followed the expiration of the patent in March 1823.[33] By September 1829 there were over 1,200 small owners.[34] Moreover, the boom itself saw an inflation of working-class earnings. Incomes of 15s–20s rose rapidly to 40s–80s weekly, while 1,500 men engaged in machine-building earned from £3 to £10 a week, fantastic wages during a period when the average earnings of framework knitters rarely rose above 12s.[35]

It has been necessary to digress into industrial history in order to explain the new housing developments of the middle 1820s. The growth in population and wealth was so rapid that Nottingham burst its medieval boundaries. The surplus population spilt over into a number of satellite communities beyond the open fields—New Sneinton, Carrington, New Basford, Hyson Green, New Radford and New Lenton. A few back-to-back terraces were built, but in general the new districts were developed as 'handsome villages', delightfully placed round the periphery of the 'green belt' formed by the open fields.[36] The new houses were typically built on three storeys, with two rooms (or more) on each floor. There was a kitchen and wash-house on the ground floor, and two bedrooms on the first. The whole of the second floor was intended for lace machines, and had workshop windows 10ft wide on each side. An attic above this floor was probably intended for storing yarn and 'brown' net, or might be used as sleeping accommodation for children or journeymen. The *Nottingham Review* was impressed by the fact that at Hyson Green, most of the houses had 'private back-yards, and gardens in front 35 yards long, which for health and comfort, are inferior to none in or near Nottingham'.[37] The details are shown in the plan and elevation (Fig. 4.3).

Hyson Green and New Basford were the most prosperous of the six new suburbs and had no back-to-back or 'blind-back' houses, though common yards (in spite of the *Review* writer) were still quite usual. It is not possible to be so categorical about building at New Radford, New Sneinton and New Lenton as these suburbs were attached to existing villages, which makes it difficult to distinguish earlier property from later. However, the reports of the public health inspectors covering these areas suggest that back-to-back housing was rare. Carrington was probably the most 'popular' of the six districts, and here only 60 out of the original 202 houses (ie about 30 per cent) were back-to-back or 'blind-back'. Clearly the standard of new housing in the Nottingham area rose during this period.[38]

The connection between the new houses and the lace manufacture can be illustrated by Hyson Green. In 1828 there were 314 inhabited houses there. A census of lace machines taken in that year shows that there were ninety-five owners in the village, having 160 machines between them. No doubt numbers of the other householders operated rented machines, or worked in one of the three or four small factories recently established there.[39]

According to Robert Mellors, the houses in Pleasant Row, Lenton Street, Saville St, Lindsay Street, and Pepper Street were built by a workmen's co-operative effort, and Club Row, Carrington, may have been built by the same means.[40] Certainly working-class building clubs were common in many industrial towns, and Hyson Green had a 'well conducted co-operative society . . . for the sale of groceries etc.' as early as 1830. Unfortunately, the deeds of this property throw no clear light on this aspect of their construction, though they do show that forty-four houses in Pleasant Row and twenty-one in Saville Street were built for £70 to £90 each, and that the capital of £5,000 was initially provided on mortgage by John Hancock, a Nottingham hosier and cotton-spinner. Possibly artisan money clubs contributed capital, as they did in the building boom of the 1790s.[41]

It is fortunate that a description of the furnishing of the house of a lace hand is available. It was written by Mary Howitt in her novel *Little Coin, Much Care*. The hero, Ford, was a lace hand who 'like many another man in those days . . . earned several pounds a week'.

The house of the Fords was exactly that of a prosperous Nottingham lace-hand about the year 20 of this century [ie c 1820]; consequently interminable would be the inventory of all that the lower room or kitchen contained. There were chairs, with and without arms, all comfortably cushioned; there was a mahogany dining table, set against the wall, covered with a new green cloth; there was a very fine mahogany chest of drawers with a secretary top; a handsome clock in a case, as good as money could buy; two work-boxes, one of rose-wood, which belonged to Mrs Ford, and another covered with red morocco, belonging to her eldest daughter . . . all of which stood upon the secretary; while a looking-glass in a gilt-frame slanted forward over the dining-table, upon which were laid a large Bible and Prayer-book, and different works taken in by Ford in numbers—Quarle's *Emblems, Henry, Earl of Moreland*, Cook's *Voyages, The Young Man's Instructor, Universal History,* and *Complete Herbal*. On each side of the glass hung a large framed engraving; another over the secretary, and a fourth over the door. White dimity curtains, duly fringed, clothed the window, and a muslin blind forbade the inspection of impertinent neighbours. Three or four toasting-forks—one of which only was ever used—a bottle brush, a red japanned hearth brush and bellows, and dozens of articles of bright tin and copper and brass, and even some plated, hung in the corners near the fireplace. On the mantelpiece above were ranged brass candle-sticks, in the centre of which stood a bright copper tea-kettle . . .; on a strong rack, which

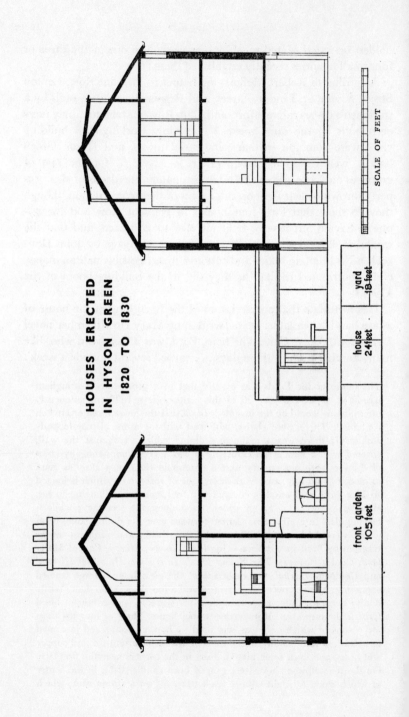

HOUSES ERECTED
IN HYSON GREEN
1820 TO 1830

front garden
105 feet

house
24 feet

yard
18 feet

SCALE OF FEET

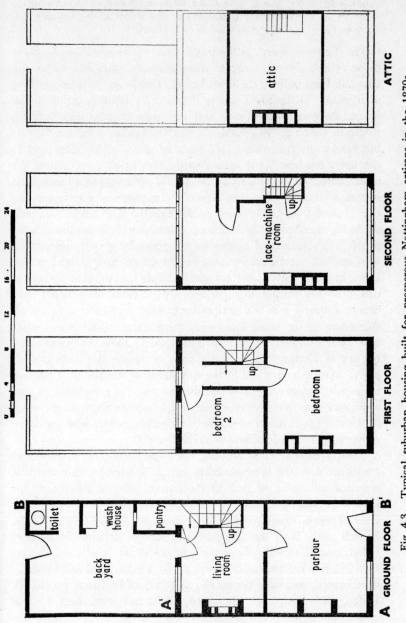

K

Fig 4.3. Typical suburban housing built for prosperous Nottingham artisans in the 1870s.

was hung to the ceiling, were laid a flitch and a half of bacon; whilst two hams, in white paper bags, hung on the staircase, lest they should grease the walls of this goodly-conditioned kitchen.[42]

The 'twist-net fever', as the trade boom of the middle 1820s came to be called, also gave rise to slum property quite inferior to any that had been built in the town before. The 'fever' attracted a flood of migrants to the town, whose demand for housing could not be immediately satisfied. Rents, and the price of land and building materials shot up. No reliable figures are available for the former, but bricks rose from 30s to £3 per thousand and building land in the town reached 36s a square yard. This situation produced the most intense congestion, as people would rather share a house than live at a distance from the hosiers' or net agents' warehouses. In one area of 9 acres surveyed at the time of the cholera outbreak of 1832, there were 883 houses containing 947 families (4,283 people). 'Thousands of houses were erected by greedy speculators, who studied, not the convenience and health of those obliged to take them, but how they might best secure 20 per cent on their outlay.' It was probably during this period, when houses were being split between several families, that cellar dwellings came into existence. According to the trade historians, garrets, stables, kitchens, cellars and the most unlikely places were converted into workshops in every quarter of Nottingham, and it sounds as though the same kind of places were extemporised for housing. During this period a number of lean-to houses were also hastily put up. They consisted of one small room surmounted by a bedroom, and were apparently run up in the corners of courts or yards, or indeed anywhere where a dozen or more square yards of land could be found.[43]

The migration of framesmiths, stockingers and other artisans and tradesmen into the lace manufacture was a selective movement; it required enterprise as well as mechanical skill to enter the new field. The framework knitters who remained in their craft suffered from depressed trade more or less continuously from the end of the French wars. Both the domestic and foreign demand for hosiery failed to expand with the growth in the capacity of the industry. By 1833 the knitters, as a group, could be described as physically deteriorated, mentally depressed, and 'too often morally debased. Ill-fed, ill-lodged, and ill-clothed, with care-worn and anxious countenances, they are a class by themselves . . .'[44] The work-men in hosiery came to constitute one of the most depressed groups in the country, while those in lace were among the most prosperous.

Inevitably this divergence of fortune was reflected in the housing conditions of the district. By the early 1830s the two social groups not only lived in houses of different size and quality, but also in different parts of the town. The lace hands lived and worked in the upper storeys of substantial houses, the lower parts of which were occupied as shops or lodging houses. Very few of them lived above the business premises round the market place, but in all the approaches and the back streets, as well as in the better houses of the lower town, the incessant thumping of the bobbin-net machine could be heard. As we have seen, numbers of them moved out to the new industrial villages. The framework knitters lived in the more obscure courts and alleys. Descriptions made in 1845 and 1850 of the tenements they lived in obviously refer to the kind of property that Blackner described—back-to-backs built fifty or sixty years earlier, in the first stages of industrialisation.[45]

Although there is an abundant literature on the plight of the framework knitters during the 1830s and 1840s, there is very little reference to their housing conditions. The most striking eyewitness description was written in 1829 by Sir Richard Phillips, the Radical journalist. It is a dramatised account of a visit to a court in Broad Marsh; the political content has been extracted in this cutting :

> The court contained an abundance of small tenements, let to many stockingers like this, and there being many families, and even extra lodgers in all, it swarmed with population. Maggots in carrion flesh, or mites in cheese, could not be huddled more closely together . . . I entered, and found a dame busy washing her floor. I will not attempt to describe the furniture—it had been better—but all was worn out or broken. The woman was in rags, which scarcely covered her and every-thing bespoke hard work and inadequate pay . . .[46]

The same story occurs monotonously over the next two decades; it has changed very little in 1850 :

> . . . there can be no doubt of the miserably depressed state of the frame-work-knitters. They appear to labour without energy, or hope, or heartiness . . . Almost without exception . . . the houses of this class of labourers are squalid and neglected looking, and in point of personal appearance and decent comfort of attire, the framework-knitters must take the very lowest rank in the social scale connected with the textile industry.[47]

The diverging living standards of workers in the hosiery and lace trades clearly illustrate the fact that slum housing and congestion were not the product of industrialism. On the contrary, the living standards of the framework knitters remained low in conjunction with their incomes, which failed to keep in step with those of most other textile workers because hosiery was an industry outside the orbit of steam-power until the mid-nineteenth century.

IV

It was not until 1832 that any systematic survey of Nottingham housing was made. The threat of a cholera epidemic caused the formation of an *ad hoc* Board of Health for the town in November 1831. The town was divided into districts in order to inspect the houses of the poor with a view to cleansing them. By July 1832 the Committee of the Board of Health was actively engaged in causing various public nuisances to be removed, and enjoying a total grant of £80 from the three parishes. Although the board was dissolved a year after its formation, when the cholera threat had disappeared, valuable information was gathered during its year's work.[48] Of about 11,000 houses existing in the town at this time, the parish officers were able to ascertain that there were '7,000 to 8,000 houses constructed back-to-back, having no means of through ventilation, and generally without other than a common convenience to several dwellings'.[49] The courts, that is to say, were invariably closed at both ends, and were entered by a tunnel 30–36in wide, about 8ft high and from 25 to 30ft long. Many of the streets in the lower part of the town were neither paved nor drained, though the parochial highways board made progress with this work after 1832.[50]

The surveys made at this time enable us to obtain a measure of the extent of inferior building. According to Felkin, 200 dwellings were found under lace dressing-rooms, heated to 80°F and upwards. This kind of property appears as an unpleasant mutation in the evolution of the kind of properties already described as characteristic of Nottingham in the first half of the nineteenth century. Two and three back-to-back terraces were surmounted by two, and occasionally three, more storeys rented to hosiery and lace manufacturers, particularly in the congested areas by the River Leen. Terraces in Currant Street and Pear Street built on this pattern are shown on the 1800 map, and similar properties continued to be erected throughout the first half of the nineteenth century. The deeds of a double row of twenty-four built by John Mitchell, 'wharfinger and fellmonger', in the early 1830s in Pool Yard Close refer to 'an extensive range of [lace] getting-up rooms running over the whole length . . . and forming an upper storey'; in 1833 Mitchell sold the terrace, with a dyehouse, for £2,000. A row of fifteen cottages built in the fields at Whitemoor (a mile west of the town) had ground and first-floor plans similar to those just described at Hyson Green, and were evidently built about the same period, but the second floor consisted of four large workshops, each of which was reached by separate staircases at the rear of the cottages. Properties on this pattern were not always bad; the Whitemoor cottages were not demolished until 1967.

Felkin's 1832 survey also recorded 200 tenements known locally as 'barracks', no doubt for sufficient reason. They were basically flats with common open staircases, along which families had one or two very small rooms each. The ends of the ubiquitous courts were frequently the site of a row of 'privies', and more than 100 dwellings were found to be built over these and other communal conveniences; Barnett said they were 'generally in a very bad state and unfit for use'. Felkin also referred to between 100 and 200 cellar dwellings, evidently similar to those that became so notorious in Liverpool. An unspecified number of houses were built over leaky sewers. If Felkin's figures can be used as a guide, the number of dwellings whose construction was inferior (excluding lean-to cottages and those exposed to sewer contamination) was about 650, or rather less than 6 per cent of the housing in the town.[51] Analysed in this way, the condition of working-class housing seems to be perhaps better than has been supposed. The justification for describing the town's housing situation as the worst of any town in the country—a charge laid against it by a government commissioner in 1844[52]—was due to the degree of congestion consequent upon the failure to break the political deadlock over enclosure.

Moreover, the picture must be balanced by noticing again the considerable numbers of excellent artisan houses that were being erected in the new suburbs during the 1820s and 1830s. Contemporaries rightly recognised the new artisan-inhabited villages as model communities. Thus White's *Directory* for 1832 recognises that 1,100 new houses have been built since 1821 in the industrial suburbs of New Lenton, New Radford, Hyson Green and Carrington, and states that these 'form several handsome villages, occupied chiefly by bobbin-net makers, and forming a number of parallel and cross-streets . . . and [with cottages] regularly built of brick and roofed with blue slate . . .'[53] The gardens and open spaces surrounding this housing compared favourably in quantity with that adjoining modern housing developments, though common yards were still quite usual.

The 1830s and 1840s were not, as we have noticed, prosperous decades in the development of the town, and apparently few developments in housing took place within it. Writing in 1845, Barnett described working-class housing almost exactly as Blackner had described it in 1812.[54] Barnett had maintained in 1836 that the 'improved tastes and habits of the working-classes were inducing them to seek out better houses than those with which they were contented twenty years ago';[55] but there is no evidence that these rising aspirations materialised in any better class of dwellings. The evidence is rather to the contrary : when the enclosure of the common fields finally released land for building, working-class income was still too depressed for framework knitters and most twist hands to be able to afford to rent any type of dwelling superior in design or construction to the pattern already described.

One of the most striking features of the chronic trade depression of 1837–42 was the abandonment of houses, shops and tenements, as extensive unemployment left families without money to pay their rent. A private census made (or sponsored) by Felkin in March 1838 ascertained that 1,155 houses were shut up, including numbers of retail shops, of which seven were capitally situated in the market place.[56] The families dispossessed usually became tenants of one or two rooms each in the dwellings of others; Mary Howitt's *Little Coin, Much Care* suggests that this need not have been an unhappy situation. At this time, the pawnbrokers were unable to receive the amount of property offered in pledge, and it was thrown away by forced sales in the streets.[57]

The *Morning Chronicle* survey of living and working conditions in Nottingham, made in 1850, confirmed that the situation in Nottingham itself had changed very little since the 1832 survey. The reporter ascertained that about three-quarters of the houses in Nottingham were occupied by the working classes, and as a rule built in courts and back-to-back. Nevertheless, some continuing improvement is suggested by statistics of population and of the number of houses. These statistics refer to Nottingham only, and take no account of the much improved conditions in the new satellite villages.

TABLE 4.1

STATISTICS SUGGESTING DIMINISHING PRESSURE ON ACCOMMODATION, NOTTINGHAM 1779–1841

	No of houses	Population	Inhabitants per house
1779	3,191	17,711	5·5
1801	5,077	28,861	5·7
1811	6,538	34,358	5·2
1821	10,327	50,026	4·8
1831	10,842	50,220	4·6
1841	12,661	52,164	4·1

There are no very reliable statistics available on rents charged to working-class tenants, or on the place of rent in working-class budgets. Nevertheless, it is possible to build up part of the picture from a few fragments of information. Table 4.2, which summarises the available information, suggests that rents remained fairly static throughout most of the second quarter of the nineteenth century. Elsewhere we learn that, though the level of rents had risen during the 'twist net fever', the growth of suburban villages, where rent levels were lower, had restored the original level by the late 1820s.[58]

TABLE 4.2

RENTS CHARGED FOR WORKING-CLASS HOUSING IN NOTTINGHAM, 1825–50

	Two-storey houses	Three-storey houses	Houses of 'better sort'
1825		2s 6d	
1829	1s 6d		
1833	2s 3d		3s 6d
1845	1s 6d	2s 2d	3s 0d
1850	1s 9d	2s 2d	

Source: *Nottingham Review*, 30 September 1825, 17 April 1829, 28 February 1845, 25 January 1850. *Nottingham Journal*, 8 November 1833.

V

The earliest legislation related to housing consisted of a series of local improvement acts promoted by municipal corporations—Leeds and Liverpool in 1842, Birkenhead in 1843, London in 1844, Manchester in 1844 and 1845, Nottingham, St Helen's and Wallasey in 1845, Newcastle, Burnley and Southport in 1846, and so on. These Acts were influenced by Chadwick's 'Health of Towns' campaign, and by the theory that overcrowded housing caused disease and early mortality because the air failed to circulate freely. The majority of them, therefore, established minimum width for courts and declared they must have openings at both ends. The Nottingham Enclosure Act is said to have been the most progressive of these pioneer acts because it compelled each house to have its own 'privy', prohibited back-to-back houses, and specified that each house must be provided with a garden or yard of not less than 30sq ft, must have three distinct bedrooms, and walls not less than 9in (two bricks) thick.[59]

Thomas Hawksley, the Nottingham waterworks engineer, who was the moving spirit behind the 1845 enclosure movement, blamed the failure to enclose on

> several influential members of the corporation [who] are extensive owners of the small houses inhabited by the working classes in the worst conditions districts, and have repeatedly avowed their hostility to the principle of enclosure, under . . . the ₹ . . . impression that their property would sustain permanent injury by the erection of better, more healthy, and more comfortable dwellings on the enclosed lands.

Probably the wealthiest, and certainly the most influential of this group was Thomas Wakefield (1791–1871), hosier, cotton spinner, colliery owner, and newspaper proprietor. For nearly a generation Wakefield was demagogue of the Whig clique that dominated the corporation both before and after the 1835 Municipal Corporations Act, and he resolutely opposed any suggestion of enclosure. His following was also responsible for defeating the first attempt to cut a new street to relieve congestion, when it threatened to involve property demolition. At a meeting of the corporation in 1845, when

> Wakefield could see the great change in public opinion in favour of . . . inclosures . . . his declaration of the way he should vote settled the question: former opponents spun round at the beck of their leader and the assent of the Council was given *nem dis* to the Bill to inclose the West Croft and only three hands were held up against the Derby Road Inclosure.[60]

The releasing of the common fields for building coincided with the prospering trade conditions of the early 1850s. Nottingham enjoyed an unprecedented building boom : 2,100 houses were built during 1851–6, and seventy-four factories and forty-one warehouses during 1851–7.[61] With more space available there was considerable demolition of old commercial property : the 'Lace Market', for instance, was rebuilt at this period. However, it was gradually realised that the housing development was making little provision for the working classes. Of the 2,100 houses just mentioned, only 845 (40 per cent) had a rental of 3s 6d a week or less. The principal cause of this failure to provide suitable low-priced dwellings was said to be the high cost of erecting houses that adhered to the regulations of the Enclosure Act.[62]

The situation might justifiably have been regarded as a necessary though unfortunate consequence of insisting on minimum standards if the quality of houses put up had fallen within the spirit of the law. This does not appear to have been the case. At the beginning of 1852, according to the *Nottingham Review*, the 'only approach to cheap houses on the newly enclosed lands are some now erecting in the Meadows, from plans prepared by Mr T. C. Hine, which adopt the back-to-back system, but obviate all its objections'. In June 1859, by which time the Meadows were built upon 'most extensively', Alderman Vickers reported on behalf of the Sanitary Committee that 'on the South side of the Tinkers Leen there are 258 houses . . . totally without any drainage having a proper outfall, and 231 of them are drained into cesspools, which are situate in the great majority of instances, but a few yards from the dwellings'. At the end of 1860 it was reported : 'There are now about 500 dwellings and some new extensive trade premises in this locality (the Meadows) quite destitute of drainage.'[63]

It may be objected that the corporation had no authority to intervene in local housing development in favour of the working classes. This, however, is not true. Lord Shaftesbury's Labouring Classes' Lodging Houses Act (1851) gave municipal corporations the power to build working-class houses, though 'the amount of new building for which they were responsible was quite insignificant'.[64] Although Nottingham was a pioneer in municipal housing, the first council housing was not opened until 1877.[65]

However, this is not intended to indicate that there was any failure on the part of Nottingham's leading citizens to appreciate the need for working-class housing. In 1841 a number of London philanthropists had established the Metropolitan Association for

Improving the Dwellings of the Industrious Classes,[66] and this model came to Nottingham via Leeds, but without much success.

At a meeting of the council held in 1852, William Eyre suggested that a company should be formed to purchase land and erect houses suitable for the operative classes, as another means of combating the high rate of mortality in the town. The mayor (William Felkin) noted, by way of commending the idea, that a private philanthropic company had been formed in Leeds for the erection of model dwellings for the poor, and £10,000 had been subscribed. The idea gave rise to considerable enthusiasm, and a group of councillors and friends took up the suggestion and formed a committee.[67] Richards, the sanitary inspector, became the honorary secretary, and about 5,000sq yd of newly-enclosed land adjoining St Ann's Well Road were bought. In May 1852 the committee advertised prizes for the best designs for single houses and blocks, the weekly rent of which was to be about 3s.[68]

A local architect won the award, and about ninety dwellings of various descriptions were erected.[69]

> But although these houses . . . readily commanded tenants, and have ever since continued to be in considerable demand, it was nevertheless felt that the rents, . . . in order to make them at all remunerative . . . were only within the reach of certain classes; and that the problem had yet to be solved of providing upon the newly enclosed land, such a description of dwelling as should supply the need of a very numerous class of persons of less adequate means.[70]

When this charitable effort failed, a number of philanthropists stepped in and tried to demonstrate that good working-class housing should yield a reasonable return on the capital invested.[71] However, none of these meritorious efforts seem to have been very successful; certainly they were not emulated by private enterprise for many years.

The work of the Enclosure Commissioners was paralleled by that of the Corporation Sanitary Committee, established in 1847 under the energetic leadership of William Felkin, an evangelical Whig who became a leading figure in the Corporation after Wakefield's resignation in 1847. In 1848 the committee began to seek the co-operation of property-owners in the dismantling of property built over 'privies' and ashpits. 'Dangerous collections of manure' were ordered to be removed, swine were removed from positions near the houses, and dwellings in unhealthy quarters were limewashed. More rapid progress was made after the first sanitary inspector was appointed in 1851.[72]

It was during the 1850s, too, that the first ideas on town planning were mooted, though with little consequence for the time being. Probably discussion originated with the laying out of the Park housing estate at this time. The most prominent figure was again Felkin. At the opening of the Arboretum (1852) he lamented the fact that the Enclosure Commissioners had not done more to make regulations for the location and design of housing, 'similar to those in force at Glasgow and Edinburgh, under which the modern parts of those cities had so wonderfully improved, and acquired so much magnificence'.[73] The commissioners did not respond to his suggestions, but the corporation were at some pains to improve the town's facilities by selling good sites to schools and churches at low prices.[74] Unfortunately, no one heeded the *Nottingham Mercury's* appeal for an industrial sector located in the Meadows away from all residential development.[75] The Enclosure Commissioners set aside 130 out of 1,069 acres for recreation and open space, and the Arboretum, the Forest, Queen's Walk, and Corporation Walk were created; and some new wide open roads were cut. But for the most part the land was built on as the commissioners apportioned it, every owner and builder exploiting the site for whatever personal or commercial advantage he could derive from it.

VI

It is not easy to draw together the changes discussed in this essay. The difficulty is partly lack of evidence, especially for the middle and later decades of the eighteenth century. If the sources were more forthcoming, we should probably recognise a striking advance in standards during this period. In the nineteenth century, the difficulty is that it becomes impossible to conceive of a general standard in view of the divergence in the fortunes of artisans employed in the town's two staple trades, hosiery and lace.

With these limitations in mind, it may be surmised that there were two significant advances in the general standard of working-class housing during our period. The first advance, coinciding with the golden age of hosiery and cotton-spinning in the town, saw working-class families move from cottages and apartments to the greater comfort of three-roomed brick and slate terraced houses. The second advance, which followed the establishment of the modern lace industry, saw the first major migration to the suburbs, and the adoption of a five-roomed house standard, with separate scullery and living accommodation and two bedrooms. The end of the period anticipates a third advance, with the erection of the first, now familiar, solid 'Victorian' terraces, built before the 1860s as model housing.

The progress of housing was retarded by two factors. The French Wars were responsible for a recession in hosiery and cotton, so that the prosperity of the town waned for more than a decade after the turn of the century. Unfortunately, the local evidence throws no clear light on Prof T. S. Ashton's belief that high wartime duties (on bricks, timber and glass) and a high rate of interest were primarily responsible for 'jerry-building'. The other retarding factor was the failure to enclose. The supply of land was so restricted that it rose from 11s per sq yd (Broad Marsh, 1792)[76] to 15s 6d in 1808 and 36s in 1825. But after this date the shift of population and industry to the new suburbs appears to have stabilised rents, and probably also the price of new houses.

NOTES

1 Charles Deering, *Nottinghamia Vetus et Nova* (1751).

2 J. R. Martin, *Second Report of the Health of Towns Commission*, Appendix, Part II. *PP*, XVIII (1845), 249–57.

3 W. Felkin, *Remarks upon the Importance of an Inquiry into the Amount and Appropriation of Wages by the Working Classes* (1837), cited in centenary edition of Felkin's *History of the Machine Wrought Hosiery and Lace Manufactures* (1867), xxix.

4 For general background see R. A. Church, *Economic and Social Change in a Midland Town. Victorian Nottingham 1815–1900* (1966); J. C. Weller, *The Evangelical Revival in Nottingham*, BD thesis, Nottingham, 1957.

5 S. D. Chapman, 'Memoirs of Two Eighteenth Century Framework Knitters', *Textile History*, I (1969).

6 M. D. George, *London Life in the Eighteenth Century*, 3rd Edition (1951), 96.

7 Scholes's *Manchester Directory* (1794), v–vii.

8 6 March 1790.

9 J. Blackner, *History of Nottingham* (1815), 50; *Nottingham Journal*, 19 May 1810, 17 Aug 1811.

10 *Factory Inquiry*, *PP*, XX (1833) SC 1, 34.

11 Quoted J. Blackner, *op cit*, 77.

12 J. Farey, *Agriculture of Derbyshire*, II (1811), 22.

13 C. Deering, *op cit*, plates facing pp 10, 138.

14 C. Deering, *op cit*, 12–13, and facing map by Badder and Peat.

15 H. H. Copnall, ed, *Nottinghamshire County Records* (1915), 125.

16 M. W. Barley, 'Farmhouses and Cottages', *Economic History Review*, VII (1954–5), 294.

17 C. Deering, *op cit*, 87–8.

18 C. Deering, *op cit*, 6; J. Blackner, *op cit*, 66.

19 For population growth in Nottingham in the eighteenth century, see J. D. Chambers, 'Population Change in a Provincial Town, Nottingham 1700–1800', in L. S. Pressnell, ed, *Studies in the Industrial Revolution* (1960), 97–124. According to this source, the population of the town was 7,000 in 1700, 12,050 in 1750, 15,340 in 1770, and 28,861 at the first census of 1801.

20 Boulton and Watt Mss (Birmingham Reference Library): T. Harris correspondence; Stretton's Map of Nottingham (1799–1800); *Nottingham Journal*, 19 April 1788.

21 On the history of the hosiery and lace manufactures, see G. Henson, *History of the Framework Knitters* (1831); W. Felkin, *op cit;* F. A. Wells, *The British Hosiery Industry* (1935).

22 According to Absalom Barnett (1773–1850), Overseer of St Mary's Workhouse and an authority on working-class life in the town. *Nottingham Journal*, 8 Nov 1833.

23 J. Blackner, *op cit*, 66.

24 M. D. Lobel, *Historic Towns. Maps and Plans of Towns and Cities in the British Isles . . .* Vol I (1969), map of Nottingham c 1800; Stretton's Map of Nottingham (1799–1800); Nottingham Corporation property deeds, particularly for Sherwin's Orchard (M 16,288–16,293), Millstone Lane (M 19,146–19,153, M 16,288–16,293) and Plat St (TC 2/38).

25 *Nottingham Journal*, *loc cit*; Osborne's papers M 16,288–16,293, M 19,146–19,153. Cp John Nixon, builder, 1792 (M 23,607).

26 A. Barnett, *The Poor Laws and their Operation . . .* (1833), 27–8.

27 *Nottingham Journal*, 26 Sept 1789. A house erected on burgess land was demolished by rioters a decade before this. G. Henson, *op cit*, 408.

28 *Nottingham Journal*, 15 Aug 1789; 14 Apr 1790; 1 May, 1790; 31 Dec 1791.

29 For subsequent legal developments, see Thomas Hawksley's collection of papers in Chadwick Mss, University College, London.

30 J. Blackner, *op cit*, 391.

31 W. Felkin, *op cit*, 204, 273, 369; Dearden's *Nottingham Directory* (1834), 86; J. L. and B. Hammond, *The Skilled Labourer, 1760–1832* (1919), 237–8.

32 J. Blackner, *op cit*, 231; W. Felkin, *op cit*, 215–17; Dearden, *loc cit*.

33 W. Felkin, *op cit*, 249. Probably a larger number were unknown to the patentees.

34 *Nottingham Review*, 11 Sept 1829.

35   J. F. Sutton, *The Date-Book of Nottingham, 1750–1850* (1852), 389–92.

36   White's *Nottinghamshire Directory* (1832), 583–4.

37   8 Aug 1828.

38   I am grateful for the help given to me in preparing this study by the Chief Public Health Inspector of Nottingham and his staff.

39   *Nottingham Review, loc cit;* census of lace machinery taken in 1828, Mss, Nottingham Public Library.

40   R. Mellors, *Old Nottingham Suburbs, Then and Now* (1914), 36, 149.

41   *Nottingham Review,* 19 Feb 1830. Nottingham Corporation Deeds, TC 2/69.

42   Pp 9–10. (1842 Edition, a composite volume entitled *The Ford Family*). William and Mary Howitt lived in Nottingham from 1822 to 1836.

43   A. Barnett, quoted *Nottingham Review,* 8 Nov 1833, 13 June 1845; also J. F. Sutton, *op cit,* 391–2; W. Felkin, *op cit,* 285–6, 330, 334.

44   W. Felkin, in evidence to *Factory Inquiry, PP,* XX (1833), 519.

45   A. Barnett, *loc cit; Morning Chronicle* report on Nottingham, quoted *Nottingham Review,* 25 Jan 1850.

46   Quoted *Nottingham Review,* 17 Apr 1829.

47   *Morning Chronicle* report, *loc cit.*

48   *Nottingham Review,* 18 Nov 1831, 27 July 1832, 16 Nov 1832.

49   W. Felkin, 'Statistics of the Labouring Classes and Paupers of Nottingham', *Journal of the Statistical Society,* II (1839), 457–8.

50   *Nottingham Journal,* 4 Oct 1849. Thomas Hawksley, in evidence to *Commission on the Health of Towns, PP,* XVII (1844), 130–48.

51   W. Felkin, *loc cit.* A. Barnett quoted in *Nottingham Review,* 13 June 1845.

52   J. R. Martin, *loc cit* (note 3).

53   White's *Nottinghamshire Directory* (1832), 583–4.

54   *Nottingham Review,* 13 June 1845.

55   Quoted in evidence to the Nottingham Corporation Enclosure Committee, *Nottingham Review,* 26 Aug 1836.

56   W. Felkin, *op cit,* 458.

57   *Ibid.*

58   A. Barnett, quoted *Nottingham Journal,* 8 Nov 1833.

59   W. V. Hole, *The Housing of the Working Classes in Britain,* PhD thesis, London, 1965, 67. Nottingham Enclosure Act, 8 and 9 Vic, Cap 7.

60   On Thomas Wakefield, see my MA thesis, *William Felkin, 1795–1874* (Nottingham University, 1960).

61   *Nottingham Journal,* 20 Nov 1857.

62   *Nottingham Journal,* 9 Jan 1857.

63   *Nottingham Review,* 24 June 1859; *Nottingham Borough Records,* IX, 148.

64   W. Ashworth, *The Genesis of Modern British Town Planning* (1955), 91.

65   J. D. Chambers, *Modern Nottingham in the Making* (1942), 51.

66 W. Ashworth, *op cit*, 82.

67 *Nottingham Review*, 19 Mar 1852.

68 *Nottingham Journal*, 8 Oct 1852.

69 These houses still stand, now merged with later Victorian developments. They occupy the area between Lamartine Street, Ferrers Street and St Ann's Well Road.

70 *Nottingham Journal*, 5 Dec 1856.

71 For example, the fifteen cottages in Robin Hood Street, built by Charles Paget, MP, and Louis Heymann in 1856 (*Nottingham Journal, loc cit*).

72 *Nottingham Journal*, 5 Oct 1849, 14 Nov 1851. On William Felkin (1795–1874) see S. D. Chapman, 'Life and Work of William Felkin', introduction to centenary edition of Felkin's *History of the Machine Wrought Hosiery and Lace Manufactures*.

73 *Nottingham Review*, 14 May 1852.

74 *Nottingham Journal*, 1 Oct 1852, 1 Apr 1853; *Nottingham Borough Records*, IX, (1946), 94–5.

75 *Nottingham Mercury*, 14 May 1852.

76 J. T. Godfrey, ed, *The Stretton Mss* (1910), 221. The figures quoted are those that attracted attention because of their high level.

CHAPTER V

LIVERPOOL WORKING-CLASS HOUSING, 1801-1851

J. H. Treble

WHEN Defoe, writing in the early years of the eighteenth century, referred to Liverpool as 'one of the wonders of Britain', he was looking at a town which had yet to experience its period of most rapid economic growth.[1] Even as late as 1768 Liverpool's built-up area was largely concentrated round the four docks then in existence. Stretching along the waterfront, its northernmost limits were marked by Queen Street and St Paul's Square, while in the south few dwellings were to be found beyond a line running from Old Dock to Hanover Street. Inland—that is due east from the Mersey—there was scarcely a building which was more than 1,000yd from the river.[2] Already, however, the town's population had begun to increase at what appeared to contemporaries to be an astonishing rate. Whereas in 1700 the borough had contained 'little above' 5,000 inhabitants, this total had soared by mid-century to 'upwards of 22,000'.[3] In 1773 numbers had risen yet again to 34,407 souls living in 5,928 houses.[4]

By the 1790s the process of urban development had been carried a good deal further. More important, much of the housing that had been erected in the intervening quarter of a century was either specifically designed to meet the needs, or quickly to become the preserve, of the 'labouring classes'. Among such areas in the southern tip of the town were Crosbie Street, first mentioned in Gore's 1781 *Directory*, New Bird Street and Jordan Street.[5] All three streets, located in Great George Ward, were to be heavily populated with unskilled and semi-skilled workmen in the early years of the nineteenth century. In the northern area of the town the predominantly working-class districts in and around Byrom Street (Exchange Ward) had been created or were in the process of completion. North Street and Johnson Street, for example, both situated in this quarter, had been laid out between 1775 and 1785,[6] though in Vauxhall Ward Banastre Street—a notorious plague-spot of the 1840s—was still only 'partially built' at the dawn of the new century.[7]

Equally significant from the viewpoint of this essay, the distinctive characteristics of Liverpool's pattern of working-class housing were by this point in time clearly discernible to the trained eyes of eighteenth-century observers of the social scene. The salient features of that pattern—a pattern which was to last for virtually the whole of the period 1780–1850—can be conveniently grouped under three broad headings. Firstly the cellar dwelling was already fulfilling an important role in providing accommodation for that section of the working-class firmly placed at the bottom of the social and economic ladder. In 1790 it was estimated that more than one-eighth of the borough's total population—6,780 out of 53,583[8]—resided in 'these subterraneous and unhealthy habitations'.[9] Moreover, unlike the cotton towns of Lancashire, Liverpool's cellars were from the first specifically built for residential purposes. As one critic of this system of house construction noted, the practice of building houses with cellar dwellings attached to them had become by 1797 a major social abuse. What, however, was even more alarming was the progressive extension of this convention to 'the houses of the mediocrity'. In these more expensive residences cellars 'are [now] generally let out by the owners of the houses to many people following trades . . . it is something extraordinary, that in houses of moderate rent the evil continues to this day'.[10] Nonetheless, despite the fact that such abodes were liable to flooding—as in Whitechapel in July 1789[11]— and despite Dr Currie's assertion of 1798 that typhus was endemic among Liverpool's cellar and court inmates,[12] they were not without their defenders. W. Moss, for example, writing in 1797, argued that such habitations possessed considerable merits. The cellar, he conceded,

> has an unpleasant appearance; yet that is the worst of its qualities; a cellar being found, from experience, a much more healthful residence than a room in a house where every room is tenanted. Being detached, a cellar can neither receive nor communicate any thing infectious in the manner that necessarily happens in the inhabited rooms of a house that all communicate by one common staircase.[13]

More powerful voices than this were to be raised in their support in 1802 when the town's property-owners, with a vested interest in the perpetuation of such dwellings, secured the defeat of a local improvement bill which, among other things, aimed at closing down all occupied cellars.[14] Thereafter no real checks were to be placed on either their construction or occupancy until 1842.

The second feature of Liverpool's housing pattern during these years was the increasing number of back dwellings which were being provided for the port's growing labour-force. According, for instance, to Simmons' survey of January 1790 almost 20 per cent—1,608 out of 8,148[15]—of the town's occupied houses consisted of this type of accommodation. In concrete terms this meant that over 25 per cent of Liverpool's population was to be found in cellars and back houses.[16] Thirdly, and lastly, chronic overcrowding was already a familiar experience in the lives of certain elements of the working classes. By the late 1790s 'many hundreds [of houses], which do not rent at more than £4 and £6 per annum, have eighteen or twenty crouded [*sic*] together, from cellar to garret, under one roof'. But resort to this expedient was rarely the result of the cupidity of the sitting tenant. Overcrowding, when and where it occurred, usually denoted the existence of families living at or below the poverty line who were 'unable [to afford] to rent a whole house'.[17]

Between 1800 and 1825 these trends continued as the physical boundaries of the town changed at a faster rate than in the whole of the preceding seventy-five years. In the southern part of the borough New Bird Street and Brick Street (Great George Ward) were extended east of Simpson Street to the shore of the Mersey itself. It was in this locality—'the whole [Wapping] district as far as Parliament Street and beyond'—that 'the erection of narrow unwholesome courthouses was . . . suffered to a most pernicious extent'.[18] In the north identical developments were taking place. In Exchange and Vauxhall Wards much of the land between Marybone and Byrom Street had been 'used as brick-yards' until 1806, when Great Crosshall Street was laid out. This was to provide the necessary stimulus for further house-building activity in that district; for due north of this new thoroughfare land was quickly used up

> principally for cottages. Some of the leading lines, Adlington Street, Bispham Street, etc., were sufficiently wide; others such as Lace Street, Henry Edward Street, and Harrison Street, were wretchedly narrow and contracted, but the whole arrangement was essentially vicious in one respect—the crowding together of too many tenements in a given area.[19]

Nor was this kind of housing confined exclusively to those wards which were contiguous to the docks. In Lime Street Ward, land to the east of Lime Street, lying almost three-quarters of a mile from the waterfront, was given over to the erection of numerous courts and narrow streets which 'did much [between 1800 and 1825] to neutralise any advantage of situation in a sanitary point of view'.[20] Thus a substantial proportion of the net addition to Liverpool's housing stock in the first twenty years of the nineteenth century— and between 1801 and 1821 the number of houses in the borough

almost doubled[21]—was catering for the seemingly relentless growth
of the labouring classes.

From 1821 to 1851, however, expansion was more erratic. Although during these three decades a net increase of 18,421 dwellings
was recorded within the boundaries of the pre-1835 borough,[22]
there is some indication that the provision of working-class dwellings
was principally the product of a series of short but intense building
booms. In the first of these booms, covering roughly the years 1827–
32, there took place a remarkable expansion in the supply of new
'very slight houses'[23] in every part of the town. Although in this
rash of building 'a great deal of money' was ultimately to be lost,[24] it
was nonetheless generally true that these six years, coming immediately after the 1825–6 slump, were very propitious for the property
developer. For one thing he was aided by a secular decline in the
construction costs of working-class housing—a fall which amounted
to almost $7\frac{1}{2}$ per cent over the decade 1824–33.[25] For another thing
there was evidence by the mid-1820s of a growing disequilibrium
between the supply of houses and the demand for them. In these
circumstances, therefore, it is scarcely surprising to discover either
substantial amounts of money being channelled into speculative
building or the willingness of such groups as shopkeepers to invest
part of their savings 'in small houses, on account of the rate of
interest yielded nominally by that property'.[26] The end-product of
this investment was the creation of additional working-class accommodation not merely in the traditional strongholds of the labouring
classes, but also in districts which were mainly the preserve of the
middle class. Significantly enough, two wards which could be placed
in this latter category had both acquired by 1841 sizeable working-
class populations. At that date 16·89 per cent of Rodney Street
Ward's total population lived in courts and a further 5·94 per cent
were to be found in cellars. The comparable statistics for Abercromby Ward were 13·54 and 6·18 per cent respectively.[27]

The second period of intense activity, beginning a little uncertainly
in 1841, lasted until 1846. During these years working-class houses
were to be erected in Lime Street and Abercromby Wards, in the
out-townships of North and South Toxteth and Everton, and above
all in Scotland Ward, the northernmost ward in Liverpool Parish.
This last-named locality, with its western limits marked by the
Mersey, had only begun to be extensively developed around 1822.
The turning point in its history had come with the completion of

Prince's Dock in 1821 and Clarence Dock some nine years later. Thereafter 'as the dock system [has] advanced northwards, [it was] accompanied *pari passu* with the extension of building'.[28] By the mid-1830s the area was still experiencing rapid economic growth; in Picton's words, 'the tide of building set in [post-1836] with considerable vigour on both sides of Scotland Road'.[29] It was only in the 1840s, however, that it underwent its period of most dramatic transformation. What this meant in terms of additional, and largely working-class, dwellings was strikingly demonstrated in the 1851 Census returns. Between 1841 and 1851 there was a net increase of 4,034 houses in the ward itself, with most of this increase being confined to the first six years of the decade. These figures represented a rise in Scotland Ward's housing stock of slightly over 70 per cent.[30]

Nevertheless, in spite of this impressive achievement the second boom coincided with the onset of a distinct shift in investment, which was to exercise a profound effect on the supply of working-class accommodation within the town. From 1838 onwards there is sufficient evidence to show that Liverpool's builders and investing public were tending to divert their money and resources away from the erection of houses for the working man to provide more expensive homes, which brought in a more secure return. In 1838 itself the building trade was largely preoccupied with constructing dwellings for the middle classes which would be let at rents of between £25 and £35 pa. The fact that such houses were 'taken up in most neighbourhoods as fast as they can be got ready for habitation',[31] indicated that at least in the short-term such a trend was likely to continue. In fact it was to last until the end of the 1840s and beyond. As Appendix 5.2 (A) shows, the percentage of new houses that could be legitimately classified as catering for the working man—ie dwellings let at an annual rental of under £12—rose above 40 per cent of the total addition to the housing stock of the greatly enlarged, post-1835 borough in only one year in the whole decade. In absolute numbers twice only during the 1840s were more than 1,000 new homes erected for the urban worker in any given twelve months. More detailed returns show that this reluctance to build new dwellings for the working classes became more marked in the second half of this decade. In 1846, 710 out of 3,460 houses were completed for letting at rents of under £12 per annum, while no fewer than 2,328 were built to let at between £12 and £25 per year. In

1847 a mere fifty-nine dwellings were built for the working classes, while 905 were erected for a middle-class clientele. A basically similar result was achieved in the following year.[32]

The factors responsible for this post-1845 pattern and the impact of that pattern on the social capital of Liverpool will be examined later. It is sufficient here to note the emergence of this potentially disastrous trend at the very time when Liverpool was about to become one of the principal ports of entry for 'Irish Famine' immigrants, and to pass on to examine the basic question of how far the working classes were subjected to overcrowding and the nature of the total physical environment in which they lived.

A tentative beginning can perhaps best be made by trying to determine the extent to which the supply of housing within Liverpool Parish—ie the pre-1835 borough—kept pace over time with the expansion of its population. For the purpose of this exercise the social historian is compelled to rely mainly on the data provided by successive censuses which, despite their limitations, enable him to construct tables showing the number of persons per house between 1801 and 1851. In the Parish itself these statistics indicate that the total population and the total stock of housing—occupied and unoccupied dwellings taken together—increased over this half century at roughly comparable rates.[33] On the other hand there was a significant difference, illustrated by the movement of the persons per inhabited house ratio, between the rate of population growth and the number of inhabited dwellings. Whereas there were 6·78 people to each occupied house in 1801, that total had risen to 7·32 in 1851. Nevertheless these statistics should not be taken to mean that there was a progressive rise in this ratio at each successive census during this span of fifty years. Between 1801 and 1811, for example, this average showed in social terms a distinct improvement, falling from 6·78 in the earlier census to 6·05 at the latter date. After 1811, however, the picture became more sombre. By 1821 this figure had reached 6.26. Ten years later it stood at 6·42, and during the course of the following two decades it followed on its upward course. By 1841 there were no fewer than 6·95 persons per occupied house; by 1851 a new peak of 7·32 had been achieved.[34]

These results, it must be stressed, were considerably worse than either the national average, which during the first half of the nineteenth century fluctuated between a low point, recorded in 1841, of 5·41 and a high point of 5·75 in 1821,[35] or the global calculations which Professor Rimmer has made for Leeds Township over slightly less than the same time-span.[36] Precisely how bad Liverpool Parish's record was in housing can in fact be underlined in two further ways. Firstly, as Appendixes 5.3 and 4 demonstrate, its population/total housing stock ratios (unoccupied plus occupied houses) were still very much worse than the national figures relating to the number of persons per inhabited house alone. Secondly, at no point during the years 1801–31 would Liverpool Parish have been able to give every family a home of its own even if it had had powers to allocate all unoccupied dwellings within its boundaries for this socially desirable end.[37] In this respect its experience again contrasts strongly with that of Leeds, which was a town of equally spectacular economic growth but with a very different social structure.[38]

Yet if in the end these statistics point to the fact that Liverpool's overall performance in accommodating its growth of numbers was poor in relation to other parts of Great Britain, they still conceal as much as they reveal. For they do nothing to point to the existence of differentials in the people per inhabited house ratio within different areas of the Parish itself. And yet it is exactly this type of information that is required to elucidate the particular problems associated with the subject of working-class housing. Were there, for instance, wide disparities in the number of persons per occupied house in the individual wards of the town? If such disparities are found to exist, can they be directly related to the income and occupational structure of the ward's inhabitants or have other explanations to be advanced? Evidence of this nature is, not surprisingly, more difficult to disentangle. To answer such questions in a completely authoritative fashion would involve a detailed examination of the Enumerators' Returns. Short of undertaking that formidable task, the historian is forced to rely on the fragmentary material, embedded in the 1841 and 1851 censuses, to obtain even a rough idea of how far, during the last decade of the period under review, there were district differences in the population/occupied housing ratio.

Broadly speaking the picture emerging from this datum is that the groups of wards with the worst records were located along the riverfront and had been amongst the earliest developed parts of the port. Into this category came Vauxhall Ward, with an average of 7·62 persons per inhabited house in 1841 and 8·36 in 1851; St Paul's – Exchange Wards (7·54 in 1841 and 7·70 in 1851); Castle

Street – St Peter's Wards (7·82 and 7·89); and Great George – Pitt Street Wards (7·76 and 8·33). Scotland Ward, the most recently built-up area in the parish, had 6·46 persons in each of its occupied houses in 1841. By 1851 this ratio had reached 7·06. Inland the middle-class stronghold of Rodney Street – Abercromby Wards experienced a slight rise in this average over the decade—from 6·47 to 6·73, while in Lime Street – St Anne's Wards (6·03 in 1841; 6·52 in 1851) an identical trend was discernible.[39] Inevitably of course there were black spots within each of these localities showing the extremes to which the practice of overcrowding could be pushed. For example, in Exchange Ward in the early 1840s Lace Street's 1,434 inhabitants were housed in a mere 109 dwellings—no fewer than 13·15 persons per inhabited house. North Street, situated in the same ward and with an average of 10 individuals per house, fared only slightly better, while in Great George Ward, New Bird Street (9·08 persons per house) and Crosbie Street (11·27) provided equally notorious examples of chronic overcrowding.[40] Significantly enough all four streets had become by this point in time almost the exclusive preserve of the Irish immigrant.[41]

At this level—looking at some of the worst 'plague spots' in the town—it is easy to see a correlation between the incidence of over-crowding and the social class of the inhabitants. On the other hand it is impossible to deduce from the census returns alone the degree to which individual wards were or were not areas of working-class settlement. This difficulty arises primarily from the form in which those returns were published. Except in the cases of Vauxhall and Scotland Wards, the population/occupied housing ratios, to which reference has already been made, relate to groups of wards rather than to the basic electoral unit of municipal government. It is, there-fore, to other sources that one must turn for guidance to the social structure of each ward; and prominent among these are the statistical tables which Dr Duncan presented to the Royal Commission on the State of Large Towns and Populous Districts. From that information it is possible to determine *inter alia* the proportion of a ward's total population that in 1841 lived in courts and cellars.

It is from such an analysis that the importance of Vauxhall Ward as a bastion of the labouring classes becomes immediately apparent. Indeed, with 56·75 per cent of its inhabitants classified as court and cellar dwellers, it could justifiably claim to be the main stronghold of the dock worker within the boundaries of the pre-1835 borough. But if it was the principal, it was by no means the only, area of heavy working-class settlement. Other wards with a substantial part of their populations situated in courts and cellars included St Anne's (40·10 per cent), St Paul's (39·94 per cent) Scotland (38·73), Exchange (36·39), Great George (30·17), Lime Street (26·42), and Pitt Street (25·19). In fact, 34·33 per cent of the inhabitants of Liverpool Parish were to be found in this kind of accommodation.[42] Nonetheless, these figures did not embrace the whole of the working-class element within the Parish or within the individual wards. Among others they specifically exclude those working men who had made their homes in 'front houses' and in dwellings which had formerly accommodated sections of Liverpool's middle classes.

In some measure, however, these gaps can be filled from an 1849 study of Liverpool rentals. The results of this investigation (Appendix 5.6) shed fresh light on the percentage of the total stock of houses in each ward which were let at annual rents of £10 and under. Once again these returns underline the relative social homogeneity of Vauxhall Ward's inhabitants. At this date no fewer than 71·48 per cent of its houses were rented at £10 and under per annum. Scotland Ward and South Toxteth, if they could not quite match this figure, were equally clearly earmarked as working-class districts. In both instances more than 60 per cent of their housing was let at this rental level. In other parts of the borough a similar pattern can be observed. For example, between 40 and 50 per cent of the dwellings in St Paul's, Exchange, Great George and St Anne's Wards came into this same category. Other districts with more than 30 per cent of their housing stock let at annual rentals of £10 and less included Castle Street and Lime Street Wards and perhaps more unexpectedly, the out-township of West Derby. There can be little doubt that accommodation of this nature was almost the exclusive prerogative of labourers, dock workers and others whose employment was either seasonal or casual. Yet in the last analysis it must be admitted that even these figures are not completely exhaustive since they omit those elements of the borough's working-class population who rented houses at above this minimum figure. Bearing this significant qualification in mind, we must now turn to examine in detail the different types of dwellings in which the labouring classes lived in the early 1840s.

I

Perhaps the most distinctive form of working-man's dwelling at this period was that associated with the court system of building. That system, tracing its beginnings back to late eighteenth-century Liverpool, was based upon the principle of packing together as many houses as possible within a given area. Partly because of the 'high value of land' and partly because of 'the desire . . . of builders and landlords to secure the most profitable investment from their money',[43] it resulted in the creation of localities of high density back-to-back housing by builders who had paid scant attention to any question of social costing. In Liverpool this usually involved the erection of two facing rows of houses, each row containing between two and eight dwellings.[44] Such houses would normally be three storeys high and consist of two rooms 10 or 11ft square and a garret, though there might often be a cellar attached, which prior to 1842 would invariably be sublet.[45] Externally the distance between each row could be as little as 6ft, and before the building controls of the 1840s was hardly anywhere as much as 15ft.[46] But this was not the worst of the drawbacks inseparably linked with this pattern of development. In many instances a court might only 'communicate with the streets by a passage or archway about three feet wide,— in the old courts, built up overhead; and the further end being also . . . closed by a high wall or by the back or side of an adjoining building, the court forms in fact a *cul-de-sac* with a narrow opening'.[47]

In other words, the end-product of the speculators' endeavours was the emergence of a patchwork of courts whose extent was only fully revealed in an 1841 investigation conducted by the town's building surveyors. According to their reports, both the North and South Districts of the post-1835 borough faced serious sanitary problems, which stemmed in part from the 'blind growth' of court housing. For instance in the North District only 117 of Vauxhall Ward's 382 courts were open at front and back—ie capable of admitting a through draught of air—while no fewer than 296 were built upon both sides. And while Scotland Ward had a slightly better record than this, with 131 of its 341 courts open at front and back, Exchange Ward in the same locality had the blackest set of results for any ward in the whole of the borough : a mere $2\frac{1}{2}$ per cent of its courts—5 out of 200—were so constructed as to permit a through draught. St Paul's and St Anne's were better, but they still between them possessed a formidable stock of insanitary housing. In the South District the largely working-class areas of North and South Toxteth and Great George's Ward again presented a picture of social suffering on the grand scale.[48]

Such suffering, however, stemmed much more from the nature of the total environment in which the court dweller lived than from the chronic overcrowding of his home, measured in terms of the number of inmates per room; for as Appendix 5.7 makes abundantly clear, only St Anne's, Exchange, Vauxhall and St Paul's Wards in the Northern District had an average of 5 persons per house. In the Southern District the same high point was reached in North Toxteth, Great George, Pitt Street, St Peter's and Castle Street Wards. These statistics are based, it is true, on the assumption of the full occupancy of every house and make no distinction between cottages with or without occupied cellars; and yet making the maximum allowance for both of these factors, there is still little to suggest that court dwelling in the Liverpool of the early 1840s was as frequently overcrowded as many contemporary commentators claimed. That there were divergencies from this pattern which were concealed by these ward averages must of course be readily admitted. But even so—and such divergencies were usually the sequel to using court dwellings as common lodging houses or the result of Irish immigrants subletting their homes to accommodate relatives and newly arrived friends—the fact remains that the persons per court house figure was in 1841 considerably below the population/occupied housing ratio for the whole of Liverpool Parish.[49] The only other point which in this context needs to be emphasised is the major role played by the court house in meeting the basic need for working-class accommodation in Liverpool at that date. In all, slightly less than a quarter of the post-1835 borough's total population—perhaps equivalent to a third of its working-class inhabitants—was to be found in such dwellings.

Court houses apart, the other principal haunt of the working man was the streets of dull, almost anonymous 'front houses', which had been specifically built for a working-class clientele. In some respects these places could claim to possess important advantages over the court dwelling. In the first place they were located in streets that were normally open at both ends. Secondly, the distance between parallel rows of these houses was more often than not around 24ft.[50]

Many of the worst claustrophobic effects of the court system of building were thus thereby avoided. To offset these good points, however, it should be remembered that 'front houses' were frequently sublet and that it was in this kind of accommodation that the bulk of the post-1835 borough's cellar population was concentrated.[51]

Exactly how formidable numerically that population had become was again vividly illustrated by the building surveyors' inquiry of 1841. At that moment in time no fewer than 7,307 cellars were occupied as separate dwellings, with an average of 3·29 persons per cellar. In aggregate terms this meant that slightly more than 24,000 people were living in these 'subterraneous abodes'.[52] Inevitably this population was unevenly distributed throughout the municipal wards. In the Northern District almost all cellar dwellings were located in five wards. Vauxhall Ward (3·13 persons per cellar) and Scotland Ward (3·26) contained between them almost half—2,011 out of 4,423—of the District's cellars. Other wards in this area with substantial cellar populations included St Anne's (2·74 persons per cellar), Exchange (3·02), and St Paul's (2·88). In striking contrast to these returns the out-townships of Everton and West Derby were scarcely touched by the problem. In the Southern District, however, the pattern is more difficult to decipher. For although the traditional working-class strongholds of North and South Toxteth (3·91 and 3·71 persons per cellar respectively) and Great George Ward (2·65) accounted for virtually 50 per cent of the District's cellar population, both Rodney Street and Abercromby Wards, with their considerable numbers of middle-class inhabitants, made surprisingly large contributions to providing accommodation for those who were at the foot of the social scale. More important, Pitt Street Ward, once almost an enclave of the mercantile community, had the highest cellar population of any ward in the South—2,103 persons in all— and the highest number of persons per occupied cellar ratio (4·63) in the whole of the borough.[53]

Some cellars, of course, housed very many more people than these ward averages tend to suggest. Among them were those cellars in the southern area of the port which were 'used for the purpose of Schools, with from forty to sixty Scholars, several of the Children apparently in the last stage of Consumption, or labouring under disease engendered by their continuance in an impure Atmosphere'.[54] Equally glaring examples of overcrowding occurred in 'double-cellars' which served as common lodging-houses. Where this practice prevailed it produced even more devastating social harm than the lodging house proper. 'Here,' it was proclaimed, 'the overcrowding is carried still further, if that be possible, and is certainly more prejudicial to the health of the inhabitants, from the still more defective ventilation of these dark and miserable abodes.' Perhaps housing at night as many as thirty Irish immigrants, this type of dwelling presented 'in miniature a picture of the Black Hole of Calcutta'.[55] Yet these exceptions to the norm notwithstanding, there is in the end scant evidence to show that the majority of cellars in the early 1840s accommodated more than a single family, though that family was usually living in overcrowded conditions—that is, more than two persons per room—since only a quarter of such abodes possessed a second or 'back' compartment.[56]

Overcrowding on this scale could only be labelled a social evil. But it was by no means the worst inconvenience to which the cellar dweller was subjected. Exercising a still more pernicious influence on his or her physical well-being was the nature of the cellar itself. Measuring between 10 and 12ft square, the floors of over one-third of these dwellings were between 4 and 5ft below the surface of the street. In a further 2,025 instances, the cellar-bottom had been laid more than 5 but less than 6ft below the level of the pavement.[57] In addition, the air in such accommodation, even where front windows were provided, would always be polluted because of inadequate ventilation and the necessity of lighting fires to keep out the pervading damp. However, as the 1841 building surveyors' reports showed, resort to this last expedient had little effect on internal conditions in those cellars which were unflagged. At that date no fewer than 2,848 of the borough's inhabited cellars were described as damp, and a further 140 as wet.[58] Exactly what these definitions meant in terms of personal hardship was strikingly demonstrated by the testimony of Mr Holmes. He asserted :

Liverpool contains a multitude of inhabited cellars, close and damp, with no drain nor any convenience . . . Some time ago I visited a poor woman in distress, the wife of a labouring man; she had been confined only a few days, and herself and infant were lying on straw in a vault, through the outer cellar, with a clay floor impervious to water. There was no light nor ventilation in it, and the air was dreadful. I had to walk on bricks across the floor to reach her bedside, as the floor itself was flooded with stagnant water. This is by no means an extraordinary case, for I have witnessed scenes equally wretched; and it is only necessary to go into Crosby-street, Freemason's-row, and many other cross streets, out of Vauxhall-Road, to find hordes of poor creatures living in cellars which are almost as bad and offensive as charnel-houses.[59]

Viewed against this background it is scarcely surprising to discover that when epidemics broke out in the borough, the cellar dweller suffered more severely from their ravages than any other section of society.

This type of accommodation and the other kinds of housing with which we have thus far dealt—the court and the 'front house'—had from the outset been built to cater for the basic requirements of the labouring classes. From 1810 onwards, however, large houses in every part of the parish that had hitherto been residences of the middle-classes were being converted into multi-occupation tenements for the working man. In Pitt Street Ward, for example, Dr Duncan drew attention to the fact that by the early 1840s the houses of the working classes were 'of a larger size than those in other districts, and of course accommodate a greater number of families or of lodgers'. This state of affairs was in large measure the product of a change in the social class of their inhabitants; as he put it, many such 'houses were formerly occupied by persons engaged in business, who gradually deserted them as the town moved eastwards'.[60] In the short term this might have involved a relatively short migration of the middle classes to Abercromby and Rodney Street Wards, though affluent merchants might stay in even these localities a strictly limited time. For as early as the 1820s there is clear indication that the more wealthy members of Liverpool society were leaving Abercromby Square itself to make their homes in villas in the surrounding countryside.[61] Lawton's examination of the 1851 Enumerators' Returns shows that this general movement to the suburbs had continued to gather momentum in the intervening quarter of a century.[62]

When and where such internal changes in the social composition of a ward's or a street's population occurred, they were invariably accompanied by a progressive degeneration of the total environment of the locality in question. In Vauxhall Ward, for instance, Maguire Street, Summer Seat and Gildart's Gardens had originally been situated in pleasant enough surroundings. But when industry began to move into this district, 'a vital change accordingly came over the spirit of the neighbourhood. The large gardens were converted into coal-yards or built over, the small ones made into pigstyes. As the manufactories increased, the only human habitations erected there were cottages of the lowest class, and the locality became abandoned to dirt and squalor.'[63] Again, in St Anne's Street (St Anne's Ward) 'old families', as they were styled, left their large and 'dignified' houses as soon as the surrounding area started to be 'encroached upon and crowded with cottages', though here the houses themselves passed into the hands of the 'shopocracy' rather than the working classes proper. This did not prevent Picton from lamenting loudly over the consequences of this change. 'Its [St Anne's Street's] aspect', he wrote 'has become entirely metamorphosed into one of a second-rate commercial character.'[64] After 1830 this pattern was to extend outside the boundaries of the pre-1835 borough to affect some of the out-townships themselves. Everton Crescent, for example, built in the out-township of Everton in 1808 and at first considered 'a very aristocratic quarter', was to undergo a similar experience sometime after 1830 : its wealthier inhabitants moved still further inland and their houses were then 'subdivided into smaller tenements'.[65]

Cumulatively these population shifts were attended with momentous consequences. By the early 1830s they were responsible for two interlinked trends, which produced widespread consternation among the more socially aware members of the community. In the first place there was a general tendency for 'the value of all large houses' to fall and 'the value of smaller houses' to rise. Secondly, the rent of formerly middle-class housing plunged sharply as and when it was taken over by groupings further down the social scale. As John Stewart cogently argued :

> Gentlemen who were paying their £100 a year, and so on, have naturally, as those immediate neighbourhoods have got more populous, gone into new large houses at the outside of the town, and therefore the other large houses have considerably sunk in value, because gentlemen would not live in them, and the consequence is, that the owners have been compelled to get a more moderate description of tenant to take a more moderate rent.[66]

The only other important contribution to alleviating the working-man's accommodation problem was made by the common lodging house. Until the erection in the late 1840s of special 'Model Lodging-Houses',[67] this kind of institution was normally merely a 'front', or court house, which was used by its owner for commercial purposes. In one sense, however, the lodging house was dealing with a much more specific section of Liverpool's population than any

M

other kind of working-class dwelling, since it almost owed its *raison d'etre* to the presence of the Irish immigrant in the town. For one thing the overwhelming majority of such establishments were owned by Irishmen. At the end of the 1840s nine-tenths of Liverpool's lodging-house keepers were thought to be of Irish extraction.[68] Pauper lodging houses, therefore—and above all those which were located in the eastern portions of Vauxhall and Exchange Wards[69] —were virtually the exclusive prerogative of Irish owners. But Irish participation in the trade did not end here; for most of these abodes were providing rest and shelter for a largely immigrant clientele. Some of these houses derived part of their income from migratory Irishmen, such as the seasonal harvesters, who would stay for two or three nights on their way to, and on their return from, the harvest fields. Others provided shelter for an element of the permanent population, while a considerable proportion of them catered for a more specialised form of demand from migrants who were seeking a temporary home before sailing to a new life in America.[70] Nevertheless, irrespective of the type of guests they attracted, they were all equally squalid. It was not without good cause that local medical opinion denounced them as '*foci* which radiate infection'.[71]

Charging 2d or 3d for a night's lodging, the proprietors of such houses rarely made any attempt to segregate the sexes.[72] The overriding philosophy of most owners was to cram as many people as posible into their 'fever dens'. This might involve trying to fit three or four persons into one bed, though as T. Fresh, the Borough Inspector of Nuisances, noted, 'in many places, even bedsteads were not to be found'. Where that situation obtained, 'the lodgers were domiciled on wretched filthy pallets of straw, which were piled side by side on the floors; and as the rooms were generally almost without ventilation, when they became filled with inmates at night, they presented scenes of wretchedness which were almost indescribable'.[73] In such an environment there could be little hope that the basic decencies of human life would be observed.

Qualitative evidence of this nature, however, invaluable as it is for highlighting the domestic economy of the lodging house, does little to answer the fundamental question of what proportion of Liverpool's total population resorted to such haunts. In some ways, of course, the question itself is beset with semantic problems. To what extent, for instance, should the seasonal worker or the would-be emigrant be considered part of the town's labour force? But a more fundamental difficulty than this stems from the paucity of the statistical material relating to, or touching on, this type of institution. Such data as are available cover only the late 1840s and then are exclusively confined to the nightly lodging house, which under the terms of the 1846 Liverpool Sanitary Act had to be registered with the corporation if the owner wished to continue in business. In December 1850, for instance, Dr Duncan reported that 1,100 such houses had been visited 'in order to ascertain the number of lodgers which each was capable of accommodating with a due regard to health'. As a result of these investigations 620 had been placed on the municipal register, and 249 of these were solely concerned with Irish and other itinerants who were planning to emigrate to Canada or America. These emigrant lodging houses were allocated a total of 2,204 persons between them, although excluded from this figure were the owners' families.[74] Fortunately the sparse nature of this information can be supplemented by the very much more detailed analysis of these establishments made by T. Fresh. According to him no fewer than 659 licensed nightly lodging houses were in operation on 31 March 1851. Of this number 286 were emigrant lodging houses which provided accommodation for 2,958 lodgers and 1,298 dependants of the owner in a total of 1,524 rooms. The 373 non-emigrant lodging houses accommodated 1,868 dependants and 2,669 lodgers in 1,723 rooms.[75] In other words, at that date rather more than 8,500 people—equivalent to about $2\frac{1}{3}$ per cent of the post-1835 borough's total population—had chosen to make their temporary or permanent homes in such places.

These official returns, however, considerably understated the size of the problem, which had worried successive generations of sanitary reformers. In the first place, as Duncan himself acknowledged, cases of overcrowding in nightly lodging houses—ie taking in numbers in excess of the allocated totals—were widespread, especially immediately after the relevant clauses of the 1846 Act came into effect. From 1847 to 1849 no fewer than 133 instances of overcrowding were reported to the authorities[76] and there were perhaps half as many again which eluded prosecution. Some hint of the scale on which such overcrowding occurred can be gauged from an examination of the difference between the number of lodgers applied for and the total ultimately sanctioned by the borough's officials. Whereas 5,627 lodgers had been allocated to the 659 nightly lodging houses in business on 31 March 1851, no fewer than 8,533—

over 50 per cent more than the total finally permitted—were applied for.[77] Yet even this wide differential did not fully reveal the incidence of overcrowding that had existed pre-1846. As Dr Duncan pointed out, 'the keepers of the worst description of Lodging houses, on finding that the powers of the Act were about to be enforced, reduced the number of their beds before applying for the registration of their houses, and did not venture to ask for more than a portion, in some cases not exceeding one-half, of the number of lodgers they were accustomed to receive'. Others who came into this same category had retired from 'the occupation' altogether because it had become no longer 'a remunerative one, under the restrictions imposed by virtue of the Act'.[78]

Perhaps the biggest defect in these returns is that they exclude the weekly lodging house, the numbers of which, it was thought, were 'twenty-fold' as great as those of the nightly type.[79] Although this was a gross overestimate of their significance, there is some indication that the system of regulating nightly houses introduced after 1846 stimulated the growth of these weekly establishments to such an extent that the whole purpose of the Liverpool Sanitary Act was in danger of being undermined, and by 1850 there was talk of amending the 1846 statute in the interests of public hygiene and environmental control. What above all was required, it was asserted, was the introduction of clauses into an amended bill which would prevent 'the unreasonable overcrowding of small rooms in court and other houses . . . by several families and persons of both sexes herding indiscriminately therein, and living together daily and nightly, in the character of lodgers, both by the week and other periods'.[80] The very fact that informed opinion could express alarm in these terms suggested that the different types of lodging house, taken together, accommodated in 1850 perhaps as much as 10 per cent of the Parish's population.[81]

Living in overcrowded conditions was thus part of the everyday experience of a substantial proportion of the town's working classes.[82] Yet this was far from the only social abuse to which they were exposed. Overcrowding itself almost paled into insignificance when contrasted with the desolate spectacle the working-class districts presented to dispassionate analysts of the quality of mid-nineteenth century urban life. In the first place a wide disparity existed almost everywhere between the number of privies built for working-class use and the number of persons they were designed to serve. An

1840–41 survey of twenty-six streets between Vauxhall Road and Scotland Road (Vauxhall, Exchange and Scotland Wards) revealed that no fewer than 804 out of a total of 1,200 'front houses' were 'without either yard, privy, or ash-pit'.[83] But even where 'out-offices' were provided with this type of dwelling they could be a doubtful boon because, in the absence of a back access road, 'night soil men' were compelled to carry 'the Soil out of the Bogholes' through the house.[84] The inhabitants of court houses were slightly better off, though even in their case the notion of 'improvement' is only meaningful in a relatively restricted statistical sense. As Appendix 5.7 demonstrates, one privy would serve between two and four court houses or between ten and twenty persons.[85] Furthermore, ash-pits and privies were only infrequently emptied. This picture of neglect, which was firmly established by the late 1840s, could be clearly related to the impact of guano imports on the price levels of urban compost. As one critic wrote :

> Prior to the introduction of guano into this country as a manure, the nightmen in Liverpool, not only emptied many of the middens free of expenses, but, occasionally, gave an equivalent for the privilege of doing so. Subsequently, however, the aspect of things, in this respect, entirely changed, and instead of paying for the privilege, the nightmen refused to discharge any middens unless *they* were paid for doing so.[86]

The sequel to this breakdown in a vital community service was predictable enough : it resulted in the formation of 'open cesspools, dunghills, or "middens" ' in the corners of courts 'as places of deposit for refuse from all the houses',[87] which was naturally a serious hazard to health. In the second place the overwhelming majority of working-class streets and courts were before 1842 undrained and unsewered, though £100,000 had already been spent on an extensive sewerage programme.[88] The bulk of this expenditure, as Dr Duncan showed, had been devoted to the middle-class districts where most of the substantial ratepayers lived. Only 56 out of 243 largely working-class streets—about 20 per cent of the total working-class area—had been in any way improved through this outlay of money.[89]

In addition the courts were never, and undedicated streets rarely, visited by the municipality's scavenging services. Undrained and unpaved as they were, 'surface water and fluid refuse of every kind' were left to 'stagnate in the street, and add, especially in hot weather, their pestilential influence to that of the more solid filth'.[90]

The working classes were also exposed to various forms of industrial nuisance, ranging from pollution of the atmosphere with smoke or fumes to noise and the 'pumping of the refuse Liquor' from Soap Works on to the street itself.[91] In many instances, even when the corporation possessed powers to prosecute offending manufacturers, it refrained from doing so on the grounds that it might thereby drive industry out of the town.[92]

Finally, the working classes suffered more than any other section of the community from Liverpool's defective water supplies. In the early 1840s water was only made available to the general population on alternate days for a period of time varying from 1 to $2\frac{1}{2}$ hours per day.[93] For the middle classes, of course, such intermittent supplies caused serious inconvenience; but for the working classes they spelt little short of social disaster. To start with, if the poor were usually supplied with piped water into their own homes, there were several localities where the working man had to share a common water tap with his neighbours.[94] Where such conditions obtained, there was little time to collect a sufficient quantity of water for his daily needs. Again, only a minority of the working classes could afford to buy enough utensils to store an adequate amount of water for a hygienic standard of life.[95] Last, but not least, supplies were sometimes only available when most of the adult population were not at home.[96] As long, therefore, as such a socially harmful system of distribution continued to operate, it was vain to expect any spectacular amelioration of the working-class environment. This much the local Health of Towns Association openly acknowledged in 1845: 'no efficient system', it proclaimed, 'for improving the habits of cleanliness amongst the Poor can be carried into effect without an ample supply of Water'.[97]

All these insanitary problems were in a sense outside the power of the working classes to remedy. It does not follow, however, that they were entirely the unwilling victims of the indifference of the middle classes. As local practitioners of social medicine were quick to point out, the working man—or more accurately the Irish immigrant—contributed in at least two specific ways to the deterioration of his environment. Firstly, the Irishman, despite the existence of local byelaws prohibiting the practice, continued to use cellars as pig-styes to the detriment of the health of his own family and that of his immediate neighbours.[98] Secondly, during any major epidemic —for example the 1832 'visitation' of cholera[99]—the immigrant patient was often reluctant to allow himself to be removed to hospital at the initial stage of the disease, thereby facilitating the spread of infection and helping to inflate sickness and mortality rates beyond the expectations of the borough's doctors. Nonetheless, too much stress should not be placed on these self-inflicted wounds; for it was interaction and interrelationship between those abuses beyond the control of the working classes which contributed most to Liverpool's unenviable record in the field of public health and which in the end produced local legislation dealing not merely with the 'sanitary problem' but also with the vexed question of the supply of working-class housing.

II

Expression of public concern over Liverpool's bad bill of health attracted no general attention until the late 1830s and early 1840s, though the town's high mortality and sickness rates had long antecedents. Dr James Currie, for instance, arguing that typhus was 'remarkably uniform among the poor' during the closing years of the eighteenth century, showed that no fewer than 3,124 persons had on average been treated annually for fever by the parish's dispensary in the decade 1787–96.[100] Periodically, however, endemic disease of this nature would reach epidemic proportions, with devastating effect. This is precisely what happened in 1801 when the death-rate, according to Smithers, reached record levels.[101] Yet in spite of the fact that this basic pattern was to continue for the next half-century, it did not prevent otherwise well informed social analysts from asserting in the 1820s and 1830s that Liverpool possessed all the attributes of a healthy town. Thus, in the 1831 *Population Abstracts*, Rickman argued that the 'great increase' in Liverpool's population since 1821 was the product of 'the salubrity of the Air, and the progressive improvement in its Trade, Commerce, Steam-Navigation, and Rail-Roads'.[102] It was not the least of the important contributions which the Registrar-General's *Annual Reports* made to the cause of sanitary reform that such value-judgments, when set against statistically expressed trends, were shown to be completely unfounded. In the *5th Annual Report* (1843), for example, Liverpool was compared with both London and the non-metropolitan areas of Surrey and implicitly indicted for her past neglect.

In Liverpool the mean duration for life was roughly 26 years, whereas the corresponding figures for London and Surrey were 37 and 45 respectively. Furthermore there were substantial differences between Surrey and Liverpool in terms of both the crude death-rate and the infant mortality rate. In Liverpool in 1841 2,087 out of 14,450 boys died before attaining the age of five. In rural Surrey, an area with a roughly comparable population, 699 of a total of 14,045 boys met with a similar fate.[103] By the early 1840s 528 out of every 1,000 deaths recorded in the Parish took place among that section of community which was five and under. Expressed in another form only 47 out of every 100 children born within the Parish actually lived until their fifth birthday.[104] But by very definition such returns relate only to average conditions. In fact, as would be expected, the incidence of mortality and sickness in the principal areas of working-class settlement was very much greater than these averages suggest. Dr Duncan, for instance, was able to point to substantial differences between the death and fever rates of the largely working-class areas of the borough and those of the middle-class district of Abercromby and Rodney Street Wards.[105] These differentials were, he asserted, a reflection of corresponding disparities in population densities; *certeris paribus* the 'prevalence of fever in any street, court or house, is generally proportioned to the density of the population'.[106] Given, therefore, this appalling waste of human resources, there was real justification for stigmatising Liverpool in the early 1840s as the 'most unhealthy town in England'.[107]

By the time, however, this assertion was made Liverpool had already taken the first tentative steps towards tackling her formidable sanitary problems. In 1842 the corporation had secured from Parliament a local improvement act which gave a newly established Health of the Town Committee sweeping powers over the development of the local environment.[108] In future no courts were to be built unless they were at least 15ft wide and open at one end, while new streets had to conform to a minimum width of 24ft. Each new house was required by law to have at least one room that was 100sq ft in area. In addition, every room with the exception of the garret was to be not less than 8ft high and to possess windows of uniform size. Equally important, all court houses, including those already in existence, were to be paved and drained at their owners' expense. Moreover, each court house built after 1845 was to be provided with a privy 'for the exclusive use of the Inmates thereof'.[109] But the act was not exclusively preoccupied with the supervision and control of future house-building. It was equally concerned with trying to remedy many of the social evils which were indissolubly linked with cellar dwellings. The panacea, however, which it produced for dealing with this particular problem was based both on a lopsided view of working-class housing needs, and on a complete misunderstanding of the market mechanism that ultimately determined the supply and erection of cottages for the 'labouring classes'. Briefly it was proposed to prohibit the use of all cellars that were located in courts as places for human habitation. Cellars underneath front houses were not to be let as dwellings unless they were at least 7ft high and their ceilings a minimum of 2ft above the level of the street surface. To allow property-owners time to adapt their cellars, where possible, to meet these basic requirements, this clause was not to come into effect until the beginning of July 1844.[110]

This statute represented a turning point in Liverpool's attitude to the sanitary question, for it was quickly to be followed by an attempt to provide a system of baths, both for personal use and for the washing of clothes, for the working man and his wife. The first such venture was opened at Frederick Street during 1842; and by the end of the 1840s elaborate plans were being drawn up to ensure that the working classes should have easy access to similar establishments in other parts of the borough.[111] In 1847 came a further local act which enabled the corporation to buy out the existing water companies and to build a new reservoir at Rivington Pike.[112] This was positive proof that the Health of the Town Committee had been in earnest when it had asserted in 1845 that it was 'a most undesirable thing' to make 'Water . . . an object of sale for pecuniary profit' and that 'so essential an element in the economy of every community should be furnished not on the competitive but on the co-operative principle.'[113] The prospect, therefore, of regular supplies at constant pressure seemed to have been brought, as a result of this measure, correspondingly nearer to realisation. There can be little doubt, however, that in the minds of most contemporaries the most significant contribution to urban renewal in the 1840s was made by the 1846 Liverpool Sanitary Act.[114] In some respects this statute remedied several of the weaknesses of the town's 1842 Health Act. It laid down, for instance, more stringent building regulations. New streets were now to be 30ft or more wide, and all cellar dwellings, with the exception of those which conformed to the 1842 statute, were to have their ceilings 3ft above the level of the pavement. Landlords could now be authorised to connect court drains to the main sewers. But this measure was not merely a more rigorous version of its 1842 predecessor. It was to be responsible for important administrative innovations, which in the long term were to have profound effects on the practice of social medicine in this country. It was to be under the terms of this statute that Liverpool appointed the first Medical Officer of Health in Great Britain—a post which was filled in 1847 by Dr W. H. Duncan. At the same time an inspector of nuisances and a borough engineer were entrusted with the task of aiding Duncan in eradicating many of the potential and actual sources of disease in the town. To this end, common lodging houses which operated on a nightly basis were to be registered and compelled to conform to a common sanitary code, while cellars were specifically to be refused licences to operate under this system.[115] Finally the pre-1846 complex of overlapping health authorities was scrapped in favour of a unitary body, the Health Committee, which was to be answerable for its conduct to the council.

Yet despite this impressive legislative record Liverpool's death rate remained obstinately high for the remainder of the period with which this essay is concerned. In part this was because some of these measures had scarcely been given time to work. This was particularly true of the reorganisation of the town's water supplies, for municipalisation did not bestow any immediate benefits on the working classes. Thus, while in August 1848 Dr Duncan was reasonably satisfied with Liverpool's general preparations to meet the threatened outbreak of cholera, he was forced to admit:

> ... the point in which the Sanatory [sic] condition of the Town is susceptible of the greatest improvement is in reference to the Water supply. At no period have the complaints on this head been more frequent or serious both in regard to the quantity and quality of the Water. During the last week numerous complaints have been made particularly by the inhabitants in the neighbourhood of Vauxhall Road and Great Howard Street of an insufficient supply, of its coming on at irregular and inconvenient hours, and of its being so impure as to emit an offensive odour after being kept a day or two in the house.[116]

The prospects of speedily overcoming such difficulties were not enhanced by the strength of the local 'economy' party, which was able to prevent any start being made on the Rivington scheme until 1852.[117] Another factor that helped to keep the death-rate high was the heavy influx of 'Irish Famine' immigrants into Liverpool. From late 1845 to 1851 this inflow of people, many of them already suffering from malnutrition and bringing with them 'Famine Fever', imposed severe strains on the social capital of the borough. In 1847, when a mortality rate of 46 per 1,000 was recorded during the typhus epidemic in Liverpool, immigrants were the main spreaders of, as well as the main sufferers from, the disease.[118] In Duncan's words, as 'the hordes of sickly and half-starved Irish continued to pour into the town', so 'Fever continued to spread, *pari passu*'. It was for this reason that he pleaded with the government to impose immigration controls. 'No Sanatory [sic] or Poor-law engine', he concluded, 'could possibly extinguish the conflagration while such combustible fuel was so abundantly supplied.'[119] Again, in the 1849 visitation of the cholera, immigrants contributed more than their proportionate share to the total number of victims.[120]

And yet if Irish immigration did exercise in the short term such a harmful influence on the total urban environment, that influence owed something in its turn to the cumulative adverse effects of the 1842 and 1846 Acts on the supply of working-class accommodation within the borough.

III

Prior to 1842 much of the housing built for the labouring classes was the work of individuals who were financed by members of the legal profession. Indeed, as John Stewart pointed out in his evidence to the *Select Committee on Manufactures, Commerce and Shipping* (1833), the very existence of this kind of speculative builder —'men who call themselves builders, and artificers connected with building, who do not get employed by anybody, but who build exclusively on their own account'—depended on a continuing flow of credit from the town's lawyers.[121] Completely different from this type of speculator but still catering for a largely working-class clientele were the groups of artisans who combined together to erect houses under the 'blood for blood' system and the 'shopocracy' which was often prepared to channel surplus funds into housing.[122] Irrespective, however, of the source of capital for such building operations, all these groups were agreed that their first priority was with the rate of return on their investment. Inevitably this meant that construction costs were kept to a minimum and that scant attention was paid to the price to the community of the social burden that was in-

separably linked with high density 'jerry-built' development. In the
words of a West Derby doctor, 'cottages are in general built more
with a view to the per centage of the landlord than to the accommodation of the poor'.[123] Yet even when operating at a time when
building controls were relatively few, bankruptcies were far from
unknown, mostly because the individual was overcommitted and
undercapitalised.[124]

It is thus reasonable to conclude that the speculative builder before
1842 was more often than not a 'small man' drawn from either the
ranks of skilled artisans or the lower middle classes. The validity
of this conclusion is supported by the 1841 Building Surveyors'
Investigation, which showed that some of the worst accommodation in the South District of the borough in the early 1840s was in
the hands of 'persons in a humble class of life, having little surplus
rent towards their subsistence after payment of interest on their
Mortgages'.[125] Similar evidence was provided by an 1849 return of
the average size of each landlord's holding of houses let at an annual
rent of £10 and under. According to these figures, the average
holding of such property only rose above eight houses per landlord
in three wards—Scotland (8·90), Vauxhall (9·51), and South Toxteth
(9·59), while in another two areas—Everton (7·67) and West Derby
(7·95)—it was between 6 and 8. In the remaining eleven wards, including the working-class areas of Great George (4·05), St Anne's
(4·36), St Paul's (4·97) and Exchange (5·21), this ratio fell below an
average of six dwellings per landlord.[126] Given this general background, it was likely that any move calculated to raise the builder's
outlay on house construction would tend to drive the small-scale
operator out of business.

There was no guarantee, however, if such an eventuality came to
pass, that his place would be adequately filled by a more substantial
class of entrepreneur. For as the larger building firms realised, the
supply of working-class dwellings was not solely governed by the
questions of construction costs and of social need; an equally important variable was the ability of the working man to pay an
economic rent for his accommodation. In the last analysis, therefore,
the pattern of house-building for the labouring classes was decisively
affected by the movement of real wages in, and the social structure
of, each urban community.

In the case of Liverpool the speculator in the 1830s and 1840s
was dealing with an essentially low-wage economy, based on 'trade

and commerce rather than . . . manufacture'.[127] In the borough itself chronic underemployment was a depressingly regular feature in the lives of those who were dependent on dock work. Frequently this might mean that unskilled labourers or porters were employed for only two or three days in a week.[128] At times, however, of cyclical unemployment, such as 1842, their customary pattern of below-subsistence earnings was replaced by the stark threat of starvation.[129] Those who worked in the building trades were also subjected to seasonal factors,[130] which undermined their ability to devote more than 2s 6d of their weekly income towards rent. As one commentator put it, 'there are always a great many straggling sort of men that cannot get regular employment, but take up with any promiscuous employment they can get.'[131] Included in this last category was the town's Irish population, which made a valuable contribution to the local economy but which was almost invariably to be found in the worst-paid jobs.[132] The strain which such Irish immigration periodically placed on the social capital of Liverpool was to be intensified from late 1845 onwards by the 'Famine' invasion. Significantly enough over 25 per cent of Liverpool Parish's population in 1851—70,194 out of 258,236—was classified as Irish-born.[133] Since, therefore, the bulk of Liverpool's working classes had to struggle to obtain a subsistence level of existence, any sharp upward movement in building costs would automatically reduce the amount of new housing available for the unskilled and semi-skilled. For as most builders knew only too well, the enhanced economic rent—the sure corollary of an increase in construction costs—would be beyond the means of most working men.

The corporation, when framing its improvement proposals in the early 1840s, was fully aware of this fact. In opposing Lord Normanby's Building Bill of 1841—a bill framed on 'the recommendations of Slaney's committee'[134]—it had concentrated on the disastrous social consequences of such a measure. In particular the council condemned the proposed prohibition of the back-to-back system of house construction on the grounds that 'the building of Court houses . . . not only . . . render[ed] the Buildings warmer and drier and more fit for habitation, but also as reducing the Cost and thus bringing the rent within the limits of the Poor'. For precisely the same reason it also criticised 'the distance between backs of the Houses as contemplated in the Bill'. If this proposition were adhered to, it would, 'where the price of Land is ten shillings or upwards per square yard . . . so materially add to the original outlay as to render such houses totally out of the reach of the working and poorer classes'.[135] Yet notwithstanding this formidable indictment of the Whig government's declaration of intent, the borough council was to secure the enactment of legislation in 1842 and 1846 which aimed at achieving exactly the same end.

This much was explicitly acknowledged by the town's surveyor in November 1842 when he asserted that two district officers would suffice to carry out all surveying duties under the local improvement act, since 'their present labours will probably be much lightened by the discontinuance of the erection of small Houses'.[136] Despite, however, the outwardly stringent nature of the building specifications laid down in this 1842 statute, there was little indication of any immediate deceleration in the provision of new housing at an annual rental of £12 and under. Indeed, as Appendix 5.2(A) demonstrates, the years 1844–45 were boom years for that section of the town's building industry catering for the working man. To some extent these returns reflected the fact that it was possible to evade certain of the more formidable building requirements. It was clear, for instance, that by early 1845 the two district surveyors were grossly overworked in trying to deal with all the *minutiae* associated with their office.[137] But perhaps of more importance, this intense building boom occurred just before the Liverpool Sanitary Act of 1846 came into force. As A. B. Foxwood noted almost forty years later, this burst of speculative building took place 'because there was an agitation then on foot for bringing in building regulations, and the builders, in order to anticipate those regulations, made a rush to provide houses of the old-fashioned and bad type'.[138] Once the detailed clauses of this latter statute were put into effective operation —in January 1847—the falling off in the construction of working-class houses at once became apparent. Although it might be argued that the housing figures for the late 1840s, embodied in Appendixes 5·2(A) and 5·2(B), are to a certain degree distorted both by the downswing of the trade cycle and by the existence as late as 1851 of many uninhabited houses in the borough, the fact remains that this trend was not confined to this relatively short time-span. Down to 1870 there remained a close and continuing correlation between a progressive tightening up of local building byelaws and a decline in the number of new dwellings built for letting at £12 per annum and under.

Such a decisive interference with market forces was not, however, accompanied by any attempt by the corporation to provide on its own account alternative accommodation for the working man. Instead, as has been shown, it intensified the pressures on the existing stock of working-class housing by introducing in 1842 a scheme for closing down certain categories of cellar dwellings.[139]

The size of the displacement of population which a rigorous implementation of this measure would involve was vividly illustrated by a February 1845 survey of occupied cellars in every ward of the post-1835 borough : there were 6,630 inhabited cellars in streets, and 6,011 of them did not conform to the minimum requirements of the 1842 Act. More important, only 2,395 could be altered to comply with the 1842 regulations. In other words, 3,616 cellars housing roughly 12,000 people were scheduled to be closed down. These returns, it must be emphasised, were taken after the closure policy had been launched. Between July 1844 and February 1845, 1,058 'front cellars', with perhaps 3,400 inhabitants, had either been emptied or voluntarily vacated.[140] Quite apart from these, there were roughly 750 court cellars, which were to be treated in an identical fashion.[141] Given, therefore, the fact that substantial numbers of the poorest workers were, if the letter of the law was enforced, about to be evicted from their 'subterraneous abodes', Sir James Graham, Home Secretary in Peel's second administration, was justified in asking the Liverpool Council if these clauses were not 'of inconvenient severity'.[142]

The town clerk's reply to this inquiry, delivered in June 1844, was optimistic, though he was unable to disguise the fact that thus early the corporation was adopting a 'gradualist' approach to the problem;[143] for although it had been decided in December 1842 that 'the separate occupation of Cellars in Courts must forthwith be discontinued',[144] it took almost eighteen months before any decisive results were achieved. As late as January 1844 a new deadline for vacating court cellars was being suggested. All such dwellings had to be closed before 1 May of that year; otherwise 'proceedings will be taken against all such Landlords indiscriminately'.[145] By February 1845, however, there were still 117 court cellars with occupants.[146]

A similar policy was followed during the latter half of 1844 and throughout 1845 in relation to 'front' cellars. As Robert Ratcliffe informed Graham, 'time must necessarily be allowed in all proper

cases before the measure can be fully accomplished . . . The worst
description of Cellars will have the attention of the Committee in
the first instance.'[147] Even so the social implications of cellar closures
were already clear. James Aspinall was compelled to admit in his
evidence before the *Commission for Inquiring into the State of Large
Towns and Populous Districts* that none of the houses then being
built 'on speculation' would serve the needs of the dispossessed cellar
dweller. 'The houses now building will be more expensive than the
abodes which they are compelled to leave, and they cannot afford
to go there; and it is very natural for them to go where they can
get the cheapest residences.' Since the weekly rent of a cellar only
amounted to 1s the result of the clearance programme would be
intense overcrowding of the worst kind of working-class dwellings.
In Aspinall's words, 'Three or four, or five families would go into a
house, where only one or two families were before.'[148] Playfair
endorsed this conclusion when he examined the repercussions of the
1842 statute on the working classes :

> The effect produced by the adoption of the measure . . . has been, up
> to the present time, one of physical inconvenience and of moral injury.
> The labouring classes who have been ejected from the cellars have, so
> far as can be ascertained, been driven into other inferior and ill-con-
> ditioned dwellings, and have suffered great inconvenience from the
> change without deriving any sanatory [sic] benefits. They cannot have
> been impressed with any other feelings than those of disrespect for
> the law which puts them to this inconvenience, apparently with so
> little purpose or benefit.[149]

It is against this sombre backcloth that the 'Famine' immigration
has to be set. Even if the building boom of 1844–6 had continued
it would have done little to help this vast influx of Irishmen and
Irishwomen, who were arriving in Liverpool with few visible means
of support. For them the cellar or the nightly lodging house was their
only hope of obtaining accommodation at a price they could afford.
Yet it was just at this time that both these types of dwellings were
being asked to conform to the more rigid sanitary controls associated
with the 1846 Improvement Act. Faced by this unprecedented situation, the council had either to turn a blind eye to infractions of this
statute and of the accompanying byelaws, or to press ahead, regard-
less of the amount of dislocation it caused, with its policy of cellar
closures.

To a certain degree this dilemma was already being solved for

Page 197 (left) The last generation of back-to-backs: no 7 Luxor Avenue, Leeds, built 1907–8. Note keeping-cellar with curtains, WC with sub-basement entrance, main living room, a kitchen (*right*), bedrooms over, and an attic bedroom; (*right*) club housing in Woodcock St, Birmingham, late eighteenth century

Page 198 (above) Narrow Marsh, Nottingham in 1919 showing typical back-to-back and blind-back housing; *(below)* Ruston's Place, Bellar Gate, a typical Nottingham Court

it by the actions of some of the town's magistrates. Mr Rushton, for example, refused to convict any person for living in an illegal cellar unless a bed had been discovered there; and 'since many Cellars are inhabited in which no Beds are found there is much difficulty in dealing with such Cases'.[150] Another factor that delayed cellar clearances was the inadequacy of the control mechanism. Duncan, for instance, estimated that by June 1847 no fewer than 3,000 cellars 'which had been closed under the provisions of the Health Act' had been reoccupied by Irish immigrants. In present circumstances, he concluded, it would be impolitic to try to shut them down again.[151] Nonetheless, in spite of such pleading the council resolved to continue with its clearance policy, though in a modified form. The worst 'plague spots' were still to be dealt with first, even if this meant depositing in the street cellar inmates who were suffering from fever.[152] In the end this 'gradualist' approach was translated into a statistical target; on Duncan's advice 'not more than 100 cellars per month' were to be cleared 'in order to give time for the supply of new habitations to overtake the demand'.[153] By early 1851 the results of this policy were clearly seen. More than 5,000 cellars had been closed, though their reoccupation remained a perennial problem for Liverpool's public health officials.[154]

The implementation of this programme had only been carried through at tremendous social cost. In the first place, far from giving any stimulus to the private builder, it had merely transferred overcrowding from the cellars to the 'front houses' and courts. As early as July 1847 this fact was openly acknowledged by the inspector of nuisances. 'The Parties', he reported, 'already cleared out of Cellars appear to have taken refuge in small houses in Courts and other places, and it is believed that not many have gone back to Ireland.'[155] Less than twelve months later the House Owners Guardian Society supported this testimony when they drew the Health Committee's attention to 'the subject of the overcrowded state of Court and other small Houses owing to the indiscriminate ejectment of the occupiers of illegal Cellars'.[156] In the second place, there was no sign that any influential social thinker in mid-nineteenth century Liverpool realised the extent to which the market mechanism had been seriously affected by building controls. Nowhere, however, even if the significance of this fact had been grasped, were the middle classes yet prepared to see councils undertake house-building on the large scale required to meet the social needs of the working man. Money in the town of Gladstone's birth was still to 'fructify in people's pockets' and until that basic precept was abandoned all future attempts at environmental improvement would continue in some measure to be frustrated by the problem of housing the working classes.[157]

NOTES

1 Quoted R. Lawton, 'The Population of Liverpool in the Mid-Nineteenth Century', *Trans of the Hist Soc of Lancashire and Cheshire*, Vol 107 (1955), 89.

2 This paragraph is based largely on J. Eyes' map, *A Plan of the Town of Liverpool with it's [sic] Docks Streets Lanes and Alleys, laid down on the 29th day of September 1768* (1769). In this article streets are related to their locations in the municipal ward system, which was created in 1835. The pre-1835 borough's boundaries were coterminous with those of Liverpool Parish. The post-1835 borough consisted of Liverpool Parish, the township of Kirkdale and Everton and parts of West Derby and Toxteth Park.

3 J. A. Picton *Memorials of Liverpool*, Vol 1, (2nd ed, 1875), 181.

4 Anon, *The History of Liverpool from the earliest Authenticated period down to the present time* (1810), 149. These figures were taken from Enfield's 1773 survey.

5 *Gore's Directories; Plan of the Town of Liverpool from a late accurate survey which includes all the new Additions and new Erections to the year 1795* [map published in 1795 by R. Phillips, Castle Street, Liverpool].

6 J. A. Picton, *op cit*, Vol II (2nd ed, 1875), 121.

7 R. Brooke, *Liverpool as it was during the last quarter of the Eighteenth Century* (1853), 488.

8 Anon, *A General and Descriptive History of the Antient [sic] and Present State of the Town of Liverpool* (2nd ed, 1797), 69. These figures were taken from Simmons' survey of January 1790.

9 Anon, *The History of Liverpool from the earliest Authenticated period down to the present time* (1810), 179.

10 Anon, *A General and Descriptive History of the Antient [sic] and Present State of the Town of Liverpool* (2nd ed, 1797), 81.

11 Anon, *The History of Liverpool from the earliest Authenticated period down to the present time* (1810), 179.

12 C. Creighton, *A History of Epidemics in Britain*, Vol II (1894), 141.

13 W. Moss, *The Liverpool Guide* (1797), 141–2.

14 B. D. White, *A History of the Corporation of Liverpool 1835–1914* (1951), 33.

15 Anon, *A General and Descriptive History of the Antient* [*sic*] *and Present State of the Town of Liverpool* (2nd ed 1797), 69.

16 *Ibid.*

17 *Ibid,* 70; W. Moss, *op cit,* 142.

18 J. A. Picton, *op cit,* Vol II, 295.

19 *Ibid,* 121–2.

20 *Ibid,* 191.

21 In 1801 the borough possessed 11,784 houses (11,446 inhabited and 338 uninhabited). In 1821 this total had soared to 20,147 (19,007 inhabited and 1,140 uninhabited). These figures are taken from the 1801 and 1821 *Censuses.*

22 The house total in Liverpool Parish—the pre-1835 borough—had reached 38,568 (35,293 inhabited and 3,275 uninhabited) in 1851. See 1851 *Census.*

23 *Select Committee on Manufactures, Commerce and Shipping, PP,* (690), XI (1833), Qq 4787–8, 4822.

24 *Ibid,* Q 4789.

25 *Ibid,* Qq 4842–3.

26 *Ibid,* Q 4792.

27 See Appendix 5.1.

28 J. A. Picton, *op cit,* Vol II, 47.

29 *Ibid,* Vol II, 328.

30 In 1841 Scotland Ward had 5,674 houses (5,491 inhabited and 183 uninhabited). In 1851 it had 9,708 houses (8,750 inhabited and 958 uninhabited).

31 *Liverpool Mercury* (14 Sept 1838) quoting *Liverpool Albion.*

32 For these trends in house-building in Liverpool, see Appendixes 5.2 (A) and 2 (B).

33 In 1801 there were 77,653 persons and 11,784 houses (11,446 inhabited and 338 uninhabited) in Liverpool Parish. In 1851 it contained 258,236 persons and 38,568 houses (35,293 inhabited and 3,275 uninhabited).

34 For these returns in tabular form, see Appendix 5.3.

35 See Appendix 5.4.

36 W. G. Rimmer, 'Working Men's Cottages in Leeds 1770–1840', *Thoresby Soc Publications,* Vol 46, 175. According to Rimmer's calculations there were 4·6 persons per occupied house in Leeds Township in 1801; 4·5 in 1811; 4·7 in 1821; 4·8 in 1831, and 4·7 in 1841.

37 The following results are compiled from the 1801–31 *Censuses.*

	Unoccupied houses in Liverpool Parish	Excess of families over occupied houses
1801	338	5,543
1811	418	4,963
1821	1,140	6,302
1831	944	7,446

38   W. G. Rimmer, *loc cit*, 176.

	Unoccupied houses in Leeds Township	Excess of families over occupied houses
1801	188	428
1811	329	210
1821	853	271
1831	1,064	555

39   For full returns, see Appendix 5.5

40   *First Report of the Commissioners for Inquiring into the State of Large Towns and Populous Districts*, Vol 1 (1844), 155–7. Evidence of Dr W. H. Duncan.

41   *Ibid*, 158. 'The districts of Liverpool, where we have seen fever to be most prevalent, are exactly those where the Irish are congregated in the greatest numbers, viz. the Lace-street district in Exchange Ward, and the Crosbie-street district in Great George's Ward.' According to the Rev Mr Parker, 80 per cent of Crosbie Street's inhabitants were Roman Catholics.

42   For full returns, see Appendix 5.1.

43   *First Report of the Commissioners for Inquiring into the State of Large Towns and Populous Districts*, Vol I (1844), 123.

44   *Sanitary Condition of the Labouring Population of England, Local Reports, PP* (1842), 284.

45   *Ibid*. For cellars in courts, see Appendix 5.7.

46   *Sanitary Condition of the Labouring Population of England, Local Reports, PP* (1842), 284.

47   *First Report of the Commissioners for Inquiring into the State of Large Towns and Populous Districts*, Vol I (1844), 126.

48   Full returns of this survey are to be found in Appendix 5.7.

49   Compare Appendixes 5.3 and 7.

50   *First Report of the Commissioners for Inquiring into the State of Large Towns and Populous Districts*, Vol I (1844), 127.

51   *Ibid*. For the cellar population located in front houses, see Appendix 5.8.

52   *Ibid*.

53   *Ibid*, for full results.

54   Minute Books of the Health of the Town Committee, 20 April 1841, Report of the Surveyor of the South District (Liverpool Record Office, Picton Library, henceforth cited as LRO).

55   *First Report of the Commissioners for Inquiring into the State of Large Towns and Populous Districts*, Vol I (1844), 131–2.

56   The statistics in Appendix 5.8 suggests that only one household on average was to be found in each cellar. That same Appendix also contains data on 'back' compartments.

57   See Appendix 5.8.

58 *Ibid.*

59 *Second Report of the Commissioners for Inquiring into the State of Large Towns and Populous Districts,* PP [610], xviii (1845), 22.

60 *First Report of the Commissioners for Inquiring into the State of Large Towns and Populous Districts,* Vol I (1844), 154.

61 J. R. Kellett, *The Impact of Railways on Victorian Cities* (1969), 355, quoting from T. Baines, *Liverpool in 1859* (1859), 8.

62 R. Lawton, *loc cit,* 101.

63 J. A. Picton, *op cit,* Vol II, 76–7.

64 *Ibid,* 312.

65 *Ibid,* 339–40.

66 *Select Committee on Manufactures, Commerce and Shipping,* PP (690), vi (1833), Qq 4838–9. Stewart, however, stressed that his conclusions about property values held true only 'as a general principle'; 'I am putting out of consideration the operation of any local circumstances.' Elsewhere he acknowledged that there were more high-rented houses in Liverpool than 'formerly'. See *ibid,* Q 4841.

67 W. H. Duncan, *Report to the Health Committee of the Borough of Liverpool on the Health of the Town, 1847–50* (1851), 64.

68 *Ibid,* 63.

69 *Ibid,* 6.

70 *Ibid,* 63–5. According to Dr Duncan shipping companies sometimes had paid for the stay of emigrants in the worst kinds of court lodgings. 'He mentioned that the [worst] court houses were those frequented by emigrants, who were accommodated for nothing, the [lodging-house] keepers receiving pay from the shipping offices.' *Liverpool Mercury* (23 February 1849).

71 *First Report of the Commissioners for Inquiring into the State of Large Towns and Populous Districts,* Vol I (1844), 132.

72 *Second Report of the Commissioners for Inquiring into the State of Large Towns and Populous Districts,* PP [610], xviii (1845), 25. According to this survey, only 33·8 per cent of 201 houses which were inspected had beds for men and women in the same room. These results, however, were so much more favourable than those recorded in other Lancastrian towns that they should be treated with the utmost caution. This same inquiry made by the local police force also gave a good impression of the internal cleanliness and health of these establishments, although 'the testimony of medical men is directly opposed to this representation'. *Ibid,* 26. More important, as Playfair acknowledged, 'there are few lodging-houses in which any classification of lodgers is attempted; the only classification ever made being a very unsatisfactory one, and it consists in placing married couples and unmarried females in the same apartment, keeping the unmarried males in a distinct room. This is thought by the keepers of such classified lodging-houses a very decent and highly becoming arrangement, and they increase the charge for this advance towards morality.' *Ibid,* 25. See also for 'persons of both sexes herding indiscriminately' in Liverpool's lodging-houses and 'living together daily and nightly, in the

character of lodgers', T. Fresh, *Report to the Health Committee of the Town Council of the Borough of Liverpool Comprising a detail of the Sanitary Operations in the Nuisance Department, 1 January 1847 to 31 March 1851* (1851), 29–30, 38.

73   T. Fresh, *op cit*, 29–30.

74   W. H. Duncan, *op cit*, 62–3.

75   T. Fresh, *op cit*, 36. According, however, to Duncan the number of licensed lodging-house in business had fallen to 507 by September 1851. This fall he attributed to 'the operation of the Bye-Laws, the opening of the Emigrants' Homes and other causes'. See W. H. Duncan, *op cit*, 62, footnote.

76   W. H. Duncan, *op cit*, 81. Over the same period 311 lodging-houses had to be dealt with for trying to evade registration.

77   T. Fresh, *op cit*, 36.

78   W. H. Duncan, *op cit*, 80.

79   *Ibid*, 81.

80   T. Fresh, *op cit*, 38.

81   The author's own estimate. The weekly 'lodging house' in 1850 was one of the main haunts of the 'Famine' immigrant.

82   The only type of working man who probably did not suffer from over-crowding—that is living more than two persons per room—was the 'average' court dweller in 1841. Significantly enough these Building Surveyors' returns were made some five years before the 'Irish Famine' immigration began. That event coupled with the impact of the local improvement acts of 1842 and 1846 on the supply of new working-class dwellings almost certainly led to a deterioration in the lot of the occupants of court housing.

83   *First Report of the Commissioners for Inquiring into the State of Large Towns and Populous Districts*, Vol I (1844), 128.

84   Minute Books of the Health of the Town Committee, 20 April 1841, Report of the Surveyor of the South District. (LRO).

85   The 'average' for the whole of the post-1835 borough was roughly fifteen persons to one court privy. In terms of wards with significant numbers of court dwellers, Exchange Ward has the lowest persons per privy ratio, with slightly in excess of ten persons per privy. North Toxteth on the other hand had the worst record with more than twenty people using each of its court privies. There were, of course, 'black spots'. Thus, one building surveyor reported the existence of 'a confined court, containing only six small houses [with] no fewer than one hundred and four Inhabitants, provided with only one privy and that scarcely fit for use'. Minute Books of the Health of the Town Committee, 20 April 1841, Report of the Surveyor of the North District (LRO). On the other hand, Mr Holmes' assertion that 'generally, a court containing 16 houses will have two single privies for the accommodation of a population averaging 80 persons', cannot be accepted as an accurate interpretation of 'average conditions'. For Holmes' evidence, see *Second Report of the Commissioners for Inquiring into*

the State of Large Towns and Populous Districts, PP [610], xviii (1845), 16.

86 T. Fresh, *op cit*, 9.

87 *Second Report of the Commissioners for Inquiring into the State of Large Towns and Populous Districts, PP* [610], xviii (1845), 14.

88 *First Report of the Commissioners for Inquiring into the State of Large Towns and Populous Districts,* Vol I (1844), 129.

89 *Ibid*, 129 and 152.

90 *Sanitary Condition of the Labouring Population of England, Local Reports, PP* (1842), 287.

91 Inhabitants of Gascoyne Street complained in September 1843 'of the Nuisance arising from the Pumping of the refuse Liquor from Messrs. Lovatt and Taylor's Soap Works into the Street'. Minute Books of the Health of the Town Committee, 11 September 1843 (LRO). On the other hand no action was taken against J. Banks' Oil Mill in Pembroke Street, though complaints had been made about the discharge of smoke and the adverse effect of the noise of machinery on sleep. It was decided that such 'nuisances' did not directly affect the health of the local community. Furthermore, 'if the Committee direct a prosecution in this case they will in all probability be called upon to adopt similar proceedings against the Proprietors of Soaperies, Saw Mills, Anchor and Smith Forges, and other important Trades affording employment to a large number of the population, and the Trade of the Town and Port might thus be seriously affected'. *Ibid*, 13 January 1845.

92 See note 91 and T. Fresh, *op cit*, 46–7 on the subject of smoke nuisances. Fresh outlines in detail the Health Committee's cautious policy towards pollution of the atmosphere by manufacturers. 'For the purpose of not unnecessarily annoying manufacturers or hampering trade, they have used considerable caution, and no case has been proceeded with until after full scientific inquiry, by a competent engineer, has been made; and wherever any practical difficulty has been found to exist, either in the construction of the furnaces or the nature of the manufacture, the proceedings have been abandoned. This is borne out by the fact that although 186 smoke informations were laid in the year 1850, only 22 were proceeded with; but the reasons for the abandonment of the remainder have been preserved and recorded in a book kept for the purpose.' It is perhaps worth noting, however, that as early as 1838 the council did take action against Muspratt and other chemical manufacturers for committing 'common nuisances', see B. D. White, *op cit*, 26.

93 *Second Report of the Commissioners for Inquiring into the State of Large Towns and Populous Districts, PP* [610], xviii (1845), 32.

94 *Ibid; Second Report of the Commissioners for Inquiring into the State of Large Towns and Populous Districts,* [602], (1845), Qq 135–7, evidence of James Aspinall. In Part II [610] of this report, it had been argued that the poor classes were generally supplied with water 'by pipes into each house, but in some courts there is a public pipe, from which the tenants of that court can draw it'. *Ibid*, 87, Q 32.

95   B. D. White, *op cit*, 32.

96   *Second Report of the Commissioners for Inquiring into the State of Large Towns and Populous Districts, PP* [602], (1845), Qq 135–7.

97   Minutes of the Health of the Town Committee, 2 July 1845 (LRO).

98   For a full discussion of this practice in a North of England context, see J. H. Treble, 'The Place of the Irish Catholics in the Social life of the North of England 1829–51' (University of Leeds PhD, 1969), 156–8. For the adoption of byelaws prohibiting pig-keepers in cellars and rooms and Irish infraction of these local statutes, see *Liverpool Mercury* 28 October 1836, 7 December 1838, and 4 February 1848.

99   J. H. Treble, *op cit*, 170–1, 173–5.

100 C. Creighton, *op cit*, 141.

101 H. Smithers, *Liverpool, its Commerce, Statistics and Institutions* (1825), 199. 'The year 1801 produced great mortality; it gave 6,593 or $6\frac{1}{2}$ persons to every 100, occasioned by a scarcity of provisions, bad bread, bad water, and the state of Ireland causing numbers to flock over to Liverpool, in such a distressed state, that a violent dysentry ensued, followed by numerous deaths.'

102 *1831 Census of England and Wales*, Vol I, *Enumeration Abstract*, 304.

103 *Fifth Annual Report of the Registrar-General* (1843), xxiv.

104 *First Report of the Commissioners for Inquiring into the State of Large Towns and Populous Districts*, Vol I (1844), 125, 141.

105 *Ibid*, 148, 150, 152–3.

106 *Sanitary Condition of the Labouring Population of England, Local Reports, PP* (1842), 289.

107 *First Report of the Commissioners for Inquiring into the State of Large Towns and Populous Districts*, Vol I (1844), 124–5.

108 All details of the 1842 and 1846 Acts, except where indicated to the contrary, are taken from B. D. White, *op cit*, 35–6, 41–3, 48–9, 62.

109 Health of the Town Committee Minute Books (LRO), 26 May 4, 16 June 1845. For the further history of this proposal, see *ibid*, 18 August 1845.

110 *Ibid*, 21 August 1843.

111 B. D. White, *op cit*, 46. Similar baths were opened in Paul Street in 1846 and Cornwallis Street (1851). Health of the Town Committee Minute Books (LRO), 25 August, 13 September, 29 December 1846; Health Committee Minute Books (LRO), 1, 7, 22 June; 5, 27 July 1848.

112 B. D. White, *op cit*, 55–7.

113 Health of the Town Committee Minute Books, 23 October 1845 (LRO).

114 B. D. White, *op cit*, 42–3, 48–9, 62.

115 For regulation of lodging houses, see W. H. Duncan, *op cit*, 57, 62–6, 80–82; T. Fresh, *op cit*, 31–6, 38–9; Health Committee Minute Books, 2 March 1848 (LRO). It is recorded in this last source that no cellars 'be Registered for the accommodation of Lodgers'.

116 Health Committee Minute Books, 10 August 1848 (LRO).

117 B. D. White, *op cit*, 56–7.
118 *Ibid*, 30; W. H. Duncan, op cit, 5–19.
119 W. H. Duncan, *op cit*, 20.
120 J. H. Treble, *op cit*, 172–3.
121 *Select Committee on Manufactures, Shipping and Commerce, PP,*
     [690] vi (1833), Qq 4787–90. It was estimated that more than half
     of the new houses which had been built in Liverpool within the last
     seven years was the work of this type of speculator alone. *Ibid*, Q
     4822.
122 *Ibid*, Qq 4792, 4814–4820. The 'blood for blood' system was defined
     thus: 'it frequently happens among a respectable class of tradesmen,
     who are occasionally contractors, and who sometimes build upon their
     own account; for instance, supposing one party to be a carpenter and
     joiner, and another a mason, the carpenter employs the mason, and
     the mason in his turn employs the carpenter'. *Ibid*, Q 4815. This
     system was given a stimulus on every occasion these workmen were
     paid 'in part' for work performed 'for a gentleman' in land; 'the con-
     sequence is, they are induced to build'. *Ibid*, Q 4820.
123 M. Flinn, ed, *The Sanitary Condition of the Labouring Population
     of Great Britain* (1965), 92.
124 *Select Committee on Manufactures, Commerce and Shipping, PP,*
     [690], vi (1833), Qq 4789, 4813, 4821.
125 Health of the Town Committee Minute Books, 20 April 1841 (LRO).
126 See Appendix 5.6 for full returns.
127 R. Lawton, *loc cit*, 94.
128 J. H. Treble, *op cit*, 71–2.
129 *Liverpool Mercury*, 14, 21 January 1842.
130 J. H. Treble, *op cit*, 57–8, 71–2.
131 *Select Committee on Manufactures, Commerce and Shipping, PP*
     [690], vi (1833), Q 4774.
132 J. H. Treble, *op cit*, Chapters I and II, *passim*.
133 *1851 Census of England and Wales, Population Tables*, Part II, *Ages,
     occupations etc of the people*, Vol II, 661.
134 M. Flinn, *op cit*, 46.
135 Health of the Town Committee Minute Books, 30 January 1841 (LRO).
136 *Ibid*, 23 November, 1842.
137 *Ibid*, 3 February, 1845.
138 *First Report of Her Majesty's Commissioners for Inquiring into the
     Housing of the Working Classes, PP* [c-4402], xxx (1884–5), Q 13, 339.
139 For precise details of these regulations, see part of the text to which
     note 110 is related.
140 See Appendix 5.9 for full returns.
141 Health of the Town Committee Minute Books, 15 January 1844
     (LRO).
142 *Ibid*, 17 June 1844.
143 *Ibid*, The Town Clerk was Robert Ratcliffe.
144 *Ibid*, 16 December 1842.
145 *Ibid*, 15 January 1844.

146 *Ibid*, 24 February 1845.

147 *Ibid*, 17 June 1844.

148 *Second Report of the Commissioners for Inquiring into the State of Large Towns and Populous Districts, PP* [602], xviii (1845), Qq 36–8.

149 *Second Report of the Commissioners for Inquiring into the State of Large Towns and Populous Districts, PP* [610], Part II, xviii (1845), 45.

150 Health of the Town Committee Minute Books, 2 June 1846 (LRO).

151 Health Committee Minute Books, 17 June 1847 (LRO). The Committee, he added, could close the reoccupied cellars if accommodation could be provided 'for even 20,000 or 30,000 of the immigrants'. He was able to show that immigrants were 'sleeping in privies, and even in the open streets. The extent to which the overcrowding of dwellings must be carried at the present time may be judged of by a fact which was communicated to me a few days ago, ie that an entire family had taken up their residence in an old boiler, found on some waste ground at the north end of the town. In different parts of Liverpool 50 or 60 of these destitute people have been found inhabiting a house containing 3 or 4 small rooms, and in more than one instance upwards of 40 have been found sleeping in a Cellar.'

152 *Ibid*, 5 July 1847, for fever victims ejected from cellars in Standish Street, Crosbie Street, Simpson Street and Brick Street and left lying on the street. An agreement was reached with the Select Vestry about arrangements for removing such cases in future to hospital, *Ibid*, 12 July 1847.

153 W. H. Duncan, *op cit*, 99.

154 *Ibid*; T. Fresh, *op cit*, 27, 29.

155 Health Committee Minute Books, 26 July 1847 (LRO).

156 *Ibid*, 22 June 1848. In July 1849 the Health Committee, after a further approach by the Home Owners Guardian Society, asserted that it was the council's intention to approach Parliament for powers to control overcrowding. *Ibid*, 19 July 1849. Down to 1851, however, nothing was done in this direction.

157 I wish to thank my colleague, Dr G. Jackson of the University of Strathclyde and Mr D. M. Jones of the University of Leeds for invaluable assistance. I am also indebted to the staff of the Liverpool Record Office, Picton Library, for their courtesy and the efficient manner in which they dealt with all my inquiries. Lastly, but not least, I am indebted to my colleagues at the University of Strathclyde— Professor S. G. E. Lythe, Dr J. Butt, and Mr J. R. Hume—for their comments on this paper.

Appendix 5.1

PERCENTAGE OF THE TOTAL POPULATION OF EACH WARD IN LIVERPOOL
PARISH LIVING IN COURT HOUSES AND IN CELLARS IN 1841

Ward	Total Population (1841)	Persons living in Courts	Persons living in Cellars	Percentage of Total Population living in Courts (A)	Percentage of Total Population living in Cellars (B)	Percentage of Total Population living in Courts and Cellars
Vauxhall	26,146	11,585	3,253	44·31	12·44	56·75
St Paul's	18,002	5,209	1,981	28·94	11·00	39·94
Exchange	17,769	3,975	2,491	22·37	14·02	36·39
Castle Street	9,691	1,829	570	18·88	5·88	24·76
St Anne's	18,882	5,588	1,983	29·59	10·50	40·10
Lime Street	18,848	4,079	900	21·64	4·78	26·42
Scotland	35,613	10,628	3,166	29·84	8·90	38·73
St Peter's	9,533	1,589	499	16·67	5·24	21·90
Pitt Street	15,263	1,742	2,103	11·41	13·78	25·19
Great George	19,645	4,590	1,337	23·36	6·81	30·17
Rodney Street	15,202	2,567	903	16·89	5·94	22·83
Abercromby	15,899	2,153	982	13·54	6.18	19·72
Total for Liverpool Parish	220,493	55,534	20,168	25·19	9·15	34·33

There are some slight, but unexplained discrepancies between the figures given for populations in this Appendix and those which are to be found in Appendixes 5.3 and 5.5.

Percentage results have in each case been calculated separately and are taken to two decimal places. This accounts for the occasional discrepancy between the figure in the last column and the total arrived at by adding together columns (A) and (B).

Source: First Report of the Commissioners for Inquiring into the State of Large Towns and Populous Districts, Vol I (1844), 148.

APPENDIX 5.2(A)

TABLE OF NEW HOUSES ERECTED IN LIVERPOOL, 1841–70

Year	Total Number of New Houses Built	Number of New Houses Built at Under £12 Annual Rental	Percentage of Total Housing Stock Built at under £12 Annual Rental
1841	1,761	628	36
1842	2,027	773	38
1843	1,390	440	32
1844	2,450	1,040	42
1845	3,728	1,212	33
1846	3,460	680	20
1847	1,220	59	5
1848	656	79	11
1849	446	90	20
1850	420	41	10
1851	837	101	12
1852	1,136	222	20
1853	924	52	6
1854	829	16	2
1855	1,355	63	5
1856	1,703	17	1
1857	1,520	124	8
1858	1,717	114	7
1859	1,758	85	5
1860	1,549	141	9
1861	1,250	46	4
1862	1,516	22	1
1863	2,015	110	5
1864	2,400	123	5
1865	1,496	–	–
1866	1,098	–	–
1867	1,227	1	0·1
1868	1,756	136	8
1869	1,224	47	4
1870	1,241	15	1
	46,109	6,473	14

Source: B. D. White, *A History of the Corporation of Liverpool 1835–1914,* (1951), 204.

Appendix 5.2(B)

RENTAL VALUE OF HOUSES BUILT IN LIVERPOOL, 1 JAN–31 DEC EACH YEAR

Year	Under £12 pa	£12 to £25 pa	£25 to £35 pa	Above £35pa	Total
1845	1,212	2,007	332	177	3,728
1846	710	2,328	236	186	3,460
1847	59	905	167	89	1,220
1848	74	506	48	28	656

Source: Health of the Town Committee Minute Books, 6 January 1846; Health Committee Minute Books, 18 January 1847, 6 January 1848 and 4 January 1849.

Appendix 5.3

POPULATION AND HOUSING RETURNS FOR LIVERPOOL PARISH, 1801–51

Census Year	Inhabited Houses	Uninhabited Houses	Population	Number of Persons per Inhabited House	Population-Total Housing (Inhabited plus Uninhabited) Stock Ratio
1801	11,446	338	77,653	6·78	6·59
1811	15,589	418	94,376	6·05	5·90
1821	19,007	1,140	118,972	6·26	5·90
1831	25,732	944	165,175	6·42	6·19
1841	32,079	971	223,003	6·95	6·75
1851	35,293	3,275	258,236	7·32	6·69

Source : *1801–51 Censuses of England and Wales*

Appendix 5.4

NUMBER OF PERSONS PER OCCUPIED HOUSE IN ENGLAND AND WALES, 1801–51

Year	Number of Persons per Occupied House
1801	5·64
1811	5·66
1821	5·75
1831	5·60
1841	5·41
1851	5·47

Source: 1851 Census of England and Wales, Population Tables I, PP [1631], LXXV (1852–3), xxxvi.

APPENDIX 5.5

POPULATION AND HOUSING RETURNS FOR DISTRICTS OF LIVERPOOL PARISH,
1841–51

District	Population	Inhabited Houses	Total Housing Stock (Inhabited Plus Uninhabited)	Persons per Occupied House	Population-Total Housing Stock Ratios
Scotland Ward, 1841	35,478	5,491	5,674	6·46	6·25
Scotland Ward, 1851	61,777	8,750	9,708	7·06	6·36
Vauxhall Ward, 1841	26,197	3,438	3,496	7·62	7·49
Vauxhall Ward, 1851	27,942	3,344	3,699	8·36	7·55
St Paul's and Exchange Wards, 1841	35,861	4,758	4,828	7·54	7·43
St Paul's and Exchange Wards, 1851	31,763	4,126	4,281	7·70	7·42
Castle Street and St Peter's Wards, 1841	19,723	2,521	2,669	7·82	7·39
Castle Street and St Peter's Wards, 1851	19,823	2,513	3,128	7·89	6·34
Pitt Street and Great George's Wards, 1841	34,972	4,507	4,619	7·76	7·57
Pitt Street and Great George's Wards, 1851	33,957	4,076	4,289	8·33	7·92
Rodney Street and Abercromby Wards, 1841	33,042	5,109	5,234	6·47	6·31
Rodney Street and Abercromby Wards, 1851	41,997	6,239	6,575	6·73	6·39
Lime Street and St Anne's Wards, 1841	37,730	6,255	6,530	6·03	5·78
Lime Street and St Anne's Wards, 1851	40,707	6,245	6,888	6·52	5·91

Source: 1851 Census of England and Wales.

Appendix 5.6

PERCENTAGE OF THE HOUSING STOCK IN EACH WARD IN THE POST-1835
BOROUGH WHICH WAS LET IN 1849 AT AN ANNUAL RENTAL OF £10 AND UNDER,
TOGETHER WITH THE AVERAGE SIZE OF EACH LANDLORD'S HOLDING OF SUCH
PROPERTY

Ward	Total Number of Houses	Houses Let at £10 and under Per Annum	Percentage of Total Housing Stock let at £10 and under Per Annum	Number of Landlords with Houses let at £10 and under Per Annum	Average size of Landlord's Holding (number of houses) of Property let at £10 and under Per Annum
Kirkdale	1,379	407	29·51	81	5·00
Scotland	10,219	6,349	62·13	713	8·90
Everton	4,418	1,250	28·29	163	7·67
Vauxhall	3,724	2,662	71·48	280	9·51
St Paul's	2,522	1,157	45·87	233	4·97
Exchange	2,295	1,142	49·76	219	5·21
Castle Street	1,495	475	31·77	96	4·95
St Peter's	1,623	123	7·58	41	3·00
Pitt Street	1,870	387	20·70	108	3·58
Great George	2,856	1,182	41·37	292	4·05
Rodney Street	3,334	642	19·26	161	3·99
Abercromby	3,394	725	21·36	181	4·00
Lime Street	3,149	1,012	32·14	176	5·75
St Anne's	3,822	1,660	43·43	381	4·36
West Derby	3,853	1,192	30·94	150	7·95
South Toxteth	5,543	3,425	61·79	357	9·59

Source: Health Committee Minute Books, 28 June 1849 (LRO, Picton
Library).

APPENDIX 5.7

COURTS AND INHABITED CELLARS IN COURTS
NORTH DISTRICT (1841)

Wards	Number of Courts	Sides Built Upon		Open at Front	Open Back	Open Front and Back	No of Houses	Cellars Occupied	No of Inmates	Privies	Persons per Court Houses
		Both	One								
1 Everton	37	30	6	7	4	16	280	4	1,121	82	4·00
2 Scotland	341	266	51	94	64	131	2,139	76	10,628	619	4·97
3 Vauxhall	382	296	60	88	93	117	2,093	34	11,585	681	5·54
4 St Paul's	196	136	53	25	30	32	979	19	5,209	359	5·32
5 Exchange	200	146	46	13	44	5	695	18	3,975	366	5·72
12 Lime St (N Dist)	83	73	6	17	7	39	445	2	2,175	155	4·89
13 St Anne's	187	119	69	36	26	50	1,112	40	5,588	365	5·03
14 W Derby (N Dist)	7	5	2	2	–	4	35	4	151	13	4·31
	1,433	1,071	293	282	268	394	7,778	197	40,432	2,640	5·20

Page 215 (left) New Tame, near Delph, Lancashire, the 1742 farmhouse built by the Buckley family. Note the change in wall construction and window design; (below) Ballgreave, Uppermill, Lancashire. The further farmhouse had the upper floor added to increase the working accommodation

Page 216 (above)   Basement loomshops in Dyehouse Lane, Smallbridge, near Rochdale; (below) Chesham Fold, Bury

APPENDIX 5.7 (*continued*)

COURTS AND INHABITED CELLARS IN COURTS

SOUTH DISTRICT (1841)

Wards	Number of Courts	Sides Built Upon		Open at Front	Open Back	Open Front and Back	No of Houses	Cellars Occupied	No of Inmates	Privies	Persons per Court Houses
		Both	One								
16 N Toxteth	149	123	27	19	48	59	1,053	197	5,494	267	5·22
15 S Toxteth	177	154	21	29	15	119	1,029	419	4,912	339	4·77
9 Great George	130	94	31	9	80	31	853	76	4,590	287	5·38
8 Pitt St	80	67	14	5	26	10	316	24	1,742	180	5·51
10 Rodney St	100	83	17	16	63	17	547	198	2,567	213	4·69
7 St Peter's	56	42	12	7	16	5	267	32	1,589	29	5·95
6 Castle St	78	58	9	7	38	1	326	26	1,829	133	5·61
11 Abercromby	80	67	13	10	41	26	548	50	2,153	146	3·93
14 W Derby (S Dist)	46	37	9	7	17	17	231	7	1,133	78	4·90
12 Lime St (S Dist)	69	48	18	11	16	14	572	26	1,904	133	3·33
	965	773	171	113	360	299	5,542	1,055	27,913	1,805	5·04
Total for the Post-1835 Borough	2,398						13,320		68,345		5·13

Source: Health of the Town Committee Minute Books, 1 April 1841. (LRO, Picton Library).

o

APPENDIX 5.8

CELLAR DWELLINGS, 1841

NORTH DISTRICT   FRONT INHABITED CELLARS

Wards	Front Cellars	Front and Back	Depth			Dry	Damp	Wet	Inmates	No of Windows To Front	Number of Persons Per Cellar
			3ft to 4ft	4ft to 5ft	5ft to 6ft						
1 Everton	24	2	7	7	10	16	7	–	87	20	3·35
2 Scotland	840	132	64	258	530	550	293	9	3,166	838	3·26
3 Vauxhall	848	191	268	342	234	547	321	21	3,253	841	3·13
4 St Paul's	508	180	161	234	111	264	286	5	1,981	510	2·88
5 Exchange	595	230	156	255	178	294	320	34	2,491	587	3·02
12 Lime St (N Dist)	117	12	9	42	66	82	34	–	375	112	2·91
13 St Anne's	559	164	95	271	175	377	210	–	1,983	542	2·74
14 W Derby (N Dist)	17	4	7	5	5	13	4	–	59	17	2·81
	3,508	915	767	1,414	1,309	2,143	1,475	69	13,395	3,467	3·03

	SOUTH DISTRICT					FRONT INHABITED CELLARS					
16 N Toxteth	267	124	55	217	118	151	244	7	1,530	365	3·91
15 S Toxteth	425	65	76	334	104	268	223	22	1,918	500	3·71
9 Great George	304	199	157	224	123	329	182	7	1,337	519	2·66
8 Pitt St	162	292	145	187	109	139	298	16	2,103	455	4·63
10 Rodney St	239	25	40	179	39	213	52	–	903	260	3·42
7 St Peter's	55	58	29	32	24	31	62	6	499	73	4·42
6 Castle St	76	62	34	52	54	26	105	8	570	143	3·85
11 Abercromby	273	24	1	153	99	161	107	4	982	242	3·31
14 W Derby (S Dist)	57	19	16	41	17	24	52	–	310	74	4·08
12 Lime St (St Dist)	101	48	43	75	29	98	48	1	525	151	3·52
	1,968	916	595	1,514	716	1,440	1,373	71	10,677	2,782	3·70
Post-1835 Borough	7,307								24,072		3·29

Source: Health of the Town Committee Minute Books, 1 April 1841.

APPENDIX 5.9

CELLAR DWELLINGS : THE IMPACT OF THE 1842 LIVERPOOL HEALTH OF
THE TOWN ACT

Wards	Inhabited Cellars in Streets	Cellars in Streets Inhabited but not Conformable to 1842 Act	Cellars in Streets and Conformable	Cellars in Streets Altered to Conform	Cellars in Streets which can be Altered to Conform	Cellars in Streets Vacated
1 Everton and Kirkdale	41	21	20	–	14	–
2 Scotland	1,123	898	222	3	330	43
3 Vauxhall	633	576	9	48	212	95
4 St Paul's	451	406	7	38	203	34
5 Exchange	570	539	6	25	219	28
6 Castle St	99	99	–	–	36	25
7 St Peter's	92	84	8	–	40	15
8 Pitt St	460	445	7	8	154	33
9 Great George	516	486	17	13	239	150
10 Rodney St	294	280	11	3	93	42
11 Abercromby	299	290	8	1	112	53
12 Lime St	262	254	3	5	86	79
13 St Anne's	519	489	26	4	160	39
14 W Derby	74	64	8	2	32	16
15 S Toxteth	731	643	88	–	282	180
16 N Toxteth	466	437	23	6	183	226
	6,630	6,011	463	156	2,395	1,058

Source: Health of the Town Committee Minute Books, 24 February 1845.

CHAPTER VI

THE CONTRIBUTION OF BUILDING CLUBS AND FREEHOLD LAND SOCIETY TO WORKING-CLASS HOUSING IN BIRMINGHAM

S. D. Chapman and J. N. Bartlett

SEVERAL of the towns whose historical housing record is examined in this book have a nineteenth-century endowment of statistical material, while others again, like Leeds and Ebbw Vale, have acquired or retained an archival record of the chronology of house building reaching back to the eighteenth century. Birmingham and its satellite towns have little to compare with this kind of documentation, but they must find a place in any work that aspires to representative coverage of urban development in the British Isles, not only on account of their size and economic importance, but more particularly because Birmingham appears to have been the home of two 'self-help' movements of considerable significance, the terminating building club (or society) and the freehold land society movement. The problem of the historian is to relate these movements to domestic welfare in quantitative and qualitative terms. Did these movements in turn contribute to a real and permanent advance in working-class housing and, if so, what proportion of the working classes benefited? There can be no precise answer to these questions, but a study of the context of the pattern of housing development in the area followed by a synthesis of the scattered evidence on these movements leads to some tentative conclusions.

I

A general impression of the physical growth of eighteenth-century Birmingham can be derived from a study of a sequence of large-scale maps of the town.[1] Westley's map of Birmingham (1731) already shows a number of unmistakable signs of infilling of gardens and orchards in the lower (southerly) parts of the town, though plots marked 'Land for Building' in Moor Street and at the end of Steel House Lane show ample provision was still being made for gardens. Westley noted that there were already 150 courts and alleys, leading off fifty-five streets, in the town at this time. Samuel Bradford's map (1750) shows numerous plots marked out for building on the north-west (Great Charles Street area) and north-east (Coleshill Street) margins of the town, each plot from 2 chains (132ft) to 4 chains in length and about 30ft wide. The size and shape of the plots was evidently not connected with the field system, and in the more mature adjacent streets, such as Temple Street, gardens and orchards are in abundance. By the time of Thomas Hanson's map (1778), the encroachment of small clusters of buildings in the gardens of these superior peripheral areas was well under way and eight years later more than a third of the houses in the town were described as 'back houses'.[2] A century afterwards the area just to the south of Great Charles Street was packed with some of the most congested small property known in Birmingham, and it seems that the deterioration originated with the process of lining gardens and paddocks with small properties; but more evidence is needed to explain this process.

The only satisfactory way of tracing the evolution of working-class housing in Birmingham is to study details of properties advertised for sale in *Aris's Birmingham Gazette* and other local newspapers for sample years over a period of a century or more from 1750. From this protracted exercise an unmistakable pattern of development emerges. It begins with the solid brick and slate merchant houses that were being built from the 1760s, when the geographical isolation that had limited Birmingham to a local market was broken by a series of canal links, which inaugurated the rapid commercial development of the town. The merchant houses were built on three (or occasionally) four storeys and were intended to accommodate a warehouse and counting house as well as domestic quarters for the family and its servants. In the 1760s newly built houses on this pattern mostly had gardens, or at any rate 'back land', sometimes with a convenient clay-pit. At the back of the house, often reached from the street by a gated arch, was also the stabling, pump, and, in course of time, workshop accommodation, known locally as 'shopping'. The back yard was frequently surrounded by a high brick wall (in the familiar manner of eighteenth-century kitchen gardens), which was the obvious site for several workmen's cottages, built up to the wall 'blind back' and sharing the communal pump and 'privies'.[3]

In 1886 a writer could still claim that there were 'houses almost in the very centre of the borough where the occupiers possess the advantage of large and fruitful gardens', and up to this time doctors and lawyers continued to live in Newall Street, Bennett's Hill, the Crescent, and other fashionable thoroughfares,[4] but for the most part such central residences were an anachronism by this time. With industrial expansion the upper rooms of the eighteenth-century houses were increasingly adapted for workshops, and were frequently offered for sale with space for 20, 40, 50, 100, 150 or 200 'pairs of hands'. Even the Moat House, Birmingham's historic manor house, was advertised for sale in 1768, being 'convenient for carrying on a large manufactory', with buildings that could have been converted to workshops for 300 men.[5] The accommodation needs of a growing population led in Birmingham, as in so many other towns, to the infilling of gardens, paddocks, orchards, and any other available land, but there was one unusual feature. The lining of yards with workmen's cottages seems to have been more highly developed than elsewhere, and is most readily identifiable as the source of the proliferation of tiny courts of blind-back houses that became so common in Birmingham. 'For Sale' reads a typical advertisement in the *Birmingham Gazette* (19 May 1788), 'three freehold tenements, one of which is fronting to Park Street and the other two in the yard at the back. There is good room in the said yard to erect three or more other tenements at an easy expense.' Anxious to press the advantages of housing in the same street, another advertiser called attention to 'a spacious yard, sufficiently large to form a court'.[6]

Changing industrial needs led to frequent conversion of backyard industrial workshops into domestic accommodation and, of course, of housing for industrial purposes. 'Five new erected tenements together with a large range of shopping which might at small expense be converted into four other tenements', reads an advertisement of 1790.[7] 'Digbeth Street. Front shop and workshops that could be converted to houses', another offered in 1813.[8] 'Ex school rooms. Five spacious apartments, three of which are 33ft by 22ft, capable of conversion to dwelling houses or factory warehouses', another offers;[9] '. . . spacious slaughterhouse that can be converted into six dwelling houses', provided another tempting offer to the public.[10] There is also plenty of evidence of multiple tenancy of 'front houses' and 'back houses', both for industrial and domestic use, from the late eighteenth century, and again the local press is the most lucid guide to common practice. In 1796, for instance, two parlours, a back parlour, and eight bed chambers in a house in New Street were offered for sale separately, with the additional expense of ground rent at £8 10s 0d a year.[11] In Woodcock Street, an open thoroughfare on the eastern periphery of the town, an advertiser offered a 'cellar, sitting room, pump, and whole yard' for sale, with the liability of $\frac{3}{4}$d a yard ground rent charges in 1813.[12] Other large houses gave over numbers of their rooms for lodgers, and the advertisements suggest they may have been rented by the men (and possibly their families) who worked in the shopping at the rear. For instance

> Paradise Street, Large dwelling house for sale, three parlours, one kitchen, six lodging rooms, cellar under the whole, and a large range of shopping and other conveniences in the yard at the back . . . (12th February 1816)

There are numerous advertisements of this kind in the Birmingham newspapers of the period.

The style of building of the greater merchants was quickly imitated by the lesser, but, of course, with proportionate economies. As the pressure on land increased, few could afford to build detached, and before the end of the eighteenth century the characteristic house on the main thoroughfares was built in a terrace, but with attempts to emulate the grander prototype, partly by preserving the three-storeyed sash-windowed style, partly by little embellishments like pillars and steps to the front door, and nearly always with access to a yard and workshops at the rear. The development of the land at the back followed the same pattern as for the bigger detached houses, which can be read into numerous advertisements in the local newspapers. This account must be limited to three examples :

> 75 PARK STREET. Freehold tenement for sale, with three dwelling houses in a Court behind and also an extensive range of shopping [workshops] standing in the Court with sawpit . . . (4th March 1816)
> GREEN STREET, DERITEND. Four dwelling houses for sale, three stories high, with shopping, stables, brewhouse, pump, and large private yard in which there is plenty of room to erect houses or shopping. (7th July 1823)
> WHITHALL STREET, near STEELHOUSE LANE. Two houses, numbers 33 and 34, for sale. Range of shopping behind, three stories high, and a court of five dwellings with a large yard, entry, pump and brewhouse, and offices ; . . (6th March 1826)

Two features are emphasised by repetition in these property advertisements. One is the availablity of an 'entire yard' with access to the road; another the existence of a clay-pit on or adjacent to the site. Both were prerequisites of further cheap building.

The invariable practice of selling properties in small clusters consisting, typically, of one or two front houses, with 'shopping' and up to six tenements in the court behind, strongly suggests that these developments represented the investment of a numerous order of people with small capitals. This impression is strengthened by a heated controversy that took place in the correspondence columns of the *Birmingham Gazette* in 1790 because of the proliferation of court houses which were rated at less than £10 a year and so exempted from the rising poor rates. William Hutton, the most vociferous of the *Gazette* correspondents, pointed out that many landlords depended on these small properties for their income.[13] Insurance policies give some notion of the value of typical holdings. For instance, in 1791, Sarah Southall, a widow of Birmingham, insured a typical small development in Balloon Street as follows :[14]

On a house, tenant, Thomas, Kendrick, builder, and known by the 'Duke and Duck'	£150
On a small house and shopping adjoining	30
On a stable and shop over and brewhouse adjoining	20
On a house adjoining the first mentioned, tenant G. Hope	70
On a house adjoining Tenant Barber	70
On a house adjoining Tenant Brandy	70
On six back houses, untenanted [just built?]	90
	£500

The investment would clearly yield 10 or 15 per cent, from which Mrs Southall could draw an income equal to the needs of a widow lady at the period. Numerous properties served both as home and factory, so it is not surprising to find that many were owned by the manufacturers who occupied the front houses.

The pioneer reports made on the sanitary conditions of Birmingham in the period of inquiries in the 1830s and 1840s add very little to our knowledge of working-class housing. Eight local doctors who made a survey in 1836 reported that there were 2,030 courts containing 12,254 tenements in the town (apart from those in the adjacent parish of Aston), and these housed most of the working population.[15] 'The courts vary in the number of houses which they contain from four to twenty', it was further disclosed in 1841 in a report to the Children's Employment Commission, 'and most of these houses are three stories high and built back-to-back. There is a wash house, an ash pit, and a privy at the end, or on one side of the court, and not infrequently one or more pigsties or heaps of manure.'[16] Evidently the working population made every attempt to retain the last vestiges of a rural image! More interesting and unusual, the average number of tenements per court was only six, reflecting the process of building by infilling of yards and gardens already described.

The 1841 report noted approvingly that it was usual for every Birmingham family to have its own dwelling, and that cellar dwellings were unknown,[17] but it does not attempt to describe the available types of accommodation. Some working-class housing was demolished in the middle decades of the nineteenth century for the building of the two central railway termini (later known as New Street and Snow Hill stations),[18] and in the 1870s for schemes of civic and commercial aggrandizement,[19] but most of the courts of the 1840s must have survived into this century. They were probably not very different, therefore, to the four basic types of tenement that was familiar to the City's sanitary inspectors early this century, and which they described and sketched in *Five Hundred Birmingham Houses* (1929). Their illustrations are reproduced here as still the best available (Fig. 6.1), but they can give little conception of the austerity of a house without internal water or drainage, or of the gloom of the steep, winding internal stairs, or of the congestion of a bedroom all but filled by one brass bedstead.

If the writers of the 1840s seem complacent, it is quite possibly because they were familiar with the much inferior conditions in which some of the nearby Black Country nailers lived. At Lye, between Stourbridge and Dudley, the squatters on the Waste lived in one-roomed huts made of fire clay mixed with straw and stubble, with thatched roofs but no windows. The mud huts, according to a writer of 1832,

> have been compared to the miserable cabins of the wild Irish (. . . having no gardens, no poultry, and too often exhibiting the sad evidence of a joyless existence, the smoke issueing from the doors and windows of the cottages), though upon a par with the inferior cottages observable in many parts of the coasts of Lancashire, Lincolnshire, Devon, etc.[20]

It is easy to forget that, in studying urban housing conditions, we are generally looking at the best that was provided for the working classes, not the worst.

When the present inner suburbs of Newtown, Ladywood, Duddeston, Nechells, Lozells, Highgate, and other working-class districts were built up in the 1860s and 1870s, the layout preserved the familiar traditions of the workshop-courts. The long sober mid-Victorian terraces, like those of Leeds, give a superficial impression of space and artisan prosperity, but the tunnel entries between alternate

TYPES OF HOUSES.

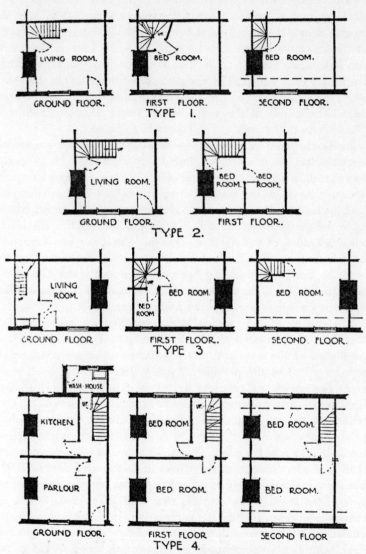

Fig 6.1.   Working-class housing in nineteenth-century Birmingham

front houses lead to numbered courts of six to eight 'back houses'. Further inspection disclosed that the 'front houses' were also built back-to-back. A single street, like that shown here (Heaton Street, Hockley) might contain more than twenty courts (Fig. 6.2). A ground floor plan of a typical block in Bishop Street (Highgate), shows how eight houses were built in one block, four on the street and four facing into the court, each house consisting of four rooms, one on top of the other. The kitchen and coalhouse was in the basement, the sitting room on the ground floor, and the bedrooms above them. The layout of the whole block reveals ingenious architect planning for the maximum use of every foot of land.

In Birmingham, as in other provincial towns, the London model working-class houses movement found only a faint echo. A company was formed in 1848 with a capital of £6,000 to erect model lodging houses in the town, but it does not appear to have done anything as nothing further was heard of it. The second attempt to introduce improved standards at economic rents did not occur until 1883, when a branch of the Artisans' Dwelling Company was formed.[21] By this time the Birmingham tradition of court development was being broken by the building byelaws introduced under Chamberlain's Birmingham Improvement Act (1876), though it cannot be said that a competitive alternative had yet been found.

The cutting of Corporation Street, provided for under the Act of 1876, led to a considerable displacement of the working-class population of the area, and this was paralleled by the commercial redevelopment of the premier shopping streets of the town, with great new stores and arcades arising in the French and Italian Renaissance style to flatter the taste of hordes of new shoppers. The failure of the corporation to provide alternative accommodation pricked the conscience of some members, and led to several experiments in municipal housing. Twenty-two two-storey cottages were built in Ryder Street and eighty-two in Lawrence Street in 1890, but the rents, respectively 5s 6d and 5s a week, clearly placed them beyond the reach of the workers that were losing their homes in clearance schemes. In 1895 the corporation attempted a cheap form of flats at Milk Street : three-room dwellings built on the ground floor, with similar accommodation above; but again it had to be conceded that corporate enterprise had not yet learned to compete with the speculative builder. Faced with the ubiquitous and, for the foreseeable future, insuperable problem of urban overcrowding,

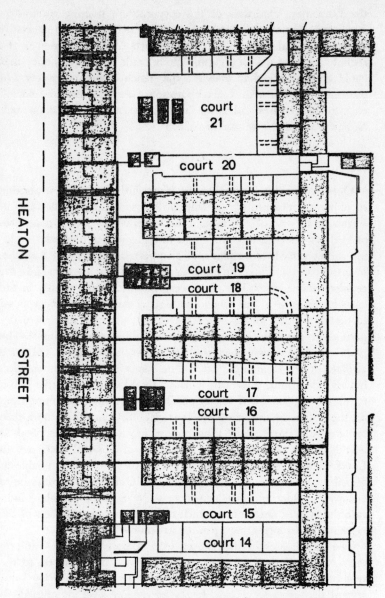

HEATON STREET

court 21

court 20

court 19

court 18

court 17

court 16

court 15

court 14

Fig 6.2. Typical Birmingham back-to-backs, built in the 1860s

the Edwardian chairman of the corporation's housing committee, Alderman Nettlefold, introduced a policy of opening up courts by demolishing end houses. 'Nettlefold' courts can still be seen in the twilight zones of the city, gaping monuments to a panic policy that could do no more than alleviate the stench of urban poverty. On the eve of World War I a corporation committee counted 43,366 back-to-back houses within its jurisdiction, rather more than there had been at the first 'census' of 1836.[22]

II

Only in the last quarter of the nineteenth century is it possible to obtain a measure of the standard of working-class housing in Birmingham. In 1876 Birmingham Corporation adopted a new set of byelaws designed to control new building and appointed a building surveyor to approve plans, to give permission to build and then to inspect the buildings at intervals to ensure that they reached the required standards.[23] The plans were retained until recently in the corporation offices, but when shortage of space led to a proposal to destroy several thousand of the earliest of them they were deposited at Dudley College of Education for preservation.[24] The plans of 522 houses whose construction was approved in the years 1878–84 have been analysed.[25] The plans relate to the smallest houses being built, those which had a total living area under 800sq ft, and were chosen as far as possible in a random manner from all the houses in the category. It is clear that many working-class families and particularly those whose incomes were described as insufficient to maintain them in a state of physical efficiency in London and York at the end of the century, would be unable to afford the rents for such a house and would of necessity continue to occupy the older and inferior property. Nevertheless the plans indicate the type of new houses which more prosperous members of the working classes increasingly aspired to occupy.

The 522 houses in the sample were almost invariably built in terraces and detached houses were extremely rare. Access to the rear of the houses was usually through a tunnel between blocks of several houses or by a passageway at ground level at intervals in the terrace—the so-called 'tunnel back' houses. Half the houses surveyed had a bay window on the ground floor of the front room, giving additional living space and a superior appearance to the house, and some 40 per cent of the sample had a small front garden averaging just under 50sq ft in area.

Inside, the house averaged 658sq ft, including attics but excluding cellars and privies and any external buildings separate from the house. The houses usually had four or five internal rooms, exclusive of pantries, privies and cellars. Houses with only three rooms accounted for a mere 12 per cent of the sample, four- and five-roomed houses accounted for 37 per cent each, and houses with six rooms for a further 14 per cent. The three-roomed houses possessed a large combined kitchen and living room on the ground floor. The four- and five-roomed houses generally had two rooms on the ground floor, one usually described as kitchen or scullery and the other as 'living room', though the term 'parlour' was also used. The six-roomed houses often had a kitchen and scullery as well as a living room downstairs, but some had simply a living room, parlour and kitchen. Additional space in the smaller houses was often provided by a small pantry, where food and kitchen utensils could be kept.

The ground-floor rooms were not dissimilar in size to those in modern suburban houses. The pantry usually had an area of less than 20sq ft, and the scullery, comparable in size to the modern kitchen, averaged just under 60sq ft in area. The kitchen was a larger room, with an average size of 100sq ft and was no doubt used as a living room—perhaps equipped with a wooden easy chair, and a couch and other chairs—as well as for eating a meal and for cooking. Living rooms or parlours were still larger, averaging 132sq ft in size, exclusive of any additional space provided by a bay window. When there was only a scullery in addition to the living room, the latter was probably in frequent use, but in other cases we may suspect that the living room was reserved for use on Sundays and special occasions or to entertain visitors who were not well known to the family.[26] The living room or parlour was usually at the front of the building, with a front door leading directly into the street or front garden, and the kitchen and scullery were at the rear. Underneath the ground floor some 60 per cent of the houses had a cellar, and this was usually 6ft high and comparable in area to a living room. However, the use of cellars as living accommodation seems to have been unusual in Birmingham,[27] and the cellar was probably used as storage space.

The houses in the sample had an average of two bedrooms, ex-

P

clusive of attics. The bedrooms averaged 113sq ft in size and were thus comparable to bedrooms in a modern suburban house, while their height averaged 9ft, giving them a greater cubic air capacity. In addition, approximately half the houses had a room labelled as an 'attic' on the plans which measured more than 110sq ft on average. This extra space must have represented a valuable supplement to the total sleeping area in the house, though in cold weather the occupants might have slept for warmth in the other bedroom in overcrowded conditions rather than in the attic.[28]

With the exception of one estate of forty-six houses, all the houses in the sample had external privies. One-third of the houses shared them with neighbours, usually one privy being shared by two houses. but sometimes the ratio was as low as one to every five houses. These shared privies were built in small blocks behind the houses and several feet away from them, a legacy of the days when privies were still ashpits and kept at a distance. Privies in the exclusive use of one household were usually built at the rear of the house and attached to the kitchen or scullery.

Bathrooms were entirely absent from the plans and only 9 per cent of houses had rooms described as 'wash houses'. No doubt when members of the family took a bath they used a tin bath or tub which had to be laboriously filled with ladles of water in the kitchen, or visited one of the public baths provided by Birmingham Corporation, and the washing of clothes was often done in the scullery or kitchen.

It is impossible to make a detailed statistical comparison of the number and size of rooms in these new houses with those in the older houses occupied by the working classes. However, there is some evidence to suggest that there had been a distinct increase in the amount of room space. Councillor Middlemore who commented on the poorer older houses in St Mary's Ward in 1884 observed: 'On entering the houses one is struck with the smallness of the rooms. I measured very many of the houses, and I find it difficult to give you the average size of their rooms. But I may mention that the largest I visited was 14ft × 9ft × 8ft [and] that the next largest was 15ft × 8ft × 7 ft 10in.'[29] Yet on the evidence above, rooms with an area of 120sq ft or more were not unusual in the newly built smaller houses of the late 1870s and early 1880s. The average parlour or living room exceeded the size of the largest room found by Councillor Middlemore and the average bedroom was only slightly smaller.

The lavatory and washing facilities of the houses in the sample were far inferior to the accepted standards of today. Their furnishings would also have seemed spartan to modern eyes, but if we allow for the absence of a bathroom the number and size of the rooms provided was not very different from that in many modern suburban houses. The space available was shared by more persons than today because of the greater family size in the nineteenth century, but in Birmingham as a whole in 1881 the average number of persons per house was only five, and though a committee of the council appointed to enquire into working-class housing in 1884 found cases of overcrowding it concluded that 'overcrowding does not exist to any great extent'.[30] Any such assessment was bound to be relative, but our comparisons with the present-day position would not lead us to object to this conclusion.

III

Having surveyed some of the characteristic features of working-class housing in Birmingham, it is now possible to attempt an interpretation of the early and vigorous development of terminating building societies and freehold land societies in the locality. Both movements were anticipated by the strong growth of the friendly society movement in the area and clearly owed something to its co-operative ideas. By the time of Daniel Defoe's well-known *Essay on Friendly Societies* (1697), the movement was already fairly popular in London, but it is not certain how early the idea found its way to Birmingham and other provincial towns. William Hutton's *History of Birmingham* implies that some of them were established by the 1730s and continued for more than a century. 'Perhaps there are hundreds of these societies in Birmingham . . .' it was noted in the 1835 edition of his book :

> some of them boast the antiquity of a century, and by prudent direction have acquired a capital at accumulating interest. Thousands of the inhabitants are connected, nay to be otherwise is rather unfashionable, and some are people of sentiment and property. There are now upwards of 400 benefit societies in Birmingham containing about 40,000 members. The payments, in case of sickness, for adult members are 6s to 14s a week, and the disbursements are supposed to amount to £200 per week.[31]

This popularity was not something new in the 1830s. Thomas Attwood, the Birmingham banker, declared in 1812 : 'There is hardly any manufacturer [artisan] in Birmingham but belongs to some club, by which he accumulates his property in prosperous times to have the advantage of it in adverse times.'[32] The Birmingham workers' strong interest in mutual self-help is confirmed by the limited statistics that are available from the early nineteenth century. They became a feature alike of public house, working, and religious life, numerous clubs being based on taverns, trade unions and chapels.[33]

The principal difference between the friendly society and the terminating building society was one of choice of benefit. While the friendly society members pooled their savings against the contingencies of sickness, old age, funeral liability or (less often) unemployment, the building club offered planned saving for house purchase. From a study of the rules of numbers of early terminating building societies up and down the country, S. J. Price's history of the building society movement concludes that shares were usually of £60 to £120, and the monthly subscriptions 5s to 10s. The subscription seems to have been based on an appreciation of the fact that 10s invested monthly at 5 per cent compound interest would amount to £120 at the end of about fourteen years.[34] Data on the cost of house building is hard to come by, but the Boulton & Watt Mss enable us to identify the kind of house that could be purchased for £120 at the close of the first major phase of building-society growth in the 1780s and 1790s. Boulton & Watt built several terraces of cottages adjacent to their famous Soho works, the earliest of which were Foundry Row, twelve houses completed in 1796, and Low Row, eight houses built in 1801–2, and details of the dimensions and costs of the second of these have survived. The row of eight four-roomed houses (two up and two down) were built for £907 which, with the cost of land, would make about £120 each. The houses were built during the French Wars, when costs of labour and timber were particularly high, and it is quite possible that building costs declined from 1815 to the middle of the century.[35] This kind of house, particularly when it was as well planned and constructed as those built at Soho, must be recognised as the best type of house available to the working classes at the period. Indeed, they would be built by Boulton & Watt to attract the kind of highly skilled artisans which were in such short supply at the end of the eighteenth century.[36]

The scattered evidence offers some confirmation that building societies in Birmingham catered only for the artisan élite and the middle classes. The rules of a building society proposed in 1781 and intending to build six streets in Deritend referred to houses of the value of £70, £140, and £200,[37] the first category probably being working-class back-to-backs. An advertisement in 1788 for another society sounds distinctly middle class.

> The United Amicable Building Society wish to contract with any builder or builders for erecting 19 houses . . . in . . . Aston . . . Front and back rooms on ground floor to be 14ft square . . . [with] Venetian windows . . . [and] Welsh slates . . .[38]

Langford, the Birmingham historian of the last century, mentions building clubs as responsible for houses in Islington Row, Cheapside, and Woodcock Street in the 1790s. Most of those in Woodcock Street (p 197) survived until 1970, part of a long row of fifty-three tall 'front houses' with a touch of Georgian elegance in the symmetry, sash windows, and front doors.[39] New John Street and Pritchett Street, just off the Aston Road and, like Woodcock Street, on the edge of the town at the end of the eighteenth century, were said to have been developed by three building clubs from 1791. They were quite elegant terraces, stucco fronted with Classical or Gothic doorways.[40] It is true that a *Birmingham Gazette* editorial in 1795, referring to recently enclosed land in Handsworth, noted that 'some of the building clubs have made a beginning upon a scale of 20 houses and gardens to an acre',[41] which does not sound particularly distinctive, and that in the same year King Alfred's Building Society was buying land for building 'contiguous to the junction of the Birmingham and Worcester Canal', but it is easily overlooked that at this period Handsworth was still a rural retreat, and the canal basin lay across the fields from the most select building sites in late eighteenth-century Birmingham. King Alfred's Place was built off the Crescent, the houses consisting of a parlour, sitting room, dining room 18ft square, four good bedrooms, under kitchen and cellaring, with large yard and garden (walled in), brewhouse, and own pump of soft water.[42]

The building societies were not exclusive bodies, for new societies often advertised for members[43] and shares of established societies were regularly offered for sale,[44] but their subscription rates clearly excluded all but those whose incomes consistently allowed a comfortable margin above subsistence. In 1835 Hutton, wishing to take the broad view, noted that 'every member subscribes perhaps two guineas per month and each house, value about £100, is balloted for as soon as erected'.[45] The membership and type of house aimed at seems to have been similar throughout the period 1775–1835.

The picture that emerges from this study of Birmingham is given further substance by evidence from Lancashire, the other important area for terminating building societies.[46] Colonies of weavers at Middleton and Chorlton (near Manchester), Longridge Fell (near Preston), and no doubt other country areas,[47] clubbed together to build terraces of cottages, but this was in the 1790s, the 'golden age' of the handloom weaver, when the advent of machine-spun yarns multiplied the demand for cotton cloth and for the work of domestic weavers and their families.[48] The chapter on Nottingham (Chapter 4) suggests that a comparable inflation of earnings in the early 1820s may have enabled some of the most energetic lace-makers to become property owners, and it seems very likely from Chapter 3 that the artisans' building clubs who paid for the earliest back-to-back terraces in Leeds in the late 1780s were also enjoying the benefit of mechanisation at a previous stage of production. The 'aristocracy of labour' in Birmingham, Manchester, Leeds and Nottingham, many of whom were able to climb the ladder to economic independence during periods of trade expansion, were also expressing their independence by helping one another to become property-owners.

There were two important connections between terminating building societies of the type just described and the growing need of accommodation for labouring families. Members of the societies could alleviate the burden of the monthly subscription by building 'back houses' to rent to their employees or to other tenants. An advertisement of 1795 illustrates the practice :

TO BE SOLD BY AUCTION . . . Lot I. One share and a half in Wilson's Building Society, consisting of three leasehold dwelling houses . . . one fronting Islington Row now in the occupation of Mr Robert Evans, butcher, and two others behind . . . subject to the payment of 15s 6d per month for subscription money until all the buildings are erected and all the engagements of the Society are discharged . . . in four years.

Lot III. One share in another Society, called Bishopsgate Street Building Society; consisting of one front and one back house adjoining in Bishopsgate Street near the Five Ways, not yet quite finished . . . Subject only to the subscription of 14s 6d per month . . . [for] six years.[49]

Building society developments at the end of the eighteenth century in Woodcock Street, Pritchett Street and New John Street also included the erection of 'back houses'. The other connection between the terminating building societies and the persistent demand for cheaper accommodation was that members evidently followed the common practice of dividing large houses for multiple occupation.[50] This practice had considerable political as well as social significance, and warrants separate treatment.

The 1832 Reform Act, by extending the county franchise to the 40s freeholder, provided a political bonus to the existing economic advantages of house ownership, and so indirectly stimulated the activity of the building clubs. Even the smallest kind of house in the four categories noted above would be valued at £40, that is, be worth 40s a year rental at 5 per cent. An advertisement in *Aris's Birmingham Gazette* in 1837 implies that much meaner properties were being purchased by clubs to qualify their owners for the new franchise :

FREEHOLD PROPERTY, Weaman Street
Which Gives Fifty Votes for North Warwickshire
To be sold by Auction by Mr J. Fallows at the Union Inn . . . a valuable freehold property consisting of two front houses, Nos 45 and 46, with 12 back houses and two shops . . . and produces a rental of upwards of £100 pa. This property would be desirable for any club wishing to make purchases for votes as it will give 50 for North Warwickshire.[51]

To create 50 votes the purchasing club would have had to put three or four families in each of the 14 dwellings, probably one family to each room. How far this practice was resorted to it is now impossible to say; one can only repeat the recollections of public-health inspectors that it was common to find a family in each room of a three-roomed house until the 1930s.[52]

The most significant limitation on this kind of development in Birmingham was probably the shortage of freehold property; most Birmingham property was (and still is) leasehold, or at any rate subject to chief rent. If a new franchise was to be created, it had to be on virgin land that could be bought cheaply. Langford mentions a society that was formed along these lines in 1837, but to judge from its advertisement, it had the middle-class trappings of the well established clubs and so attracted little popular support.[53] The setting for a popular movement was not created until the late 1840s, when Rev George Dawson (1821–76), the creator of Birmingham's civic gospel, and the town's best known herald of the post-1851 spirit of progress, began his independent evangelistic

career in the town. Dawson's pulpit at the Church of the Saviour
attracted immense congregations, and his newspaper, the *Birmingham Mercury*, sold 10,000 copies on its first appearance in December 1848. Apart from his youth, eloquence, and radicalism, Dawson's
attractiveness lay in his contrast with other nonconformist ministers
of the town. While they were characteristically dour, heavy, and
gospel thumping, Dawson gave the impression that he had the
vision of a new heaven and a new earth, and by tireless advocacy
of every radical cause—free trade, early closing, popular education,
temperance, universal franchise, and other mid-Victorian crusades—
he intended to take his people there.[54] Such a preacher immediately
attracted zealous young nonconformists like James Taylor (1814–87),
already a popular preacher in the temperance movement, and ready
for a new crusade in the cause of working-class self-help.

The political context for the launching of Taylor's Freehold Land
Society was provided by the success of Joseph Sturge's Complete
Suffrage Union in reconciling the political differences between
artisans and the radical middle class in Birmingham between 1842
and the end of 1845. Sturge built up cordial relations with the
Christian Chartists, obtained ascendancy over Fergus O'Connor's
'revolutionary' Chartists, and made the extension of the franchise
a centre party issue in the town. In 1847 G. F. Muntz and William
Scholefield were adopted as Liberal candidates for the Birmingham
constituency because, alone among the contestants for nomination,
they declared themselves in favour of extension of the franchise,
and their subsequent election, as they no doubt appreciated, was
due in no small measure to their acceptance of this principle.[55] At
the same Parliamentary election, the Liberal candidate in North
Warwickshire was defeated, and the two Birmingham MPs immediately gave their support to Taylor's scheme, the *Birmingham
Journal* following with an enthusiastic editorial. The similarities
with O'Connor's National Land Company were as obvious to contemporaries as they are to historians today, and Taylor was taunted
as 'Little Fergus'. But while O'Connor was anathema to the middle
classes, Taylor's more gradual scheme, and his religious noncon-
formity and deference to the Liberal manufacturers, assured him
of adequate support. Middle-class visions of a scheme of social re-
generation of the working classes appealed to idealists, and the
improving trade conditions and 'New Model' trade unionism of the
1850s provided an additional impetus. As the movement gathered

momentum, leading Liberal MPs like Cobden, Bright and Villiers were glad to lend their eloquence to open-air meetings.

Taylor himself was an evangelist with boundless enthusiasm and energy for his cause, and he intended his movement to have the widest possible appeal. 'If eloquence be the power of moving the people to action and thought,' commented the *Brighton Herald* after Taylor had addressed a meeting in the town, 'Mr Taylor is eloquent, for we never saw a meeting so excited and kept on stretch for more than two hours as he kept it; his language is that of the people, his illustrations homely and striking, his gesticulations grace-ful, and his eyes and countenance betray an earnest, sincere heart.' The Birmingham FLS subscription was fixed at 1s entrance fee and 3s a fortnight. At this rate, it would have taken a member eight years to buy a £30 share (nearly half the period to buy a house with one of the terminating building societies), but following the established building-club practice, ballots of members were held from the first. In January 1848, the first plot of land was bought at Handsworth, and in May the first of many well advertised processions was held to take possession of the site. Branches were already being formed at Dudley (by Rev J. Palmer), Walsall, Stour-bridge, Wolverhampton and West Bromwich, and before long Tay-lor was preaching his cause further afield. A second plot of land was bought at Perry Bar (a mile north of Birmingham) and in July there was a grander parade and band, with workmen taking posses-sion of what was proudly to be named Franchise Street. Encouraged by widespread enthusiasm, the society paid £5,000 for its third site of 60,000sq yd at Bloomsbury. Subscriptions were mounting rapidly —£4,802 was received in 1847–8, £8,644 in 1848–9, and £11,533 in 1849–50—but not sufficiently fast to cover a series of capital out-lays of such magnitude. An approach was successfully made to the bank, and with such solid support, Taylor and his committee went from strength to strength in the early 1850s. The *Ninth Annual Re-port* (1856) noted that £92,000 had been subscribed to the Birm-ingham FLS and that twenty sites had been purchased and divided for building, the largest of which, Great Lister Street (1852), had been divided into 376 plots. There was some slackening of pace in the later 1850s, but five more estates were opened by 1860.[56]

The earliest estate development plans of the Freehold Land Society have been lost, and information about the quality of hous-ing and background of members has to be gleaned from other sources. In the 1865 prospectus it was tacitly admitted that some of the earliest owners had built 'in an irregular and reckless manner', but this was soon checked by insistence on a building line and on minimum value for properties erected. The status of the Birmingham FLS can be best appreciated by studying one of its early and major developments, Aston Park.

The Holte family, who had been lords of Aston Manor from the Middle Ages, sold the fine Jacobean Hall and Park in 1818 to Greenway, Greaves & Whitehead, a banking house. The land was retained as a private park until 1851, when the owners began to sell small plots by auction at carefully regulated intervals. At this time the existing housing in Aston consisted for the most part of large detached dwellings with extensive gardens, similar to those being built at Edgbaston. In 1852 the best plots in the park were commanding nearly £3,000 an acre. Nevertheless, the Birmingham FLS succeeded, in 1855 and 1860, in acquiring three large sites between what is now Victoria Road and Albert Road. The favoured position of the society is suggested by its purchase of large parcels of land overlooking the retained part of the park at a period when speculative builders could only secure small plots in the area.[57] The houses on Victoria Road were built with substantial gardens at the rate of 9·65 houses per acre (a low density even for this favoured locality), and the ordinary market value of the land on which each of the houses were built must have been of the order of £200 to £300. Victoria Road was built in terraces on the 'tunnel-back' principle, each house having a parlour, living room, scullery, three bedrooms and outside offices. This type of house, as we have already shown, did not become general in Birmingham until after the 1876 byelaws became effective, and in Aston back-to-back building was not prevented by the local Board of Health byelaws until 1882, by which time nearly a third (29 per cent) of houses in the parish had been built on this pattern.[58]

From the 1861 Census enumerators' returns it is possible to identify the occupations of heads of households in Victoria Road. Sixty-four houses appear in the returns, nearly all occupied by skilled artisans or independent manufacturers in the Birmingham metal trades. One was occupied by a surgeon, another by a superintendent of police. A quarter of the sixty-four households had one or two servants living in with them.[59] What seems abundantly clear, without further analysis, is that those who benefited from the activities of the Freehold Land Society were hardly working class in the commonly accepted sense. The main achievement of the society in Aston Park, apart from obtaining Parliamentary votes for its members, seems to have been to have set a superior standard of housing, and, because they had been able to buy building land at bargain prices, to obtain this better quality at a lower price.

This conclusion is given additional substance by the evidence of the surviving deed polls, the oldest dating from the late 1860s, which invariably include four carefully defined conditions for site development. The distance from the footpath to the front of the house is specified, or shown in a site plan, in such a way as to insist on a generous front garden. The earliest deed poll, that for fifty-four plots at Trinity Road, Handsworth, signed in 1869, insists that 'Each house shall be set back 20 yards from the footpath on the north side and 10 yards on the south side,' and this regulation was maintained with variations to suit the site. Secondly, a minimum price was laid down for each site, varying from £130 to £400, according to the value of the site. If to these figures we add the value of the land, we are in a price range which would not normally be considered working class. Thirdly, it was stipulated that no trade or business was to be carried on in the houses and, further to repudiate the main tradition of the evolution of working-class housing in Birmingham, the final condition was that no 'back or small dwelling house or dwelling houses of the description of a labourers or poor person's house' was to be built on the land, 'or any workshop or building for carrying on any trade or manufacture whatsoever, or any beer house, public house, refreshment house, or ale house'.[60] It is interesting to notice that these conditions look like an elaboration of regulations in existence twenty years earlier for the development of the Calthorpe estate at Edgbaston.[61]

Most of the houses on the estates developed between 1869 and the end of the century are still there, and though nearly all now fall within the inner suburban area, the most casual inspection leaves no doubt of their solid middle-class origins.[62] It is impossible to resist the conclusion that the Birmingham Freehold Land Society, which was born and grew rapidly as a radical democratic organisation in the early 1850s, was quickly taken over by the artisan élite and small manufacturers. After 1850 the rate of growth slowed down and by the period of the Second Reform Act (1867), the Society had become a sedate middle-class movement. The period of its vigour as a popular movement was so brief that its contribution to the development of working-class housing cannot have been important.

NOTES

1 Most conveniently studied in *Birmingham before 1800. Six Maps in the Local Studies Library, Birmingham Reference Library* (1968).

2 J. A. Langford, *A Century of Birmingham Life* (1868), I, 201.

3 J. A. Langford, *op cit, passim*; illustrations in nineteenth-century directories, and surviving buildings in the Black Country; W. B. Stevens, ed, *Victoria County History, Warwickshire*, VII, 51–7.

4 Quoted in A. Briggs, *History of Birmingham*, II (1952), 14–15; M. J. Wise, 'Birmingham and its Trade Relations in the early 18th c.,' *Birmingham University Historical Journal*, II (1949–50), 54–7.

5 J. A. Langford, *op cit*, 109.

6 *Birmingham Gazette*, 9 April 1798. This newspaper subsequently abbreviated to *BG*.

7 *BG*, 18 October 1790.

8 *BG*, 12 July 1813.

9 *BG*, 8 March 1824.

10 *BG*, 16 January 1826 (premises at Dudley).

11 *BG*, 8 February 1796.

12 *BG*, 3 May 1813.

13 *BG*, 11 October, 4 November 1790.

14 Royal Exchange registers, policy no 24093, Guildhall Library, EC2.

15 Quoted in *Children's Employment Commission Report*, Parliamentary Papers, 1842, fol 176.

16 R. D. Grainger's report to Children's Employment Commission.

17 R. D. Grainger, *loc cit*.

18 J. R. Kellett, *The Impact of Railways on Victorian Cities* (1969).

19 A. Briggs, *op cit*, 19, 82.

20 W. Scott, *Stourbridge and its Vicinity* (1832), 93–5; cf Rev D. Robertson, 'Recollections of the Lye Parish' (Ms, 1914, at Lye Vicarage), reprinted Stourbridge *County Express*, 31 December 1960.

21 *The Builder*, VI (1848), 357, and XLV (1883), 324, quoted in W. V. Hole, *The Housing of the Working Classes in Britain*, PhD thesis (London, 1965), 284.

22 A. Briggs, *op cit*, 83–6; Reports of Birmingham Housing Committee 1902–7; J. S. Nettlefold, *A Housing Policy* (1908).

23 W. B. Stephens, ed, *op cit*, 54. Borough of Birmingham, *Bye-laws for Regulating the Construction of New Street and Buildings* (1876). Previously builders had been required to submit plans to ensure that proper drains were provided (C. Gill, *History of Birmingham*, I, 425), but none of these earlier plans seem to have survived.

24 We are greatly indebted to Miss M. Lawton, a former student, for drawing our attention to the plans, and to Mr N. Borg, City Engineer and Surveyor, for assistance in saving them from being sent to salvage.

25   The analysis of the plans was carried out by Dr Bartlett with the aid of four former students, Miss M. Lawton, Miss J. Dainton, Mr D. Garnett and Mr G. Ratcliffe. Dr Bartlett has contributed this section of the chapter, the editor the other two sections.

26   See for example, B. S. Rowntree, *Poverty: A Study of Town Life* (1901), 148.

27   J. H. Clapham, *An Economic History of Modern Britain* (Cambridge 1932) II, 492; C. Gill, *op cit*, I, 367, and 1836 'Doctors' Report' quoted above.

28   Borough of Birmingham, *Report of the Artisans' Dwellings Inquiry Committee* (1884), 72.

29   Borough of Birmingham, *op cit*, 54.

30   J. H. Clapham, *op cit*, 492; Borough of Birmingham, *op cit*, 12–14.

31   W. Hutton, *History of Birmingham* (6th edition, 1835), 294–6.

32   *Minutes of Evidence of Committee of Whole House Concerning Petitions against the Orders-in-Council of 1812*, 4 (BRL).

33   'List of Friendly Societies in the County of Warwick', Warwicks CRO.

34   S. J. Price, *Building Societies, Their Origin and History* (1958), 102.

35   Boulton & Watt Mss (BRL). Cost data in Box 43 (reference from Dr J. Tann) and plans in portfolios marked 'Houses at Foundry' and 'Plot Plans, Foundry'.

36   E. Roll, *An Early Experiment in Industrial Organisation* (1930), 60, 66.

37   J. A. Langford, *op cit*, I, 201.

38   *BG*, 24 March 1788.

39   J. A. Langford, *Modern Birmingham and its Institutions* (1877), II, 164; A. Musgrove, *The History of Lench's Trust, Birmingham* (1926), 42.

40   S. J. Price, *op cit*, 60; W. B. Stephens, ed, *op cit*, VII, 54.

41   *BG*, 26 January 1795.

42   *BG*, 23 February 1795, 20 April 1812.

43   eg, *BG*, 24 March 1785 (Saracen's Head Building Society).

44   eg, *BG*, 23 February 1795, 9 March 1795.

45   W. Hutton, *op cit*, 296.

46   S. J. Price, *op cit*, *passim*.

47   S. J. Price, *op cit*, Ch 3; S. Bamford, *Early Days* (1848–9), 98–9; D. Bythell, *The Handloom Weavers* (1969), 94; P. M. Giles, *Economic and Social Development of Stockport 1815–36*, MA thesis (Manchester 1950), 47–8; below 269–71.

48   W. Radcliffe, *Origins of Power Loom Weaving* (Stockport, 1828), 10, 55, 62.

49   *BG*, 9 March 1795. Cf similar developments in New John Street and Pritchett Street, *BG*, 12 April 1813, 3 May 1813.

50   eg, in Woodcock Street where cellar, sitting room and pump offered for sale, *BG*, 3 May 1813.

51   *BG*, 23 January 1837. (Italics in original.)

52   We are indebted to Mr W. H. Nock, former chief public-health inspector, for advice and information.

53   J. A. Langford, *Century of Birmingham Life*, II, 570–1; S. J. Price, *op cit*, 49.

54 Dawson Mss, Volume 17 (BRL).

55 T. R. Tholfsen, 'The Origins of the Birmingham Caucus', *Historical Journal*, II, 1959.

56 'Biographical Sketch of James Taylor junior of Birmingham, the Founder of Freehold Land Societies', *Freehold Land Times and Building News*, 1 October 1854; 'The Birmingham Freehold Land and Building Societies', *Building Societies' Gazette*, December 1889; Birmingham FLS Prospectuses, 1851 and 1865; *Birmingham F.L.S. Fifth Annual Report 1851–2*, and *Ninth Annual Report 1856* (other early reports lost); Birmingham FLS Minute Books (1847 onwards) and Deed Polls (1869–98) in possession of Birmingham Incorporated Building Society.

57 Albert Road (overlooking park) was not developed by FLS until 1875, sixty-three plots for houses of £200+ (Deed Poll, 1875).

58 R. Anderson, *Anatomy of Aston*. City of Birmingham College of Art and Design School of Architecture dissertation, 1969, Chapters 2, 3.

59 *Ibid.*

60 Birmingham FLS Deed Polls, Birmingham Inc Building Society.

61 Rawlinson's *Report on Sanitary State of Birmingham* (1849).

62 Birmingham FLS Deed Polls. The twenty-three estates recorded are:
    1869 Coventry Rd (60 plots).
    1871 Grosvenor Rd, Wellington Rd, Westminster Rd (30). Houses to cost £150+.
    1872 Brighton Rd, Moseley (75), £130+.
    1872 Erdington (78), £250+.
    1872 Greenhill, Moseley (87), £300+.
    1873 Beoly Rd, Arrow Rd, Prospect Rd (121), £100+.
    1875 Albert Rd, Aston Park (63), £200+.
    1875 Milton Rd, Wednesfield Heath (63), £100+.
    1875 Woodfield Rd, Cambridge Rd, Clarence Rd, King's Heath (123), £300+.
    1876 Stirling Rd and Carlyle Rd off Hagley Rd (66), £300–£400+.
    1876 Stanmore Rd (9), £300+.
    1877 Sparkhill (194), £150+, £250+.
    1879 Murdoch Rd, Linwood Rd, Whately Rd, Handsworth (268), £150+, £200+.
    1887 Gordon Rd and Heathfield Rd, Handsworth (23), £200+, £300+.
    1890 Alcester Rd (127), £150+, £250+.
    1890 Northfield (57), £300+.
    1890 Antrobus Rd, Handsworth (130), £150+, £200+.
    1892 Row Heath Rd, Middleton Hall Rd (N side), King's Norton (110), £150+, £250+, £300+.
    1894 Midland Rd and Row Heath Rd, King's Norton (41), £150+.
    1895 Grange Estate, King's Heath (448), £130+ to £300+.
    1896 Shirley Estate (33).
    1898 Grove Estate, Yardley (294).

CHAPTER VII

THE ARCHITECTURE OF THE DOMESTIC SYSTEM IN SOUTH-EAST LANCASHIRE AND THE ADJOINING PENNINES

W. J. Smith

THE chapters of this book on the history of working-class housing in Leeds, Birmingham and Nottingham have identified an artisan élite responding to greater economic opportunities and higher earnings by investing their savings in recognisably superior types of dwellings. In Leeds the handloom weavers built the first back-to-backs in the fields in the 1780s and 1790s, in Nottingham the lacemakers took advantage of inflated wages in the boom of the early 1820s to build new suburbs, in Birmingham building clubs sprang into existence whenever trade conditions seemed to offer the promise of a margin of income for regular saving. But clearly no collection of essays on working-class life in the Industrial Revolution could hope to be representative without devoting some attention to Lancashire and the industrial north-west generally, for in this period cotton seized and retained the lead in economic growth and organisation, a lead that had been made possible through inventions enabling the output of spun yarns to be greatly increased to meet an elastic demand for cheaper textiles.

Kay's fly-shuttle, invented as early as 1733, did not come into general use until the 1760s, when the resulting increase in output of the handlooms led to an ever increasing scarcity of yarns and so acted as a spur to inventors intent upon the construction of machines which would spin several threads at one time. Hargreaves' spinning jenny made its appearance in 1767 and was followed by Arkwright's water-frame and Crompton's mule; the jenny helped to increase production and also reduce costs primarily in the cotton trade, but within a short space of time it had been adapted for the woollen industry of the Pennines. Increased demand for textiles made possible by the increased output of cheaper yarns multiplied the demand for the skills of the handloom weaver, for, until the 1830s, there was no reliable and widely used technique of weaving by power. The years between 1788 and 1811 were the 'golden age' of the handloom weavers; one estimate suggests an increase in cotton looms from 75,000 to 225,000 between 1795 and 1811.[1] These were the years when, as Radcliffe recalled, wages 'rose to five times the amount ever before experienced . . . every family bringing home weekly 40, 60, 80, 100 or even 120 shillings a week ! ! !',[2] and though many weavers' families did not earn anything like these incomes, there can be no doubt that high piece-rates enabled an industrious minority to earn unprecedented wages and acquire their independence.[3]

After the practical experience of a few years, any young man who was industrious and careful, might then from his earnings as a weaver lay by sufficient to set himself up as a manufacturer, William Radcliffe claimed. Those who succeeded as independent (or master) weavers were soon at work improving and extending their workshops and, at length, rebuilding the entire house and workshop accommodation; as Radcliffe describes :

> while the old loomshops being insufficient, every lumber room, even old barns, carthouses and outbuildings of any description were repaired, windows broke through the old blank walls, and all fitted up for loomshops. This source of making room being at length exhausted, new weavers' cottages with loomshops rose up in every direction, all immediately filled . . .[4]

These new buildings were developed to house both family and workshop (loomhouse) with the greater consideration given to the latter. They are not to be confused with the cottages and houses in which some or all of the processes of textile production were sometimes carried out within the domestic accommodation.

The following work is part of a study of the vernacular architecture of south-east Lancashire and the adjoining Pennines, the basis of which is to relate the regional traditions of domestic building to the architecture of the domestic system. Three areas have been selected for close study, the woollen producing regions of Rochdale and Saddleworth, and Middleton where the specialisation in silk and fine cottons ensured the continuation of handloom weaving until the 1860s.[5]

The vernacular building traditions of the Pennine region were generally established by the early seventeenth century, at the conclusion of the period of the 'great rebuilding'. Many of the earlier timber structures had been partially or wholly rebuilt in stone supplied from local quarries. In the greater part of the north and north-west carboniferous sandstone from both upper and lower levels of the millstone grits was used; the upper strata could be riven and split into flagstones easy to handle and work but friable whereas the lower strata gave a harder, granular and less bedded stone. This was used for those parts of the building where the greatest strength was needed—the quoin (corner) stones, window jambs, mullions, sills and lintels. Because of the hard intractable nature of the gritstone, the decoration was of the simplest kind, the interplay of contrast between the two types of stone, the section given to the mullions—splay, cavetto or ovolo—the window structure recessed into the thickness of the wall, and the doorways usually bearing a heavy lintel often carved with a date and initials of the builder or owner and with the under side of the lintel being shaped to a four-centred or segmental arch. The most common plan form was that of the hall house—the room laying along the main axis of the house—where the 'house part', the equivalent of the medieval hall, became the principal living area. These traditions were easily adapted to the requirements of a domestic industry such as hand-loom weaving in the late eighteenth century, when the loomhouse made its appearance. The local style then developed to create a functional industrial-cum-domestic unit; the long rows of mullion lights were retained and frequently extended from three or five to as many as fifteen. In the process of development some of the character of the domestic vernacular style disappeared, structure was simplified, mullions were made of flagstone and became rectangular in section, the doorframes and lintels were made from the more easily obtained long narrow flagstone and were unrelieved by any decoration, and in the internal planning the workroom was given priority over the living accommodation.

A region which shows an early intrusion of the domestic system into a vernacular idiom is centred on Kendal. In this district spinning galleries are to be found, once more numerous than at present; these ranged from Coniston in the west to Dent in the east and Patterdale in the north. Spinning galleries were first floor balconies built of wood with a rail sometimes supported by turned wooden balusters but more usually quite plain in character. They were placed in an angle of the farmhouse facing on to the yard away from the prevailing winds, and here in suitable weather the wool would be spun and knitted, the maximum use being made of the available light. A fine example is to be seen at Pool Bank in the Winster valley, Westmorland, which was built on to the 1693 wing. Nearby at Hodge Hill is a more sophisticated version.[6]

A group of yeoman-clothiers' houses in the Hebden Bridge region shows the first change brought about by the domestic system in the plan form of the buildings. This was the addition to the rear of the hall of a room which appears to have been used as a kitchen. At Greenwood Lee, Heptonstall, the extension is clearly a kitchen, with the large arched fireplace in the east wall, and similar arrangements can be seen at Birchen Lee Carr (extension dated 1673), Old Edge, Hippins and Stannery End.[7] Presumably these kitchens replaced the originals, which would have been on the main axis of the building, but why? In the late seventeenth century the wool cloth trade expanded and many clothiers altered their homes to accommodate some of the processes of woollen manufacture. In these examples the original kitchen became a workshop, the old through-passage serving to isolate the noise and smells from the main part of the house and also help to keep the living quarters more private from the journeymen workers. At Greenwood Lee there is a most intriguing feature at the east end of the old kitchen wing, a narrow room extending from several feet below ground up to the roof, the possible site of a waterwheel. There are the remains of a water-race under the yard by the house and Crump records a scribbling machine driven by water-power for sale near Huddersfield in 1779.[8] Some alterations made to the former tail-race certainly show late eighteenth-century characteristics of construction.[9]

There are several loomhouses in Saddleworth parish which show their growth and development from the farmhouses of the region. New Tame, near Delph, was a farmhouse built in the early eighteenth century (datestone 1742) by the Buckley family in the vernacular idiom, the windows having splay section mullions and hood moulds. Towards the end of the century the upper floor of the farmhouse was taken down and rebuilt, the roof heightened to make a loftier workroom, and new windows were installed, but they were quite different in style from those built forty years previously. The mullion section is rectangular and the lights are larger in proportion, and the centre mullion of each pair of lights is recessed, so carrying on some traditions of the past. The new walling is also different, larger blocks of stone being used and laid as 'water-shot' masonry[10] (see below p 260). From 1760 other families settled at New Tame, Wrigley, Brierly, Heginbottom, Carter and Platt, all clothiers,[11] and as a result the existing buildings were extended and added to, materials from the earlier farm buildings being incorporated. At the end of the row the fully developed loomhouse can be seen—a three-storey building incorporating two houses, back-to-back on the ground and first floors, but with a workshop on the upper floor extending the full depth of the building.[12] Mullion windows with square section mullions are used throughout and in rows of six lights. On the exposed north-west side of the loomhouse at first-floor level are the remains of a now blocked doorway, which was the taking-in door where the raw material was unloaded on to the lower workroom floor for the initial processes of carding and spinning, a feature common to nearly all loomhouses in rural areas. The staircases of loomhouses were narrow and space-saving, having an average width of 27in; it would be difficult to manhandle bales of raw wool up such stairs besides being inconvenient to have to pass through the 'house part'. The yarn prepared on a lower floor ready for weaving could then be taken up, by the staircase this time, to the loomshop on the top floor (p 215).

The rows of mullion windows did not result in an excessive charge being made by the Window Tax. From 1747, two or more lights in one frame, or opening, were to be charged as one window provided that the mullions or partitions between were less than 12in wide, and as the average width of a rectangular mullion was 5in—well below the limit—the owners or tenants of loomhouses rarely paid for more than seven windows, containing as many as thirty lights, which cost 6s in 1780.[13]

At Ballgreave, Uppermill, the farmhouse built in the early eighteenth century was enlarged as the Radcliffes, who were clothiers, increased production. The building was enlarged in two phases, first a new wing was added to the south end of the farmhouse and later a complete upper storey was built running the full length of the building, which had a long range of twelve lights facing west to illuminate the loomshop. At the rear of this upper storey is the 'taking-in' door (now blocked) between two rows of windows, the sharp rise in the ground behind the building allowing direct access to the loomshop by means of a flagstone bridge, which has long since been demolished (p 215).

Nearby, Load Clough is a fine example of a three-storey loomhouse 'lately erected and built at his own Proper Costs and Charges' by George Garlick, a clothier, shortly after 1786.[14] The two upper storeys are each lit by a row of eight-light square section mullion windows with two additional two-light windows in the west gable giving cross lighting to the loomshops. There is only one two-light window in the east gable, which gives light to the upper floor. The taking-in door is at the rear and leads directly into the upper loomshop. As with New Tame, all the mullions are recessed from the face of the wall.

In all these examples it can be seen that the vernacular traditions inherited by the late eighteenth-century clothiers formed the ideal functional style for the domestic system. The mullion windows provided the necessary horizontal illumination for the weavers working close to the window, the thick stone walls helped to keep the atmosphere of the loomshop constant and so keep the warps in even tension, and the hall house planning allowed family life to continue in the one main room.

The loomhouse became part of the urban and suburban scene over a period of thirty to forty years, during which time it was modified by changing economic circumstances and fashion. Three phases can be identified in the Rochdale area, the first represented by the loomhouse described above, one in which all the windows were of the square section mullion type. At Smallbridge, Rochdale, there was a very fine example of the first-phase loomhouse in an urban area, numbers 309–11 Halifax Road, a square block built in 1806 by James Leach, a machine-maker, to the 'clear annual value' of £11.[15] This block consisted of four dwelling units each having a single room per floor, the two fronting the main road having a connected basement, ground floor and first floor, and the two rear units having ground floor and first floor only. The basements must have been used for domestic purposes only, for the firegrates were small and decorative and did not have cooking ranges; perhaps the journeymen or junior members of the household lived here. The top floor workrooms ran from front to back over two adjacent units separated by a dividing wall, and were accessible only from the rear houses. The western loomshop was lit by a row of six-light mullion windows at front and rear, some side light being provided by a two-light window in the west gable. The east loomshop had a six-light window at the front and a similar window in the east gable wall with a small two-light window in the rear wall. There was no taking-in door, confirming that by this period the primary processes in the preparation of the yarn were carried out by the manufacturers in their mills, leaving the work of preparing the warp and weaving the cloth to the domestic worker. The narrow twisting staircases would be no obstacle to taking warps and finished yarns up to the loomshop and the completed bolts of cloth down again. Over both workshops were 'cocklofts', which stopped short of the front and rear walls by 7ft, so allowing access from the loomshop. The yarn and cloth would be stored here and windows high in the gable provided light. In this particular loomshop it was possible to see indications of blocks once fixed to the floor in order to steady the looms and stop them 'walking' when in operation. The heads of the looms were braced by struts to the joists supporting the cockloft (Fig. 7.1).

At New Delph is the tallest loomhouse in the area, rising to four storeys. The upper three floors each have seven-light mullion windows facing south, and the two top floors have two-light windows in the gable ends, giving cross lighting, and these provided the only means of light, the rear of the building being built into the sharply rising ground behind. There is no strict orientation in the positioning of loomhouses and while the above example faces south many others face other points of the compass. The position of the loomhouse relative to the lay of the land was the qualifying factor. At Hough Square, Milnrow, is a row of six loomhouses dated 1805—two storey houses with the main windows of five lights at the front facing north-west.

In the second phase, the mullion window on the ground floor was replaced by a sash window, but in other respects there was little change. A group of three loomhouses on Henry Street, Rochdale, are typical examples, built three storeys high and in brick, except for the rear elevation, where flagstone has been used. The mullion windows on the first and second floors are of six lights and have stone lintels, sills and mullions, but the ground floor at the front has a sash window with a narrow stone lintel and sill. The loomhouse was becoming 'respectable'! In a town where brick was the predominant material used, the street elevation conformed to the local pattern set by the elegant rows of Regency terraces on nearby Drake Street. There are three similar loomhouses on Ramsden Road, Wardle, near Rochdale, but unlike the Henry Street example, these are built of stone throughout and may reflect the way in which ideas moved out from the town to the surrounding areas. Further examples are to be seen at 25–29 Charles Lane, Milnrow, which are built from squared sandstone laid in water-shot courses.

Bent Meadows, Rochdale, is a row of small two-storey brick loomhouses with sash windows on the ground floor at the front but with mullions still being used for the three-light first floor windows and those at the rear. This forms a contrast with rural Saddleworth where the traditions of recessed mullions was maintained, the loomhouses in the Rochdale area having the mullions flush with

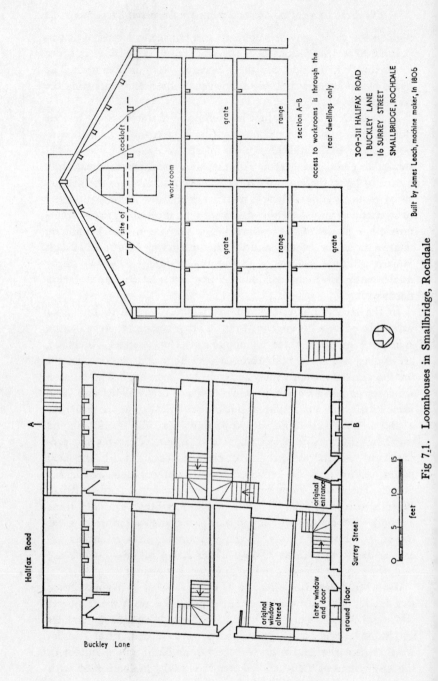

Fig 7.1. Loomhouses in Smallbridge, Rochdale

Halifax Road

Buckley Lane

Surrey Street

ground floor

original window altered

later window and door

original entrance

0 5 10 15

feet

309-311 HALIFAX ROAD
1 BUCKLEY LANE
16 SURREY STREET
SMALLBRIDGE, ROCHDALE

Built by James Leach, machine maker, in 1806

section A–B

access to workrooms is through the rear dwellings only

grate

range

workroom

site of

cockloft

grate

range

grate

the outer face of the walls. This can be considered as the conclusion of a change in window design in vernacular buildings of the north-west. Towards the end of the seventeenth century it became the practice to bring the splay mullions forward in the upper-floor windows so that they were flush with the outer face of the wall; Old Bent House, Littleborough, built in 1692 is a fine example of this change, which coincided with a change in walling construction, when building techniques permitted walls of a narrower section than formerly.

The third phase saw the use of sash windows extended to the first-floor level. At Hamer Place on Halifax Road, Howarth Cross, Rochdale, built in 1811, the three-storey brick loomhouses have mullion windows on the upper floor and basement only, while the first and second floors have sash windows at the front. These are Regency buildings displaying some characteristics of Neo-grecian revivalism, the plain well proportioned windows and plain surfaces relieved only by the continuous string course, which also doubles as the sill for the upper workroom windows and can be seen as an example of an increasing awareness of architectural sophistication. At Clegg Hall, a mile away to the east, stands a block of eight back-to-back loomhouses built in the local gritstone but following the fashionable style of Hamer Place. These are rural loomhouses but there is no sign of a taking-in door, so by this time the primary processes of woollen production were being carried out in the adjoining mill, leaving the handloom weaver to ply his craft and complete the process of manufacture.[16] This third and final phase lasted until the 1820s, the decade that saw the rapid decline of the domestic system in the face of the more efficient competition of the power looms and weaving sheds.

Many loomhouses had been built adjoining woollen spinning mills as a development in the organisation of the industry. Chesham Fold on Rochdale Old Road, Bury, is a terrace of ten loomhouses fronting the main road, behind which is the woollen mill. The row consists of three-storey houses built in squared sandstone, each with a loomshop on the top floor running the full depth of the house. The rooms on the first and second floors are quite generous in size and a central boxed-in staircase gives access to all floors. At the front are sash windows on the first two floors with mullion windows at the rear. The workroom still has mullion windows above the continuous sill and each house has a five-light window with the centre light being wider and fitted with a small sash window to allow some control over the ventilation of the loomshop. The rainwater heads at Chesham Fold are particularly fine and are typical of the early nineteenth century, and clearly this row of loomhouses was meant to display some architectural pretentions (p 216).[17]

A variation on the third phase can be discerned in the two-storey loomhouse with two adjoining rooms on the ground floor, each with a sash window, such as that which stood on Sand Street, Smallbridge, Rochdale. This variation, which also heralded the declining importance of the loomshop, was a row of back-to-back houses, those facing on to Halifax Road being entirely domestic in purpose and having sash windows on both floors, while behind were loomhouses in Sand Street with first-floor loomshops having a six-light range of windows, which included one small sash window. The loomhouse occupies the greater floor area of each pair (see Fig. 7.2). In the domestic unit the fireplace/cooking range was the most important feature and was the centre of family life, providing warmth, comfort, cooking facilities and a certain amount of light. It followed that the area in front of the fire was of prior importance and must not be blocked at any cost. Consequently, the staircase was placed at the opposite end of the room to the fireplace and boxed in. But here it faced the doorway to the street, and to keep down the draughts to the upper floor a door was provided at the foot of the stairs. In the loomhouse, however, the staircase was placed against the inner dividing wall where it did not interfere with the most important area in this house—the working area in front of the windows, which was thus kept clear for the looms. At 21 Sand Street and its adjoining unit in Halifax Road, the inhabitants enjoyed a convenience to be envied by their neighbours—an external privy built up against the chimney breast where it could take advantage of the warmth from the kitchen fire! There are a number of loomhouses of similar plan—but without the toilet accommodation—between Rochdale and Littleborough.

At Flock Hall on Halifax Road, Smallbridge, is a block of five pairs of back-to-back houses, stone to the main road and brick to the rear; the northernmost three pairs were built in 1813, the other two belonging to the first phase, but the front windows were later altered to conform with the rest of the block.[18] The houses are three-storey plus a cellar below the rear units only, and

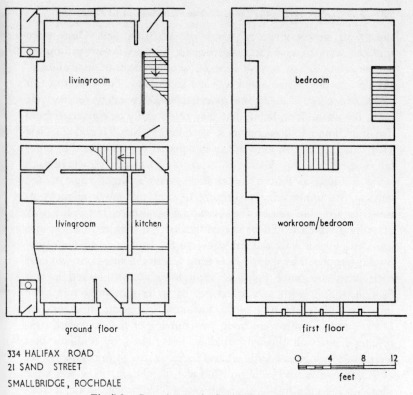

ground floor   first floor

334 HALIFAX ROAD
21 SAND STREET
SMALLBRIDGE, ROCHDALE

O   4   8   12
feet

Fig 7.2.   Loomhouses in Smallbridge, Rochdale

the workrooms on the upper floor, which extend the full depth of
the block, are lit by rows of six-light mullion windows. The cellars
are self-contained with no access to the rooms above and may have
been inferior workrooms. A most interesting feature is the construction of the floor above the cellars of tongue and groove floorboards
supported by standard joists; laid on the floorboards is a 1in layer of
sand and finally a closely laid flag floor of 1in flagstones. Why such
an elaborate floor? The most likely explanation is soundproofing,
the layer of sand acting as an efficient sound insulator. The same
arrangement was also to be found in several loomhouses in Middleton.

   With the introduction of the power loom, manufacturers gradually ceased to employ handloom weavers, and the unemployed loomshops were closed down, often by blocking up single or ranges of
lights. This was less for reducing the amount of window tax than
a means of creating more comfort and warmth, a good brick or

stone wall having much greater insulation than glass. Quite often mullions were removed to make way for a sash window, so improving ventilation, but not all blocked windows are an indication of the decline of the handloom weaver. Some loomhouses built at this period of decline, 1820–26, incorporated blocked windows as they were built, the assumption being that they could easily be converted from dwelling house to loomhouse if necessary.[19] Nos 21 and 23 New Hey Road, Milnrow, are built from squared flagstones laid in regular courses in a way known as 'water-shot stonework', where each stone is tilted so that its outer face makes a slight angle to the vertical, its upper edge projecting beyond the lower edge by as much as 1in. The reason for this tilting is obscure, but it is a way of walling which would be very difficult for a builder to insert into an opening in a wall and still preserve the continuity of the coursing, as happened in these two houses, where the first-floor windows each have the outer lights of six-light windows blocked in this fashion, that is with regular courses of water-shot stonework. The only logical interpretation of this technique is that the windows were blocked as the walls were built, the coursing of the stonework continuing from wall through window, interrupted by mullions that were built in together with sill and lintel. A row of four loomhouses at Rakewood near Hollingworth Lake, Rochdale, show the same idea, but here the two-light openings are filled in with stone, including both centre mullions and recessed lintel. On Cross Stone Road, Todmorden, is a further example, two adjoining loomhouses of three storeys built in square gritstone blocks with fine joints. The upper floor, the intended loomshop, has an eight-light window stretching over both houses, but the two centre lights are blocked with the same masonry as the walls. While the party wall between the houses is substantial the loomshop is divided by a wooden framed wall, easily removable if the loomshop was ever to be used.

The number of loomhouses that can be interpreted in this way is small compared with those loomhouses whose windows were later blocked with either brick or stone, but it is evident that some self-employed weavers still had the capital and faith in the future of their craft in spite of the advent of the power loom. The building of loomhouses in the woollen areas came to an end by the 1830s, though in Middleton they continued to be built until well into the 1860s.

As a substantial town Middleton dates from 1776. Sir Harbord Harbord, later Lord Suffield, succceeded to the manor on the death of his father-in-law, Sir Ralph Assheton, in 1765, when the estates inherited by his wife, Mary, were vested in him. The Harbords were from Gunton in Norfolk, which remained their principal seat, while Middleton Hall became neglected and was largely taken down in 1805. But before this the Harbords, not being resident, began to dispose of plots of land to the north of the parish church, a locality called Barrowfields, and also land in front of the hall, an area known as Little Park.[20] The first lease was dated 1 March 1776 and was for a plot of land along the turnpike road, now Long Street. A covenant written into all the earlier leases made it obligatory for the lessee to erect within the ensuing twelve months a substantial dwelling, which had to conform to minimum standards, including a stated yearly value. The houses erected were usually two rooms deep, with brick walls and flagstone roofs and dressings, materials that came to be associated with the urban Georgian style. Door and window frames were of wood with flat arched brick lintels or flat stone lintels, the stone being local flagstone, which was rather friable; the windows were of small 5 by 9in panes set in frames, one of which could slide behind the other—so called Yorkshire lights, a common type being a three-light window with the centre light sliding left or right.

Industry came to Middleton in 1780 when John Jackson built a cotton factory at the lower end of Wood Street powered by a waterwheel;[21] later the concern was taken over by Daniel Burton of Manchester and the premises extended. It was at this period, close to the end of the eighteenth century, that the first known loomhouses were built in Middleton. Many of the early leases were to weavers, who are shown to be mainly local men in the indentures of conveyance, and presumably they built houses which also accommodated a loomshop, but most of the earlier houses were demolished during the last thirty years and no proper records were kept of their appearance. However, sufficient remained until recently to give some idea of the range of design.

From its early industrial beginnings Middleton had specialised in weaving silk, with intermittent periods when cotton took priority, particularly in the 1820s when Edward Baines mentioned that the 'cotton trade is carried on in this township and parish to a considerable extent'.[22] By 1840, after the introduction of power looms, the silk trade had 'revived and extended to a much greater amount than was previously the case', so that 'it prevails to a considerable extent, and there is also cotton weaving by hand and power'.[23] Cotton was mainly muslins, nankins and ginghams, delicate fabrics for which, together with silk, there was no mechanical substitute for the skill of the handloom weaver. This was the principal reason why handloom weaving continued in Middleton until well into the latter half of the nineteenth century, even though cotton mills for spinning, weaving and printing were built in and around the growing town.

The delicate nature of silk and fine cotton necessitated a specially designed loomshop isolated from direct contact with the dusty streets. The silk was handed out and returned by weight, and contact with the open air changed the moisture content and weight. Smoke was damaging, and the ordinary weaver had to work all through the winter without a fire.[24] At 68 Boarshaw Road, built in 1798 by Samuel Ogden, a weaver,[25] the living room opens directly into the street, and behind this room is the small kitchen, which also contains the staircase. The workroom connects only with, and runs the full depth of, the adjoining living room, and a three-light window on the front and a two-light window at the rear provide the necessary light. The windows had no provision for opening and so preserved the isolation of the loomshop (see Fig. 7.3). This loomhouse was similar to the one described in the autobiography of Samuel Bamford :[26]

> My uncle's domecile, like all the others, consisted of one principal room called 'the house'; on the same floor with this was a loom-shop capable of holding four looms, and in the rear of the house on the same floor, were a small kitchen and a buttery. Over the house and loom-shop were chambers; and over the kitchen and buttery was another apartment, and a flight of stairs. The whole of the rooms were lighted by windows of small square panes, framed in lead, in good condition; those in front being protected by shutters.

Before the use of tar-macadam the danger of broken windows from stones flicked up by passing carriages made shutters essential in the smaller houses and cottages of this period. Inside the house there were

> a dozen good rush-bottom chairs, the backs and rails bright with wax and rubbing, a handsome clock in mahogany case, a good chest of oaken drawers, a mahogany snap-table, a mahogany corner cupboard, all well polished; besides tables, weather glass, cornish and ornaments, pictures of Joseph and his Brethren.

Signs of some prosperity in a weaver's home, c 1800.[27] A similar loomhouse is described by D. Smith in *Industrial Archaeology of the*

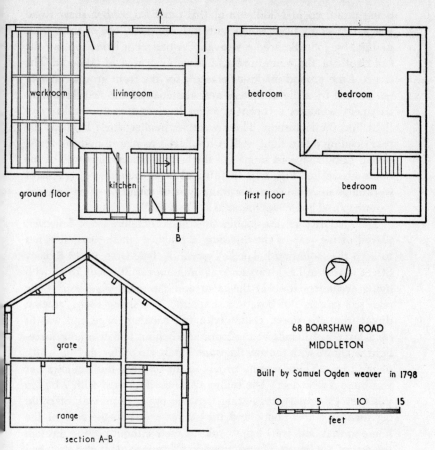

Fig 7.3. Loomhouses in Boarshaw Rd, Middleton

East Midlands (1965)—a framework knitter's cottage at Calverton, Nottinghamshire—and the similarity is due to the same basic influences, the building materials of the area and the function of the building.

An earlier loomhouse built in 1782 and also on Boarshaw Road,[28] had a basement workshop lit by a three-light window that originally faced into a light well. The area of this loomshop was 140sq ft, while that of 68 Boarshaw Road was 132sq ft, the living room being 190sq ft. From the turn of the nineteenth century the loomshops became larger, presumably because of increased demand for the fabrics being produced in Middleton at this time. No 93 Boarshaw Road was a two-storey brick house with sash windows, one of three built in 1802 by John Brearly, a weaver.[29] A basement loomshop ran the full depth of the house and had a working area of 300sq ft. The slope of the ground made it necessary for the front ground floor to be reached by a flight of steps and also enabled the two three-light basement windows to open at street level and so allow plenty of light into the loomshop. There were six smaller single lights at the rear opening into a light well. A fireplace was placed midway and a strong 12 by 15in joist supported the brick inner dividing wall of the house above (see Fig. 7.4). In this and other examples of basement workshops in Middleton, the same type of sound proofing between loomshop and house was found as at Flock Hall.

The majority of the loomhouses in Middleton were, however, placed at the rear of the building, a practice which made it easier to keep the loomshop isolated. Typical of these were 43–49 Brassey Street, a row of brick two-storey loomhouses built about 1850, with living accommodation at the front and the main workshop at the rear (containing the boxed-in staircase). The living room, entered direct from the street, contained a full cooking range and was lit by a large sash window; the loomshop behind had two long three-light windows with narrow flagstone lintels, stretching the full width of the room. There was no provision for opening the windows nor was there a rear door. The ceiling was heavily joisted with 7 by 5in joists set 13in apart, suggesting that the upper room was, or could be, used as a loomshop; and the staircase was in the rear of the house so that both workshops could be used without passing through the rest of the house. The windows in this upper room also stretched the full width of the room, but here the centre light of one of the windows only could slide to provide ventilation. This would be necessary if, as was most likely, these upper rooms were also used for sleeping, the beds being placed between the looms. The sliding windows could be tightly closed to prevent draughts, but perhaps the height above the street outside prevented much dust from getting in (see Fig. 7.5). Privies and the water pump were in the court behind the row, and were shared by a similar row behind on Wagstaffe Street. Access to the court was by a 'ginnel', which would be essential as there was no rear entrance to the loom houses.[30]

In the above example the loomshop was a little smaller than the living room, but this was not always so. At 52 and 54 Fielding

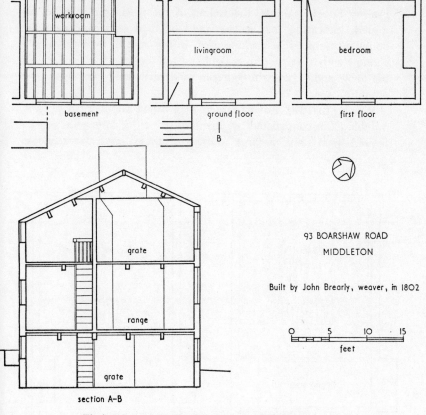

basement   ground floor   first floor

93 BOARSHAW ROAD
MIDDLETON

Built by John Brearly, weaver, in 1802

section A–B

Fig 7.4. Loomhouses in Boarshaw Rd, Middleton

Street, built about 1850, the loomshops were larger than the house part. The two houses formed a square block with 52 on Fielding Street and 54 behind facing on to a small court (see Fig. 7.6). The loomshop of 54 had a working area of 190 sq ft and was alongside the living room, which had an area of 170sq ft. The workroom was lit by three large three-light windows, two along the front and one

R

at the side giving cross lighting. A particular feature of the window frames of many Middleton loomhouses is the fineness of the glazing bars, those at number 54 being ⅜in wide and beautifully made with carefully mitred joints, to allow the maximum amount of light to pass into the workroom, a practical consideration rather than a display of the skill of the joiner. The boxed-in staircase leads from the living room and occupies a corner of the workroom. As with the Brassey Street example, the ceiling of the workroom was heavily joisted, indicating that it too could be used as a workroom, so doubling the possible working area, in this case lit by a three-light window with a centre sliding light and a three-light fixed window in the gable end. The main bedroom was reached through this upper room.

Writing in 1840, Edwin Butterworth called attention to the 'admirable loom constructed by Jacquard [which] is in general use for figured goods, and a large number of these looms are made in

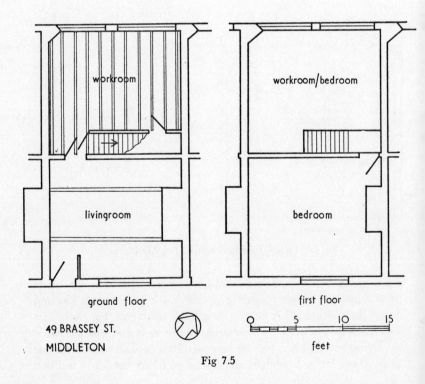

ground floor   first floor

49 BRASSEY ST.
MIDDLETON

0   5   10   15
feet

Fig 7.5

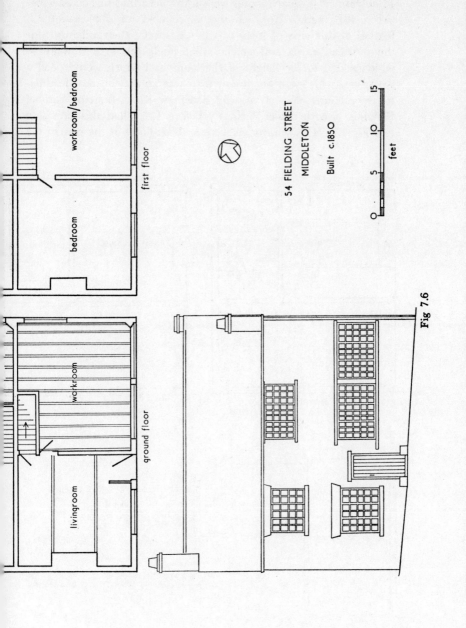

workroom/bedroom

bedroom

first floor

workroom

livingroom

ground floor

54 FIELDING STREET
MIDDLETON

Built c.1850

0   5   10   15
        feet

Fig 7.6

Middleton'.[31] Jacquard looms were introduced into this country between 1816 and 1820 when they were used for silk weaving. A feature of this type of loom was the 'harness'—the mechanism for the punched cards and needles that made the figured weave— which added to the height of the loom, and which would need a workroom with more headroom than was normal in most Middleton loomhouses. Nos 50 and 52 Boarshaw Road, built by Samuel Fielding, a corn dealer,[32] shortly before 1846, had this provision (see Fig 7.7). The workrooms were on both floors at the rear of the

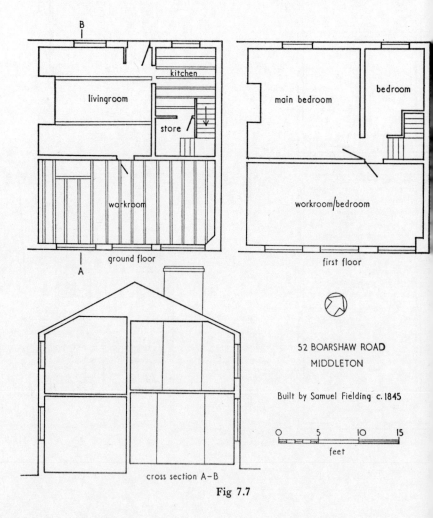

Fig 7.7

houses and extended the full length of each house, each workroom having a floor area of 220sq ft. At the front were two rooms—a kitchen of 97sq ft and a living room of 160sq ft—with the staircase leading from the kitchen. The loomshops were entered from the living rooms and were kept free of any obstructions, and whereas the living rooms were just short of 8ft in height, the workrooms were 9ft 3in, the difference in height being helped by the fall of the ground at the rear of the houses. In November 1846 the two loomhouses were leased to James Fairbrother of Middleton, a silk weaver.[33]

An arrangement formerly widespread in Middleton consisted of a row of loomhouses with rear workrooms but with the end house having the loomshop extended to the rear, so increasing the working accommodation above that of its neighbours. At 106 to 110 Sandy Lane, built in 1832 by a weaver,[34] the former had such a workroom, but with an area of 225sq ft as opposed to 140sq ft of the adjoining loomhouses (see Fig. 7.8). During demolition a blocked door once linking the workrooms of 106 and 108 was discovered, but this had not been an original feature and there are no other signs of the other workrooms interconnecting in this way. The grandfather of the late occupier of 106 had two looms working in the loomshop towards the end of the nineteenth century. A similar arrangement was to be seen on John Street where there was a terrace of six loomhouses built about 1852,[35] with the corner house having the extended workroom. This was the longest terrace of loomhouses of one build in Middleton at that time.[36]

The loomhouses were the weavers' own property, Robert Rawlinson claimed in 1854,[37] while admitting that his statement could be disputed. The origins of this remark can be traced to the early cottages and loomhouses built in Middleton by the cottagers and weavers. A lease of property on King Street dated 1794 mentions 'that part of Middleton . . . called and known by the name of Clubhouses', and Bamford enlarges on this by explaining that in the late eighteenth century 'all the houses and buildings . . . on the north side of St Leonards Square' was a 'mass of buildings called "The Club Houses" '.[38] Increasing prosperity during the 'golden age' of the handloom weavers resulted in the formation of building clubs in many parts of the county to help meet the housing shortage. The clubs were properly speaking terminating building societies, ie when their purpose had been realised they ceased to exist. According to

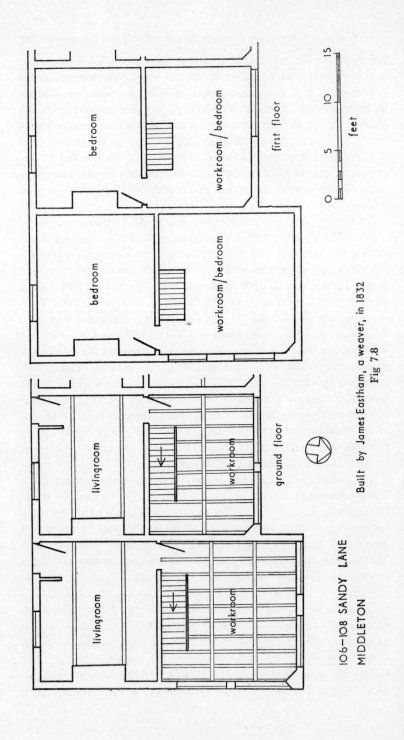

106–108 SANDY LANE
MIDDLETON

Built by James Eastham, a weaver, in 1832

Fig 7.8

Edmund Ashworth, giving evidence in 1840, building societies 'prevail considerably among the working people, but more fully among the shopkeepers and better class of people'.[39] But Edwin Butterworth writing of such matters in Middleton in the same year mentions that the building societies were 'composed chiefly of the working class' and adds that 'the town increased rapidly'.[40]

Evidence of how such clubs were conducted in Middleton has not yet come to light but some idea of how building was financed can be deduced from some of the early property deeds. At 50 and 52 Boarshaw Road the land had been leased by Lord Harbord to Joseph Fielding, a weaver, in 1799. In 1838 his widow, Betty Fielding, sold the plot for £5 to Samuel Fielding, a corndealer and possibly also a relative, who then built two substantial loomhouses, which he sold for £228 in 1846 to James Fairbrother, a Middleton silk weaver.[41] This appears to be a straightforward case of development by a person who obviously had some capital. On Boarshaw Road two adjoining plots were leased by Lord Harbord in 1802 to John Briggs and John Brearly, both weavers from Middleton.[42] John Briggs built two houses (87 and 89), each to the clear annual value of £8, and John Brearly built three houses likewise (91 to 95), one of which he occupied, the other two being let to William Bailey and George Wood, weavers. The latter two loomhouses were sold in 1817 to James Harrison, innkeeper of the Masons Arms, Middleton,[43] for £150, subject to a ground rent of £2 10s 0d; in 1821 Harrison also bought the two houses built by Briggs for £128 subject to a ground rent of £4. Harrison then built five houses at the rear of the plots—fronting on to Brassey Street—and in 1825 sold the whole to Samuel Topp of Middleton, a weaver, for £700. However, in order to raise the purchase price, Topp had to mortgage the properties, but was unable to repay the loan within the specified time and so forfeited the property. In 1828 he was listed as a tenant of Richard Millat of Staley Bridge, a joiner, the mortgagee.

Here was an unsuccessful speculation but not surprising considering that the later 1820s were a time when the prosperity of the handloom weavers was on the wane. Briggs and Brearly both built at a time when the handloom weavers were enjoying unprecedented wealth, the trade of muslin weaving being 'the trade of a gentleman', and the weavers bringing home their work 'in top boots and ruffled shirts, they had a cane, and took a coach in some instances, and appeared as well as military officers of the first degree'.[44]

Charles Hulbert also comments on the sartorial display of wealth shown by handloom weavers of south Lancashire at the turn of the nineteenth century.[45] Harrison, then, bought and improved the property just before the decline of the handloom weavers' position, and was able to dispose of it to the luckless Samuel Topp just when the trade cycle passed its meridian.

But while the handloom weavers, both in cotton and wool, were being eclipsed by power looms and factories, in Middleton they were able to continue in their livelihood alongside the mills and weaving sheds. Specialisation was their strong weapon and while some members of the household worked at a local mill or down the mines, the head of the household often continued to practise his craft of fine weaving in his own home. Such was the position up to the 1860s, when the Anglo-French Treaty made it impossible for silk weavers to compete with the cheaper imported French silk.

Among the last of the Middleton loomhouses were 108 and 110 Brassey Street built shortly after 1864.[46] From the front there was nothing to distinguish these two from the adjoining terrace of domestic houses, but at the rear the two three-light small paned windows on the ground floor clearly indicate loomshops. The rear first-floor room was lit by a single three-light window with a centre sliding frame and the plan of the houses followed the usual two-up and two-down, with the rear workrooms being the largest, very little change in fact from loomhouses built forty and more years before. The windows at the front and the doorway had deep stone lintels with skew-cut ends, far more substantial looking than in earlier houses, but the long narrow flagstone lintels persisted for the loomshop windows. The simple vernacular traditions were still maintained for the workrooms while a more sophisticated architectural style was beginning to change the character of the terraces of domestic dwellings.

A group of houses built on Townley Street in 1857 showed an even greater sophistication in architectural style. The group of houses formed a hollow rectangular block of fifteen dwellings, the main front being on Townley Street and continuing along Preston Street, Hall Street and Thorne Street. The architectural treatment of the main front was of a high order : the sash windows had deep stone lintels with skew-cut ends with a decorative panel cut along the lower edge of the stone, and the doors had a deep stone arched lintel with a large bold keystone, the whole resting on stone moulded imposts. The architecture was of a more simple style on Thorne Street where the skew-cut lintel was the only decorative feature, and between 4 and 6 there was a ginnel leading into the courtyard, which was normally entered through an entrance at the rear of number 8. All the houses except two had rear doors opening into the courtyard, where there were the privies. The two exceptions were 4 and 6 Thorne Street which were both loomhouses with the workrooms at the rear on the ground floor; both were 3ft deeper than the adjoining houses, the extra room being for the workrooms, each of which was lit by two large two-light windows with small panes and deep stone lintels. Originally there had been no rear doorway and the ginnel would have been necessary to give the occupants easy access to the yard. This Townley Street group is evidence of the decline in the building of loomhouses. Thirty years before four out of five buildings had been loomhouses, but by the late 1850s the proportion had dropped to an average of one in six and after 1865 no more loomhouses were built in Middleton.

From this brief study two points emerge : first, that the so-called traditional 'weaver's windows'[47] so much associated with loomhouses, were part of a regional style of building going back to the sixteenth century and are not necessarily found in other cloth-producing regions, where such windows were not part of the building tradition. In the Cotswolds for example, windows in the smaller stone houses and cottages were often of two or three lights; these were often grouped two or three to a loomshop, and in later examples were represented by window opening divided by wooden mullions set in a wood frame. Many examples can be seen at Wotton-under-Edge, Gloucestershire. Secondly, while the loomhouses of the north-west gradually adopted façades showing an awareness of current architectural fashion,[48] the functional design of the loomhouse arising from the vernacular tradition proved to be so well suited to its purpose that no fundamental changes were ever made.

NOTES

I am grateful to Messrs O. Ashmore, B. E. Meadowcroft and P. F. Sutcliffe for their help and assistance, especially in helping to measure a multitude of loomhouses.

  1 S. D. Chapman, 'Fixed Capital Formation in the British Cotton Industry 1770–1815', *Economic History Review*, XXIII (2) (August 1970).

2 W. Radcliffe, *Origin of the New System of Manufacture commonly called Power Loom Weaving* . . . (Stockport, 1828), 66.

3 S. J. Chapman, *The Lancashire Cotton Industry. A Study in Economic Development* (Manchester, 1904), 39; Cp D. Bythell, *The Handloom Weavers* (Cambridge, 1969), 130–1.

4 W. Radcliffe, *op cit*, 65.

5 Loomhouses particularly associated with the cotton industry, such as are found at Cromford in Derbyshire, are not featured in this study, but most of the observations made hereafter can be applied to them.

6 M. Hartley and J. Ingilby, *The Old Hand-knitters of the Dales* (Clapham, 1951), 64–6.

7 See C. F. Stell, 'Pennine Houses: an Introduction', *Folk Life*, 3 (1965).

8 W. B. Crump and G. Ghorbal, *History of the Huddersfield Woollen Industry* (Huddersfield, 1935), 68.

9 Examples of clothier's communities, ie the clothier's house and dependent weaver's cottages, are to be seen at Baldingstone, north of Bury, and Newhouses, Scouthead near Oldham. The cottages belong to the first-phase loomhouses.

10 F. Atkinson, 'Water-shot Stonework: A Building Technique', *Lancashire and Cheshire Antiquarian Society*, LXIX (1959), 141–3.

11 J. Radcliffe, ed, *The Parish Registers of St Chad, Saddleworth, 1751–1800* (Oldham, 1891).

12 The building is now one house.

13 S. Dowell, *History of Taxes and Taxation in England*, III (1884), 168–77.

14 I am grateful to the owner, Dr G. Gooberman, for allowing me to see the original deeds to the property.

15 Deeds in the Town Hall, Rochdale. I am grateful to the Town Clerk for permission to examine documents in his custody.

16 Remains of a waterwheel have recently been found in the mill.

17 An unusual arrangement of a block consisting of loomhouses and a warehouse complete with loading bays on each floor is to be seen on Littlewood St, Rochdale.

18 Deeds, Town Hall, Rochdale.

19 In this connection, cp the hat factories on Annan and Law Streets, Denton. See also D. M. Smith, 'The Hatting Industry in Denton, Lancashire', *Industrial Archaeology*, vol 3, no 1 (1966).

20 E. Baines, *History, Directory and Gazetteer of the County Palatine of Lancaster*, II (Liverpool, 1825), 430.

21 Deeds in the Town Hall, Middleton. I am grateful to the Town Clerk for permission to examine and make extracts from the deeds now held by the corporation. Future references will be abbreviated to MTH, followed by the reference number of the parcel in which the relevant deeds are to be found. Jackson's Mill is in MTH 105. See also the *Suffield Rental c 1784* in Middleton Reference Library.

22 E. Baines, *op cit*, 429

23 E. Butterworth, *Historical Notices of the Town and Parish of Middleton in the County Palatine of Lancaster* (Middleton, 1840).

24 J. Prest, *The Industrial Revolution in Coventry* (1960), 75.

25 MTH Archives B 3.

26 S. Bamford, *Early Days* (1849), 98–9.

27 *Ibid.* See also W. Radcliffe, *op cit*, 67

28 Built by James Kent, this was one of the very few houses in Middleton to have a datestone, now preserved in Middleton Public Library. In 1784 the house was described as the 'Methodist Meeting House', *Suffield Rental, op cit.*

29 MTH Archives B 67; also see MTH 681.

30 In the later nineteenth century nearly all the loomhouses had one of the rear windows partly bricked up and a rear door built in, but the presence of the stone lintels and the vertical joints in the brickwork clearly showed where the original windows were situated.

31 E. Butterworth, *loc cit.*

32 MTH Archives B 44.

33 In this connection it is interesting to compare the illustration from the Mansell Collection reproduced in N. Bentley, *The Victorian Scene* (1968), 225. This shows an interior of a handloom weaver's home in which the Jacquard loom breaks through the ceiling into the chamber above.

34 MTH Archives S 16.

35 MTH Archives J 21.

36 In Middleton there was no evidence of the cottage factories such as described by J. Prest, *op cit*, 96.

37 R. Rawlinson, *Report to the General Board of Health on a Preliminary Inquiry into the Sewerage (etc.) . . . of the Township of Middleton in the County Palatine of Lancaster* (1854).

38 S. Bamford, *op cit*, 33 and 98.

39 *Select Committee on Health of Towns* (1840), 3.

40 E. Butterworth, *loc cit.*

41 MTH Archives B 44.

42 MTH Archives B 67. In 1821 John Briggs had removed to Lincoln, Maine, USA, where he was described as 'clerk'. There is no evidence that he ever returned to this country.

43 The Masons Arms later became the registered offices of the Middleton Building Society, fl 1846. MTH Archives B 44.

44 Quoted by S. J. Chapman, *op cit*, 39

45 C. Hulbert, *Memoirs of Seventy Years of an Eventful Life* (Shrewsbury, 1852), 87, note.

46 MTH 749.

47 J. Tann, *Gloucestershire Woollen Mills* (1967), 20.

48 A very fine example of an elegant Regency street façade with 'weaver's windows' at the rear is to be seen on New Street, Uppermill.

CHAPTER VIII

HOUSING IN AN INDUSTRIAL
COLONY: EBBW VALE, 1778-1914

F. J. Ball

ALMOST completely encircled by hills, Ebbw Vale lies in the north-western corner of Monmouthshire at the head of the Ebbw Valley, bounded on the east by the Nantyglo-Blaina and Abertillery Urban Districts and on the west by the Tredegar, Bedwellty and Abercarn Urban Districts. The northern boundary of the urban area forms the county boundary with Brecknockshire. The town owes its existence to the economic changes of the Industrial Revolution, for, until 1778, it was only a hamlet consisting of a few scattered farms. As industry developed within the valley, there followed a steady increase in population until today almost 30,000 people live within the urban district area. The town extends from Beaufort and Rassau in the north to Cwm in the south, and the urban district covers an area of 6,869 acres, measuring $7\frac{1}{2}$ miles from north to south and approximately $1\frac{1}{2}$ miles from east to west. The main section of the town lies between 900 and 1,000ft above sea level, forming a letter 'T' with Rassau and Beaufort as the horizontal and the central districts as the vertical. To the south lies the mining district of Cwm, lying between 700 and 800ft above sea level. This area is roughly rectangular, measuring approximately $\frac{3}{4}$ mile long and $\frac{1}{4}$ mile wide, as shown in the adjoining map (Fig. 8.1).

The land which was to be industrialised was typically Welsh upland farmland, with farms and cottages scattered along the slope of the hills and generally placed above the line of the trees. They faced southwards and nestled against the hill slopes as protection against the winds. These houses were usually built of stone and timber and hence differed from the typical Welsh farmhouse, which was made of earthen sides and timber. Describing the neighbourhood, Archdeacon Coxe wrote :

> It is impossible to travel without being struck with the appearance and cheerfulness which results from whitewashing the houses; on account of the abundance of lime this operation is performed annually, both within and without, and contributes to the health of the inhabitants. The white colour of the dwellings, scattered along the summit and sides of the hills, and surrounded by foliage of different hues, considerably heightens the picturesque effect of diversified landscapes.[1]

The houses of the more prosperous farmers or freeholders usually possessed two entrances, the servants' entrance being at the junc-

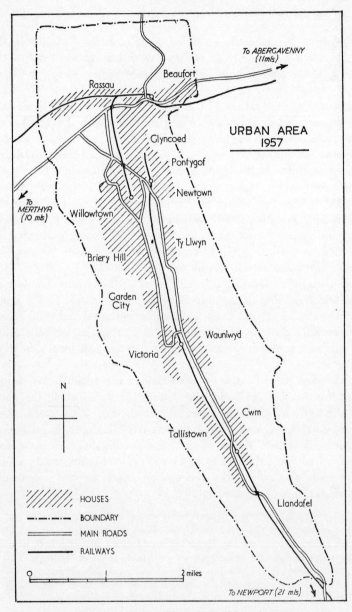

Fig 8.1. Map of Ebbw Vale Urban Area

tion of the cowhouse and the kitchen, and the master's entrance by
the porch at the junction of the kitchen and the hall. This hall was
so raised above the level of the other rooms that all these rooms
could be easily surveyed from it. Ty yn y Llwyn might well have
been such a house, described as 'a delicate House, both the Kitchen
and Hall. A person delighting in study, and being alone, need not
desire a better place than the Hall, with the delightful garden
before it towards the South . . . and the delightful woody prospect
about it.' In the same passage Edmund Jones also referred to a 'well
built house at Aber-mythve, the habitation of a respectable Freeholder. And lower down by the River Side, near Pontrhiwgyngi, is
an excellent place to build a delightful habitation.'[2]

Bon-y-dderwen (Fig. 8.2), one of the oldest farmhouses still stand-
ing, retains evidence of an earlier layout, consisting of three rooms
on the ground floor, three rooms upstairs, and an attic where provisions were stored. Outside the main structure are small buildings
in which bull rings are still to be found. The house was taken over
by the Harfords, who knocked down part of one wall to add a
kitchen, altered the direction of the stairs and made a new front
entrance.[3] The cottages of the small farmers were usually built upon
a most 'frugal plan, and of no longer dimension than is necessary
for the accommodation of a small family'. Attached to these cottages were gardens of sufficient size to supply the family with common vegetables.[4]

It is most difficult to estimate the number of inhabitants living
within the urban area at this time. In the parish of Aberystruth,
according to Jones, there were about 150 houses, 'but as several of
them are at present without Inhabitants, in others only one woman,
in others two persons, and in others but three or four, though there
are some large families, yet I cannot think that all the Inhabitants
together do exceed 500 in number'.[5] If we assume these figures to
be fairly representative of a mountainous district, then the urban
area with sixty-five cottages would contain about 220 inhabitants.

The roads in the valley were little more than footpaths. On a
fourteenth-century map of South Wales, there were two tracks
leading into the valley, the first to the parish church at Bedwellty
and the second to the parish church at Aberystruth. By the middle
of the eighteenth century many new paths had been constructed,
linking together many of the farms. The state of these paths can
well be imagined when we recall that Sir John Phillips took two

s

days in summer to travel from Llandovery to Hay, a distance of 35 miles.[6] Williams wrote :

> Private roads and lanes except those approaching the houses of Gentlemen, are untouched, or touched by the rude hand of Negligence and Waste. High banks, ragged roots, large sheep holes, random stone and rubbish, trees stretching their branches across, or hacked into decay, form charming studies for picturesque painters, but dreadful means of intercourse, compared with toll roads, rail roads and canals.[7]

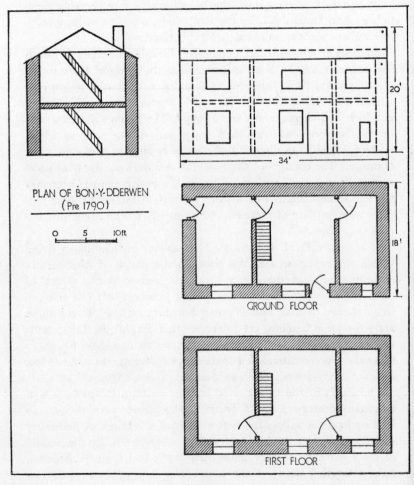

PLAN OF BON-Y-DDERWEN
(Pre 1790)

0   5   10ft

20'

34'

18'

GROUND FLOOR

FIRST FLOOR

Fig 8.2

The regard for the local paths might well be imagined when Watkin Evans, a yeoman, was brought to trial in 1750 'for digging a cole-work and pitt in the highway leading from Pont Ebboth Vawr towards Abergavenny on the King's highway, here called Heol y Hendre'.[8] On an average £12 4s 0d was expended annually on the upkeep of the roads and bridges within the parish of Aberystruth during these years.[9] As in other mountainous areas, no provision was made for sanitation of any kind, while water for drinking and other purposes was obtained from springs and rivers.

Although deposits of slag and ashes have been unearthed to reveal possible sites of very early furnaces at Briery Hill, Troedy-rhiwclawydd and Cwm Merddach and although 'scouring rites' had been granted by manorial documents dating from 1697, industria-lisation really began in Beaufort when Edward Kendall leased land in 1778 from the Duke of Beaufort for the purpose of 'erecting one or more furnaces'.[10] He constructed his first furnace in 1780 on the farmland known as Gwaun Ebwy and built his house on the site of the old farmhouse. Although Walter Watkins had mined coal and ore in Ebbw Vale since 1768, it was not until 1786 that he signed an agreement with the Miles family whereby he was per-mitted to erect a furnace on the Penycae estate.[11] Later the works passed by way of Jeremiah Homfray into the hands of Harfords, Partridge and Company, with the Harfords as the managing direc-tors.[12]

As industry grew and more workers were attracted to the valley, it became imperative to provide houses and cottages for them. It soon became necessary for the ironmasters to assume responsibility for this work, and they attempted to meet the housing shortage by compelling their labourers to take in lodgers, whose interests were protected by written agreements. In 1796 a labourer would rent a house plus 'firing' (fuel) for 1s a week, or 8½ per cent of his weekly wage, provided he would take in lodgers and never charge more than 9d a week for providing a flock or feather bed or more than 6d for any other type of bed. In cases where the lodgers were man and wife, the tenant could charge 1s 6d or 1s according to the type of bed provided. If the lodger were single and a labourer, this would constitute approximately 17 per cent of his weekly wage.[13]

Among the first cottages to be built were the thirteen in 'Y Rhanc Gam' in 1787.[14] A ledger of 1791–6 gives us an insight into the building programme of the company. In 1791, William Phillips received from the Ebbw Vale Company £54 2s 6d for building houses. In February 1792, Andrew Maund received £500 12s 6d for building offices and houses, and in the July of the same year Thomas Jones received amounts totalling £231 18s 0d for erecting houses in Penycae. The following year, John Richards received wages for work done on cottages in Ty Llwyn and also twelve guineas for converting a barn into four cottages. In May 1796, 6,580 bricks were imported into the area, and in July 1796 David Jones and his son were engaged on the repair of houses at Ty-ar-y-nant and in putting in grates, in pointing the ridge of a roof and in replacing broken tiles at the Lower Hendre. In the same year Williams, a tiler, received 1d a yard for pointing the houses at Penycae. For all these houses, the paving stone was brought to Ebbw Vale from Crumlin and the tilestone from Aberbeeg. These cottages probably included the seven at Ty Nant, seven at Ty Llwyn, twelve at River Row, five in the Old Brickyard and eight at Pontygof.[15]

The repair work and conversion of the farm is evidence of the process, known in several industrial colonies, of improving existing cottages and any other suitable property for a new tenantry. Richard Arkwright took over a declining lead-mining colony at Cromford (Derbyshire) to build his famous cotton-spinning works, but his first workers' houses were not built until 1778, when the second mill was under construction, and it is clear that he must have utilised existing cottages. At another 'model' industrial community, that built by Samuel Greg at Styal (near Manchester) from 1785, the first nineteen dwellings were made from a divided farmhouse, dairy, Dutch barn and shippon, and it was not until 1790 that the first row of new houses was ready for families to occupy. This temporary expedient was certainly better than the Scottish makeshift of reserving the ground floors of cotton mills for accommodation of workers.[16]

Relatively little is known about the houses erected in the first phase of new building in Ebbw Vale because 'Y Rhanc Gam' was demolished in 1913, but two terraces built in the first years of the nineteenth century survived until recently. By this time a style of building sometimes referred to as 'double houses'—an adaptation of the familiar back-to-back plan to hilly country—had come into existence. The term is used to describe houses built one above the other into the side of a slope, the lower house being entered from one side, and the upper one from a higher level on the opposite side. In South Wales examples of this practice have so far been documented at Blaenavon (Staffordshire Row and North Street), Clydach Ironworks (Ynys-y-garth cottages, 1800), Abernant, and Ebbw Vale.[17] Another variant on the theme was familiar in parts of the Pennines, particularly around Todmorden and Hebden Bridge (West Riding).[18]

In 1802 sixteen cottages called 'Y Rhanc Cae'r Glyn' (later known as Furnace Row) were built near 'Y Rhanc Gam', and in 1811 twelve cottages known as 'Y Rhanc Clach' (later known as Limestone Row) followed. These cottages were low-roofed with stone-tiled floors, and the rooms were small and badly ventilated. No sanitary arrangements were provided and water had to be obtained from mountain springs. Meanwhile, in 1805, eight new cottages had been erected in Pontygof near the site where Anthony is reputed to have built a bridge across the river. In 1811, the cottages on the Sychffos were erected, and shortly afterwards those on the Gantre Isaf.

The Gantre cottages (Fig. 8.3) were originally numbered 1–28, of which thirteen contained basement flats and two were of two storeys only. The basement consisted of three rooms—a living room 11ft by 12½ft containing a grate and one window, a bedroom 6ft by 8ft 8in with one window, and a pantry 6ft by 3½ft. It opened out on to a garden which fell away to the Gantre stream and was not connected in any way with the upper storeys. Above the basement was the house proper, consisting of two storeys, the lower a replica of the basement, save that the pantry had one small window, and the upper containing two bedrooms. The larger bedroom was 11ft by 12½ft and the smaller 6ft by 12½ft. Both these rooms had only one small window (2ft 8in square) and sloped from 11ft at the centre to 5½ft at the outside walls. The stairs were spiral and made of wood. The outside walls were made of stone and were 2ft thick, and the outside doors, resembling stable doors, could be opened in halves. The headroom in all the rooms, other than the bedrooms on the second storey, was 6ft 10in.[19] The Sychffos cottages were originally numbered 1–18, of which nos 9–16 formed the basements of nos 1–8, while nos 17 and 18 formed 'back-to-back' houses. These cottages were in every way similar to the Gantre cottages. There were gardens on both sides of the cottages, one for the family living in the basement, and one for the family above. Like the tenants of the Gantre cottages, these tenants would obtain their water from the Gantre stream.

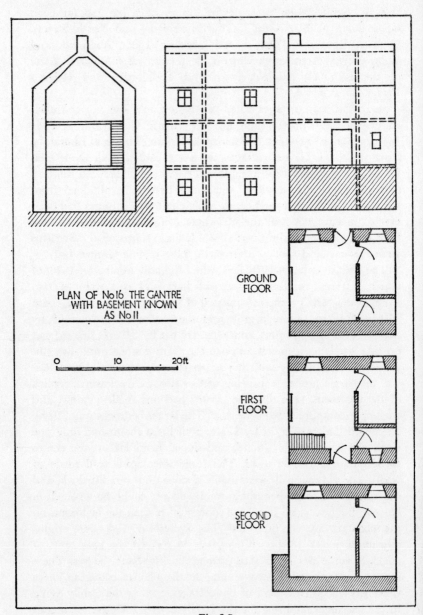

PLAN OF No 16 THE GANTRE
WITH BASEMENT KNOWN
AS No 11

0   10   20ft

GROUND
FLOOR

FIRST
FLOOR

SECOND
FLOOR

Fig 8.3

In 1814 the Harfords valued the Sychffos cottages at £1,373 0s 8d, the Hendre cottages at £1,484 19s 10d, the cottages near the Company Shop at £290 18s 7d and the cottages in the Ty-nant area at £724 1s 2d.[20] This would give an approximate individual value of £36 per house for the very early houses, £52 per house for the period 1802–5, and £55 per house for those erected after 1811.

There seem to have been no cottages erected by the Harfords between the completion of the Sychffos cottages and those constructed in the early 1820s. In 1818, they obtained possession of the Sirhowy Ironworks and between 1818 and 1820 extensive furnaces, bar and plate mills were erected. Once more there was an urgent need for houses, which was met by the construction of four rows of cottages on the Hendre site, later to be known as Trenewydd to distinguish it from the older cottages of the Gantre and Sychffos. The first of the rows was completed by 1828. In construction these houses were similar to the older ones, being made principally of local stone, with small windows, poor ventilation, and no water supply. When completed there were eighty-three houses in the rows and seventeen others in the vicinity. They were built in such a manner that their backs faced the roadway, while access was by way of a lane running between the doors and the gardens. In winter these backs were reputed to be dangerous to the unwary as they became piled up with dirt and ashes. Latrines were not provided until 1884, when C. B. Holland, as general manager, ordered the construction of dry closets. Before that, all that had existed were holes dug in the garden, screened by sheets of corrugated iron. On this estate there were two bakehouses under the supervision of a full-time baker whose duty it was to see that all the tenants had the use of the baking facilities at their allotted time, a feature of industrial colonies found elsewhere.[21]

In 1824, the Harfords possessed 103 cottages in the parish of Bedwellty whose total rateable value amounted to £30 19s 4d, averaging 5s 10d per house.[22] These rows of cottages would be the Gantre, the Sychffos, Old Tunnel, Wesleyan Place and the ones near Bony-dderwen, the Forge and the Rising Sun Inn. Old Tunnel comprised ten back-to-back cottages, of which one was considerably smaller than the other. These cottages ceased to be occupied in 1960 and at that time formed but five houses.[23] There were fourteen cottages in Wesleyan Row, eight near Bon-y-dderwen, seven near the Forge and four near the Rising Sun. The rents of these houses originally varied between 1s 6d and 2s a week, that is, between 10 per cent and 13 per cent of a miner's pay.[24] At this period a cottage at Llwyd Coed was sold by William Lewis to Edmund Henry for £9. A year later, in 1824, Edmund Henry bought another house for £25, but allowed the tenant to remain in possession for a further two months at a rent of 10s a month;[25] in other words, it seems likely that the Harfords provided better accommodation at lower rentals than was available to those employed in agriculture.

In the parish of Bedwellty, the building of cottages restarted early in 1829. By the end of 1831, over 100 new cottages had come into being.[26] This progress was maintained down to 1842, when the number of Harford cottages amounted to 407, an increase of 304 in thirteen years. These new rows were called Colliers' (82 cottages), School (24), Pond (46), Armoury (47), Church (10), Old Pit (11), Nursery (23) and Chapel (45). There were also eight new cottages near Penual Chapel.[27] These cottages were either four-roomed and consisted of two storeys, or were two-roomed with a loft above. As with the general run of cottages within the valley, they were constructed without sanitary provisions of any kind or water supply. The two-roomed cottages were provided with a ladder that led into a windowless attic. These ladders were often concealed in a cupboard that had to be opened before ascent into the attic was possible. Larger houses were constructed at the end of each row for the foremen and lesser officials. As with Trenewydd, there were communal bakehouses. By 1843, the Harfords owned 604 workmen's cottages and six agents' houses.[28] These cottages were rented at 3s a week, ie between 12 per cent and 15 per cent of a collier's wage. In the case of a labourer, this rent would be 17 per cent of his pay.[29]

According to the 1841 Census, six of the company's cottages were unoccupied and the remaining cottages housed 3,379 inhabitants; so each cottage was occupied by 5·7 persons, or 0·1 less than the average for the whole area. This average also compared most favourably with the average for the parish of Aberystruth (6·1 per house), but not so favourably with that of Bedwellty (5·6 per house). At Varteg and Blaenavon, two towns not far distant, the averages were respectively 5·9 and 6·3 per house.[30]

The Ebbw Vale House, the home of the ironmaster, was built of stone and slate. On the first floor were the dining room, the parlour, the entrance hall and staircase, the butler's pantry, two kitchens, the scullery, the cellarage, and all the other necessary offices. On the second floor were four bedrooms and a drawing-room, and above these five attics. Attached to the house were the coach house, the four-stall stable and other outbuildings. The house itself stood in its own grounds and was surrounded by lawns and shrubbery.[31] The house was built before 1796, for in that year William Saunders had pointed the roof of the company's house, the stables and the privy house.[32] It would, therefore, seem that the masters had made provisions for their own sanitary arrangements, and they also did so for the agents' houses that stood in their own grounds.

Building commenced in Victoria late in 1836, and by the October of the following year, the Victoria Iron Company had expended £4,857 13s 6d in constructing dwelling places. As well as building new cottages, the company converted an old barn and another building into four houses and added two more wings to an old public house. Two private builders, by name Jones and Davies, were also erecting houses, the former having completed two and the latter sixteen. They had also another sixty houses in the course of erection.[33] Later, Davies converted two of his cottages into a temporary shop for the company. By the following October, there were 150 cottages occupied and another sixty in the process of erection and scheduled to be completed within three months. At this time the company employed 650 labourers. It was hoped, also, to complete the surgeon's house by the November. (The surgeon, a Mr Coles, was expected to pay a rent for this house and was to receive his wages on a percentage basis.[34]) By 1838, eighteen more cottages had been completed and occupied, and twenty-eight remained unfinished as a result of a reduction in expenditure on the part of the company.[35] Six months later, in October, these twenty-eight cottages had been finished and work was progressing on twelve in Lethbridge Terrace which were being converted into twenty-three dwellings. Six more in Queen's Street were nearing completion. As the company did not contemplate building any more cottages, it was prepared to lease land to any private person who wished to do so. This resulted in the completion of six more houses.[36] In 1842, the cottages within the area numbered 255, of which 183 were owned by the company.[37]

According to the slope of the ground, these cottages did or did not include basements. Where the slope was suitable for a basement to be included, these cottages were built on a plan similar to those of the Gantre, but otherwise they were two storeys high. They were all built of local stone with exterior walls 18in thick. The two storeys consisted of two rooms downstairs and three rooms upstairs. On the ground floor facing the main road was a room 15½ft by 10½ft, and that included the stairway. The back room was 15½ft by 9½ft. Both these rooms possessed grates, originally big open ranges with two ovens, the smaller one on the right and the larger one for baking bread on the left. The front room contained one window and the back room two, and the headroom was 8½ft. On the next floor there were three bedrooms : the first, into which the stairs came, 15ft by 10½ft containing two windows, one of which had been bricked up; the second, also with one window, 9½ft x 7ft; and the third, also with one window, 9½ft by 8½ft. The headroom of these bedrooms sloped from 8ft to 5½ft. Outside was a yard, 8ft by 4½ft, where coal was stored under an arch in the back retaining wall.[38] Jones, a mason and builder, reported that he had built 50 of these cottages at a cost of £4,000, an average of £80 per house.[39]

The rents of these cottages varied between 1s 6d and 3s a week, only one being listed at 1s 6d, 38 at 2s, 28 at 2s 6d, and the rest of the company's houses at 3s.[40] If we consider the wages paid at this time, the lowest paid, the unskilled labourers, who in all probability would rent the cheapest cottages, would pay about 12 per cent of their wages in rent; the collier, receiving between 20s and 22s a week, would pay between 12 per cent and 15 per cent; and the highest paid, the refiners, puddlers, and other skilled men, about 11 per cent. In 1841, the average number of persons per house was 6·5, a figure well above the average for the urban area.[41]

The Tithe Map of Rassau reveals a number of cottages scattered along the tramroad, and one row of houses. These houses were similar in structure to those of Augusta Street (Fig 8.4), Victoria, and accommodated on an average 4·6 persons.[42] In the Beaufort area, there was a cluster of cottages about Carmel Chapel, another on the hill, and a third near the works. River Row, consisting of twenty-three cottages similar to the one described in Victoria, was in existence in 1802.[43] Other cottages built in the early days of industrialisation were Shop Row (19), Gantre Row (7), Lower Yard Row (8), Upper Yard Row (13) and those in the Waungoch area. In 1824, we learn that this company had twenty-three houses in the parish of Bedwellty, with a rateable value of £5 13s 4d.[44] This number had increased to forty-two by the end of 1831.[45] In 1841, there were 472 houses in this district (60 in Bedwellty and 412 in Llangattwg), with an average of 5·8 persons per house.[46] There were also at this time three blacksmiths, ten butcher-grocers, nine inn-keepers, three carpenters, a saddler, a surgeon, a tailor and a watch-maker.[47] In Cwm, then called 'Abermythve' or 'Cwm Mythve', there

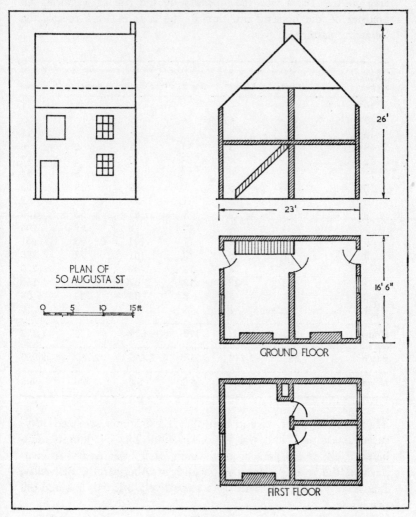

PLAN OF
50 AUGUSTA ST

GROUND FLOOR

FIRST FLOOR

Fig 8.4

were a few houses in the vicinity of the tramroad and one or two scattered homesteads on the hill slopes.[48]

The immediate result of this industrialisation was a rapid increase in population. Between the years 1801 and 1841, it multiplied itself eleven times, with the most startling rise between the years 1818 and 1833 in the Ebbw Vale area, as evidenced by the increase in the 'Rent and Firing Account'. A temporary setback in the Beaufort area in the 1830s was recompensed by the rise of Victoria. An analysis of the housing situation in the area in 1841 reveals the following pattern :

No of persons per house	Drysiog	Victoria	Rassau	Ebbw Vale	Beaufort	Total
19					1	1
15		1		1		2
14		2				2
13		3		1	2	6
12		4		5	4	13
11		8		11	5	24
10	1	16		30	19	66
9	5	16	3	37	21	82
8	5	39	5	65	55	169
7	4	34	10	98	62	208
6	5	43	11	107	85	251
5	1	46	23	101	77	258
4	3	28	32	92	65	220
3	2	22	15	67	43	149
2	5	5	8	38	29	85
1	2	1	3	6	4	16
Houses	43	268	110	659	472	1,552
Pop'n	238	1,749	510	3,846	2,747	9,090
Average	5·5	6·5	4·6	5·8	5·8	5·8

Thus in 1841, there were in the valley 1,552 houses occupied, fifty-three unoccupied, and two in construction. The inhabitants numbered 9,090 or 5·9 per occupied house, or 5·7 per house. In comparison, the averages for the parishes of Aberystruth, Bedwellty, Llangattwg and Llangynidr were respectively 6·1, 5·6, 5·3, and 4·9 per house.

It is only by inference that we can deduce the sanitary conditions prevalent in the valley. 'The houses occupied by the collier population', reported Thomas Felton of Blackwood, 'in this vicinity are generally built on sloping grounds, where one habitation is above another, and are very rarely drained, although it must be obvious from the side land situation that drains are much required.'[49] It was reported in 1845 that accumulations of filth at Merthyr were removed about once in five years. The report said :

> Liquid refuse was either thrown into the river or allowed to soak into the subsoil, leading to offensive smells in warm weather and to deterioration in health. In some cases forty to fifty persons shared one privy and often as a last resort tips . ⸱ . were frequented by persons of all ages and sexes, who managed the best way they could.[50]

In such conditions, it is not surprising that cholera invaded the area in 1832, 1837, and 1850. Rowlands reported :

> The amount of sickness is greater than in the agricultural country, among the young especially from two years of age and under. The surgical cases among the children are not at all prevalent with the exception of accidents. But fevers are very prevalent from the smallness of their houses and the number of persons residing in them.[51]

Tremenheere wrote :

> The houses of the workers are ranged round the works in rows, sometimes two to five deep, sometimes three storeys high. They often contain from one to six lodgers in addition to the members of the family, and afford most scanty accommodation for so many inmates. It is not unusual to find that ten individuals of various age and sex occupy three beds in two small rooms. The surface of the soil around is frequently blackened with coal, or covered with high mounds of refuse from the mines and furnaces. The road between the rows is so imperfectly made as to be left often, in wet weather, ankle deep in black mud. Flat pavement is rarely seen, except in some new works now in erection. Volumes of smoke from the furnaces, the rolling mills and the coke hearth are driven past according to the direction of the wind. Gardens are few, and almost entirely neglected.[52]

With the collapse of the Harfords, the first stage in the industrialisation of the valley came to an end. As in other districts, material progress outran the limited resources of the parochial authorities to organise social life. Although living conditions were primitive, it must be remembered that the Ebbw Vale and Victoria Companies alone provided close on 700 cottages within the span of seventeen years when the population must have trebled itself, and this in itself was no mean achievement.

The ironworks assumed a new lease of life when purchased by Messrs Darby of Coalbrookdale in 1844. This company later bought the Victoria Works in 1844 and the Abersychan Ironworks and Collieries in 1852. It also bought up the works in Pontypool and Abercarn. The company modernised its processes and was thus enabled to survive the period during which many of the old ironworks, such as Beaufort, were closed for ever. It also modernised its business methods and became known, first as the Ebbw Vale Company Ltd, and later as the Ebbw Vale Iron, Steel and Coal Company, taking advantage of the limited liability acts.

As the population within the central zone of the urban area was rapidly increasing, it become impossible for the company to provide sufficient cottages for all its employees. Hence in the early 1850s it adopted the policy of leasing land to any worker or group of workers who might like to erect their own dwellings. Meanwhile building was also taking place on much of the freehold land within the area. Thus, on the Drysiog Estate, there grew up the little community of Briery Hill. There can be no doubt that the first cottages erected on this estate were for the better paid workmen and for those who were willing to form Building Clubs; it is not without significance that one of the early terraces was known as Club Row. By 1884 the district was a thriving community of some 600 houses, twenty-nine shops (including a pawnbroker's), ten inns and thirteen beer retailers.[53] However, freed of company control, there was little planning in the project. Many of the early houses, as in Spencer Street, were made of wood.

It was during this period that the fields of Willowtown began to be covered by houses. In 1866, because of overcrowding, the company was forced to build three rows of wooden cottages in Tredegar Road.[54] Other houses built in this area by independent contractors tended to be larger than the cottages built by the company. In the 1880s the scattered settlements between Briery Hill and Colliers' Rows were being joined together by a long street, variously known as Armoury Terrace, Bethcar Street, Ida Place, Market Place and Libanus Road. The two hamlets of Cwm and Waunlywd grew rapidly in size towards the end of the century. Between 1874, when the colliery was opened, and 1914, 391 houses were erected in Waunlwyd,[55] a district situated on the hill slopes facing Victoria. The houses were larger than those of Victoria, but contained no bathrooms. They were built in rows, provided with wash-houses in the rear, but with no communal bakehouses as the art of baking bread was dying out. The opening of the Marine Colliery in the 1890s led to a rapid development of Cwm, where over 1,000 new houses were erected by 1914. The village really consisted of one long street, Canning and Marine Streets, with roads leading from it. The houses contained no bathrooms and suffered from land subsidence.

The surveyors' books for the period 1893 to 1907 reveal the extent of the building programme in Ebbw Vale during those years, when 1,766 new houses were erected.[56] Offset against this was the demolition of older houses, for between 1905 and 1907 as many as seventy-two houses were pulled down. It was during this period that the old Forge Rows were replaced by new terraces. The extent of the housing problem is revealed by the rapid increase in population, which almost doubled itself between 1891 and 1911 :

	1891	1901	1911
Ebbw Vale	13,736	17,401	26,261
Beaufort	2,754	2,761	3,291
Rassau	822	832	989
Totals	17,312	20,994	30,541

An examination of the population figures during these decades reveals a substantial increase in the North Central Ward (Willowtown) and the South Ward (Cwm and Waunlwyd), with a small increase in the South Central Ward (Briery Hill).[57] During the period 1881 to 1911, there was a slight increase in the number of persons per habitable house, the figures being : 1881, 5·39; 1891, 5·57; 1901, 5·49; and 1911, 5·6. This average is somewhat higher than that for the county (4.9), and also for that of England and Wales (4·39) for the year 1911.

However the Census Reports reveal a slight easing in the housing problem in respect to the size of tenements. In 1891 in this area 59 per cent of the tenements had less than five rooms per tenancy, but in 1901 this had fallen to 48·9 per cent and in 1911 to 47·3 per cent. The 1901 percentage figure compares quite favourably with many of the industrial areas within the county, being lower than those of Aberystruth, Blaenavon, Nantyglo-Blaina, Rhymney and Tredegar, but higher than those of Abercarn, Abertillery, Panteg, and Pontypool.[58] In 1911, also, the percentage of families living more than two persons per room was 7·5 in Ebbw Vale as compared with 9·1 for the rest of the county.

According to the census of 1911, the percentage of families living more than two persons per room was 7·5 in Ebbw Vale as compared against an average figure of 9·1 for England and Wales. In terms of human habitation there was also a slight improvement, for in 1891 58·8 per cent of the population lived in tenements of four rooms or less, while in 1901 the figure was 44·5 per cent and in 1911 it was still further reduced to 40·1 per cent. Details of the final census at the end of the period under review are as follows:

	Inhabited houses	Tenements	Population
Ordinary dwellings	5,051	5,593	28,470
Shops	235	252	1,288
Hotels, inns, etc.	56	58	368
Offices, etc	4	4	22
Institutions	4	4	188
Others	7	7	37
Barns, sheds, etc.	0	5	168
Totals	5,357	5,923	30,541

At this time there were 133 houses, ten shops, and one other build-building in the course of construction. There were also thirty-seven places of worship, seventy-nine shops and sixteen theatres and places of amusement. There were 168 persons living in barns, sheds, caravans, tents, or the open air.[59]

One of the greatest obstacles to progress within the valley arose from the insularity of the four parishes. 'Ad hoc' bodies had helped to overcome parochialism, and there was a steady growth in area after the formation of the council in 1874. Originally the local board of health exercised control over Victoria, Briery Hill, the Forge Rows and Colliers' Rows. Newtown was brought under its control in 1877, and Beaufort in 1878. In 1891 and 1893 it was further enlarged by the addition in the South Ward of several areas formerly within the parishes of Aberystruth and Bedwellty. Unfortunately for progress, it seems that in its early days the local board was dominated by the Ebbw Vale Company, who insisted that the rates were kept low; it is reported that until 1893 the rate was not allowed to exceed 1s in the pound. This in itself was sufficient to hamper the progress of the town and its housing programme. Nevertheless, under growing pressure from the local Trades and Labour Council, the UDC had commenced its programme of demolishing the older houses and replacing them by new ones. The Forge Rows disappeared between 1898 and 1910, while Newtown was due for demolition when World War I broke out.

Discussion of the possibility of building council houses began in 1903 when John Lee, a local builder, submitted a sequence of plans for cheap four-roomed houses. Inevitably there was tension between the need for economy on the one side, represented by the builder's realistic assessment of land and building costs, and aspirations after space and improved standards suggested by the local surveyor and by civic pride. Sixty-four cottages were completed in 1910, consisting of living room, scullery (containing a bath) and three bedrooms, with outside offices and a large garden. The average price was £164, a figure only achieved by building leasehold. Rents were fixed at 6s 6d weekly, plus £1 a year ground rent. The Ebbw Vale Company had increased the rent of their houses by 6d weekly in 1904, and the average rental at the period, according to the Trades and Labour Council, varied between 6s and 7s weekly. If this can be accepted, the new council house rents were in step with the general upward trend. Average wages within the valley rose from 30s to 35s weekly in 1875 to 40s to 45s weekly in 1914, so that the average workman was paying 14 to 16 per cent of his wages in rent.[60]

To summarise : the detailed evidence available from Ebbw Vale indicates one very significant trend. The houses erected by the company at the end of the eighteenth century probably represented better value than those available to farm workers, but the accommodation was crowded by the common habit of taking in lodgers and the Harfords' encouragement of this practice. It was not until the second half of the last century, when terminating building societies and private builders attempted to provide a better standard of accommodation that there was a significant overall improvement, at least so far as this can be measured in terms of the proportion of houses of more than four rooms. The first local-authority housing was built in 1910, but only sixty-four cottages were completed. The cost of building workmen's houses rose steadily throughout the period

T

from £36 in the late eighteenth century to £164 at the end of the nineteenth century. This, of course, followed an increase in the number of rooms and sanitary amenities, but rents increased from 8½ per cent of a labourer's wage in 1796 to a fairly consistent 12–14 per cent in the first half of the nineteenth century, and by the end of the period it had risen again to 14–16 per cent. In short, there was clearly an improvement in standards of domestic accommodation over the period from the foundation of the industrial colony to World War I, but the workman paid for it by devoting an increasing proportion of his income to paying his rent. The rising cost of building in the second half of the last century, noticed in Chapters 1 and 2, suggest that this conclusion might also hold in other places than Ebbw Vale.

NOTES

1   W. Coxe, *Historical Tour of Monmouthshire* (Brecon, 1904), 176–8.
2   Edmund Jones, *History of the Parish of Aberystruth* (Trevecca, 1879), 57.
3   Plan of Bon-y-dderwen.
4   C. Hassall, *General View of the Agriculture of the County of Monmouth* (1812), 27.
5   Edmund Jones, *op cit*, 60.
6   T. Jones, *History of Brecknockshire* (Brecon, 1898), 145.
7   D. Williams, *History of Monmouthshire* (1796), 355.
8   Monmouthshire CRO, *Process Book*, 216.
9   Parish Records, Aberystruth, Surveyor's Accounts.
10 National Library of Wales, Maybery Papers, deed 16 Oct 1779; also deed 3 Oct 1779. Scouring rights can be seen in documents B/1/0005, B/1/0011 and B/1/0032 at Monmouthshire CRO.
11 Monmouthshire CRO, B/1/0032, B/1/0011, B/1/0007, B/1/0005; Richard Thomas & Baldwins (hereafter RT & B), Ebbw Vale Ledger 1791–6, 76–80.
12 F. J. Ball, *The Growth of Industrialism in the Valley of Ebbw Vale*, unpublished MA thesis (London, 1959), 48–51.
13 RT & B Memorandum Book, 1796–1818.
14 C. Parry, *History of Ebbw Vale*, unpublished manuscript in Newport Public Library, 16. This name was later anglicised to 'Crooked Row'. In 1913 they were demolished. Present row of houses known as Louvain Terrace.
15 RT & B, Ledger, 1791–6.
16 S. D. Chapman, *The Early Factory Masters* (1967), 157–9. W. C. Lazenby, *The Social and Economic History of Styal*, MA thesis (Manchester 1949), 98–113; Marshall Mss 63/31 (Brotherton Library, Leeds)

and Scottish Record Office U/P 1 Currie Dal C/9/1 (Dr Butt's transcripts).

17 D. M. Rees, 'Industrial Archaeology in Wales: an introduction', *Archaeologia Cambrensis,* CXIII (1964), 139–41; J. M. Lewis, 'Some examples of 19th century Working-Class Housing in South Wales', *Journal of the South-East Wales Industrial Archaeology Society,* I (2), 30–33; see also Harold Carter, *The Towns of Wales* (Wales UP, 1965).

18 M. W. Barley, *The House and Home* (1963), plate 217; above 254–6.

19 C. Parry, *op cit,* 16, for date of erection.

20 RT & B, Ledger, 1814–15.

21 C. Parry, *loc cit.*

22 Bedwellty Parish Records, Poor Law Account, Manmoel Division, third rate, 1824.

23 National Coal Board, Ebbw Vale, Rent Books. Width of smaller cottage 10ft 4in, of the larger 15ft 10in. They were united in 1907.

24 Bedwellty Parish Records, Poor Law Account, Manmoel Division, Disbursement of 1824.

25 Monmouthshire CRO, Hanbury Papers 0270, November 1823 and September 1824.

26 Bedwellty Parish Records, Poor Law Account, Manmoel Division. Fourth rate of 1831. Average number of persons per house for Manmoel, 5·9.

27 C. Parry, *op cit,* 16; PRO, Census Returns, 1841, Bedwellty 107/750. *Children's Employment Commission Report,* 1842, evidence of Evan Jones, 250; Ebbw Vale, 407 houses, 2,300 people.

28 Harril's Sale Catalogue, Newport Public Library.

29 *Children's Employment Commission Report* (1842), 627, evidence of Hannah Hughes.

30 G. S. Kendrick, *The Population of Pontypool and the Parish of Trevethin* (Pontypool 1840).

31 Harril's Sale Catalogue, Newport Public Library.

32 RT & B, Ledger, 1791–96 (June 1796).

33 Monmouthshire Iron and Coal Company, Prospectus and Accounts, 1836–9, Newport Library, px M000 672, 25 Oct 1837.

34 *Ibid,* 31 Oct 1838.

35 *Ibid,* 28 Apr 1839.

36 *Ibid,* 31 Oct 1839.

37 *Ibid,* also Hoggart's Sale Catalogue, London 1842.

38 Photographs and plan of Augusta Street.

39 J. Jones, *Victoria Ironworks and Joint Stock Company* (1853).

40 D. Mushet, *Victoria Ironworks and Mining Ground* (Bath, 1841), 9.

41 PRO, Census Enumerators' Returns, 1841; PRO, HO 107/750.

42 Census Enumerators' Returns 1841; HO 107/1366.

43 National Library of Wales, *Journal of the NLW,* Vol VIII, No. 4, 406.

44 Bedwellty Parish Records, Poor Law Account, Manmoel Division, rate for 1824.

45   *Ibid*, fourth rate, 1831.

46   PRO, Census Enumerators' Returns 1841; PRO, HO 107/1366.

47   Slater's *South Wales and Monmouthshire Directory* (1844).

48   Parish Records, Tithe Maps for the parishes of Aberystruth, Bedwellty, Llangynidr and Llangattock. National Library of Wales, Aberystwyth.

49   *Children's Employment Commission Report* (1842), 490.

50   *Second Report of the Commission on the Health of Towns* (1845), 318–19.

51   *Children's Employment Commission Report* (1842), 624. It was an outbreak of cholera in the 1860s that lead to the opening of the first public cemetery, as the dead were being buried on open land.

52   *Ibid*, 208–9.

53   Kelly's *South Wales and Monmouthshire Directory* (1884).

54   *Monmouthshire Merlin*, 6 Oct 1866.

55   J. Kegie, *County Development Plan (Part II). Town Map No 7, Ebbw Vale* (1953), 89.

56   Surveyors' books. Housing given in years from 1893 to 1907 inclusive: 63; 67; 81; 77; 77; 153; 23; 60; 176; 137; 120; 180; 176; 174; and 202.

57   Census Reports:

	1901	1911
North Central Ward	4,090	7,752
South Central Ward	7,660	8,696
South Ward	5,651	9,813

58   Census Reports, 1901.

59   Census Report 1911.

60   Ebbw Vale UDC Surveyors' Reports, 1909–12; Trades and Labour Council Reports, esp 16 May 1904.

INDEX

Page numbers in italics indicate photographs